To
Margaret
With thanks and
all good wishes
from
Philip

ON THE MOVE

ON THE MOVE:

ESSAYS IN
LABOUR AND TRANSPORT HISTORY
PRESENTED TO PHILIP BAGWELL

EDITED BY

CHRIS WRIGLEY AND JOHN SHEPHERD

THE HAMBLEDON PRESS
LONDON AND RIO GRANDE

Published by The Hambledon Press, 1991

102 Gloucester Avenue, London NW1 8HX (U.K.)
P.O. Box 162, Rio Grande, Ohio 45672 (U.S.A.)

ISBN 1 85285 060 4

A description of this book is available
from the British Library and from the
Library of Congress

Printed on acid-free paper and bound in
Great Britain by Cambridge University Press.

Contents

Philip Bagwell: An Appreciation

John Shepherd

In his inaugural lecture at the London School of Economics, on 12 October 1932, R.H. Tawney defined history as being 'concerned with the study, not of a series of past events but of the life of society and with records of the past as a means to that end'. Philip Bagwell's life and career have been a fine testimony to this description of the historian at work in society. The publication of this *Festschrift* provides the occasion for his colleagues, former students and friends from academic and public life to recognise his many talents as a teacher, scholar, reviewer, supervisor and examiner who has made a particular contribution to his local community and beyond.

Until his retirement in 1977 Philip spent most of his teaching career at the Polytechnic of Central London, starting at its predecessor institution, the Regent Street Polytechnic in 1951. At that time there was only one other historian on the staff to cope with the general outline history courses, so Philip and his colleague literally divided the world between them. From this beginning, he became well-known as a specialist in transport and labour history. After earlier research published in the *Journal of Transport History*, the National Union of Railwaymen invited Philip to write their official history to mark the union's fiftieth anniversary. Published in 1963, *The Railwaymen* was the first part of a classic two-volume study of trade union history (the second volume appearing in 1982). His *Transport Revolution, 1770–1985* is now in its second edition and has long been essential reading on undergraduate economic and social history courses.

Living in Finchley near the Northern Line of the London Underground, Philip is a constituent of a former British Prime Minister. Margaret Thatcher has canvassed him regularly (at general elections) and has always been on the end of erudite and searching questions on Conservative transport policy. Philip has had a longstanding interest in the welfare of the Northern Line and his efforts were instrumental in preventing the partial closure of West Finchley tube station. His monograph *End of the Line?* is a well-reasoned and convincing critique of Conservative transport policies in the Thatcher era. Philip is an authority on transport workers and has made a number of appearances on radio and television in that capacity. On 28 January 1991 Television South (TVS) broadcast a major interview between Alec Harvey and Philip on the state of British transport and the nature of the reforms needed for the future. Also in 1991 Philip published *Doncaster: Town of Train Makers*, a carefully researched and illuminating study of the Doncaster Railway Works and those railway people the travelling public rarely see. Another achievement is his work on the hitherto neglected subject of coastal shipping in the nineteenth century.

Philip Bagwell was born on 16 February 1914 at Ventnor on the Isle of Wight into a family with religious and socialist principles. His parents were devout Baptists. He was two years of age when, with his sister Joan, he watched the police take away his father, a conscientious objector who spent two years in prison for his beliefs. Philip was educated at the Quaker Bembridge School, then at Wigton in Cumbria, before studying for his B.Sc.[Econ] and Teachers' Certificate at Southampton University in the 1930s. He took a wider interest in politics, participating in a hunger march and fighting the twin evils of unemployment and fascism. Like many of his generation, he joined the Communist Party. Following wartime service in India and Burma in the Royal Corps of Signals, Philip supported himself by part-time teaching while completing his Ph.D, on German Disarmanent Policy, 1919–1934, at the London School of Economics under the supervision of Professor Manning. After the war he left the Communists and joined the Labour Party.

His other main academic interest as a historian has been in the field of labour history. He has been an enthusiastic supporter of the Society for the Study of Labour History since its foundation and has made a major contribution to the research and teaching of labour history. He served for five years as Secretary of the Society and is now one of its Vice-Presidents, along with J.F.C. Harrison, Royden Harrison, Eric Hobsbawm, and John Saville.

Philip Bagwell

Philip has produced many journal articles on trade union and agricultural history, a case study on transport history in Chris Wrigley's *History of British Industrial Relations, 1875–1914* and a collaborative work with Gordon Mingay, *Britain and America, 1850–1939*. His *Industrial Relations in the Nineteenth Century* is a valuable guide to source material in parliamentary papers for students and researchers alike.

He has also had a long association with the Christian Socialist Movement and one of its founders, Lord Soper. His involvement has included service on its national committee and being a leading member of its central London branch. He has written the history of the West London Methodist Mission, entitled *Outcast London: A Christian Response*.

In 1972 Polytechnic of Central London recognised his contribution to research and teaching by conferring on him one of the first awards of a professorship in the polytechnic sector. On his retirement the Polytechnic established the Philip Bagwell Prize as an annual award to the student on the Diploma in Labour Studies course who has shown the greatest all-round development. Philip has been associated over many years with this course, which has been popular with trade unionists and mature adult learners entering or returning to higher education. On the publication of the second volume of *The Railwaymen* in 1982, Len Murray made a special presentation to him of an illuminated address on behalf of the NUR at a well-attended gathering at its Unity House headquarters.

During his time at the Polytechnic of Central London countless undergraduate and postgraduate students have been tutored with skill and wisdom by Philip. His colleagues could always turn to him as a courteous and supportive ally. As a young and inexperienced lecturer organising my first history conference, I was very grateful for Philip's active participation and unobtrusive help; especially when, after speaking himself, he quickly filled a crucial gap caused by a missing keynote speaker. Chris Wrigley's admiration of Philip's work on the railwaymen grew ever deeper as he researched the role of the government in industrial relations in Britain in the late nineteenth and twentieth centuries. Philip is a kind, caring and unassuming person who would be the first to acknowledge the strength and support he has gained from the long and happy marriage with Rosemary, his wife and his closest ally in all endeavours. They are active in their local community in voluntary work and have many friends in this country and Europe.

No appreciation would be complete, however, without some observations on the 'Bagwell Style' which has characterised his research and teaching. With good humour a subject is thoroughly and painstakingly researched, no document left unturned and notes methodically recorded in copper-plate handwriting on a multiplicity of index cards, carefully filed and stored in the Bagwell household. However, the 'temperamental typewriter', mentioned in at least one Bagwell production, now appears to have been superseded by modern information technology in the form of a computer and xerox copier. From this resource Philip produces a regular output of articles, reviews and books. Over ten years after his retirement he is more active than ever. His latest project is assisting his sister Joan produce an account, based on their parents' correspondence in the First World War, of their father's experience as an imprisoned conscientious objector.

Philip's generosity and willingness to share his knowledge and expertise at any time are well known to his colleagues and fellow researchers. We are now able to mark Philip's unique contribution with this set of essays on labour and transport history. In producing this volume the editors would like to acknowledge the support of their fellow contributors, Lord Soper, Jimmy Knapp of the RMT and Martin Sheppard of The Hambledon Press in helping to make this *Festschrift* possible.

Philip Bagwell: Tributes

1. *Donald Soper*

Philip Bagwell has been a friend of mine for nearly fifty years and I count it an honour to be able to pay this testimony to someone for whom I have throughout those years not only regarded with affection but with deep respect. My contacts with Philip, unlike those of other contributors to this festschrift, have been almost entirely within the framework of the church. I have of course known of his contributions in other spheres and reading his books reminded me that he was a man, for many, if not all seasons. Nevertheless his companionship in the work of the West London Mission where I was stationed for over forty years, was the opportunity of getting to know and to admire a genuinely good soldier and servant of the Christian faith. In particular I would put on record his commitment to Christianity not only as a personal faith, but just as clearly as a political and social obligation. His politics, with which I so heartily agree, are rooted in his Christian allegiance and it has shone through all the years in which I have had the privilege of being involved with him in the work of the church. Not least in commendation of this lay ministry (for that is what it has been) is the contribution of his wife, Rosemary, in their happy and enduring marriage.

2. *James Knapp*

I did not have the pleasure of meeting Philip until 1972 after my election as a full time union officer. Philip was a regular visitor to Unity House – the union's headquarters – and I am delighted to say he is still a regular and most welcome caller at the office. Like many other members of the old NUR I first became aware of Philip's special talents following the publication in 1963, of his book *The Railwaymen*, the official history of the NUR. This book remains an invaluable reference source and on numerous occasions, discussions about past events in the Union have ended with someone asking, 'What did Baggie say?'

In addition to the official history of the Union, Philip has written a number of other books for the old NUR. I was particularly pleased to invite him to produce a record of our epic struggle with BR and the London Underground in 1989. Philip has also been a regular contributor to the Union's newspaper, *Transport Review*. Inevitably, after a visit abroad Philip will turn up – much to the editor's delight – with a 1,000 word article on railways in Sweden, the USSR or wherever his travels have taken him. Philip Bagwell has given enormous support to the NUR over very many years, and he continues his association with the new union, RMT. I am certain that members everywhere are delighted to be given the opportunity – through their General Secretary – to be associated with this special tribute.

Philip Bagwell

Bibliography of Philip S. Bagwell

Chris Wrigley

BOOKS

1 *The Railwaymen: The History of the National Union of Railwaymen* (London, Allen & Unwin, 1963), pp. 725.

2 *The Railway Clearing House in the British Economy 1842–1922* (London, Allen & Unwin, 1968), pp. 320

3 *Britain and America: A Study of Economic Change, 1850–1939* (London, Routledge, 1970), pp. x + 312. Reprinted 1971, 1987, pp. x + 318. Japanese edition (Japan UNI Agency, 1970). (Joint author with G.E. Mingay)

4 *Industrial Relations* (Government and Society in Nineteenth Century Britain. Commentaries on British Parliamentary Papers, General Editor: P. Ford) (Shannon, Irish University Press, 1974), pp. vii + 166

5 *The Transport Revolution from 1770* (London, Batsford, 1974), pp. 460. Second, extended edition (London, Routledge, 1988), pp. xiv + 474

6 *The Railwaymen*, vol. 2, *The Beeching Era and After* (London, Allen & Unwin, 1982), pp. xxiv + 459

7 *End of the Line: The Fate of British Railways under Thatcher* (London, Verso, 1984), pp. xi + 208. A Japanese translation for Kokuro, the Japanese National Railway Workers' Union, 1985

8 *Outcast London: A Christian Response. The West London Mission of the Methodist Church 1887–1987* (London, Epworth Press, 1987), pp. 174

9 *Doncaster, 1853–1990: Town of Train Makers* (Exeter, Doncaster Books, 1991)

BOOKLETS

1 *NUR Golden Jubilee Souvenir, 1913–1963* (London, NUR, 1963), pp. 46

2 *Transport: Private Privilege or Public Service?* (London, Central London Branch of Christian Socialist Movement, 1974), pp. 14

3 *75 Years of Industrial Trade Unionism (1988)* (London, NUR, 1988), p. 96

4 *The Summer of Discontent (1989)* (London, NUR, 1989), pp. 48

CONTRIBUTIONS TO BOOKS

1 'The Triple Industrial Alliance, 1913–1922' in A. Briggs and J. Saville (eds.), *Essays in Labour History, 1886–1923* (London, Macmillan, 1971), pp. 96–128

2 'The Left in the Thirties', in D. Rubinstein (ed.), *People for the People* (London, Ithaca Press, 1973), pp. 224–33

3 'Walter Hudson, 1852–1932, Trade Unionist and Labour M.P.' in J. Bellamy and J. Saville (eds.), *Dictionary of Labour Biography*, vol. 2 (London, Macmillan, 1974), pp. 197–200

4 'George James Wardle, 1865–1947, Trade Unionist and Labour M.P.' in J. Bellamy and J. Saville (eds), *Dictionary of Labour Biography*, vol. 2 (London, Macmillan, 1974), pp. 373–76

5 'The Impact of Steam', in *Mitchell-Beazley Encyclopaedia* (London, 1977), pp. 154–55

6 'The Decline of Rural Isolation', in G.E. Mingay (ed.), *The Victorian Countryside*, vol. 1, (London, Routledge, 1981), pp. 30–42

7 'Transport' in Chris Wrigley (ed.), *A History of British Industrial Relations, 1875–1914* (Hassocks, Harvester Press, 1982), pp. 230–52

8 'Coastal Shipping' in D. Aldcroft and M. Freeman (eds.), *Transport in the Industrial Revolution* (Manchester, Manchester University Press, 1983), pp. 142–76. (Joint author with John Armstrong)

9 'Coastal Shipping' in D. Aldcroft and M. Freeman, *Transport in Victorian Britain* (Manchester, Manchester University Press, 1984), pp. 171–217. (Joint author with John Armstrong)

10 'The New Unionism in Britain: The Railway Industry', in W.J. Mommsen and H.G. Husing (eds.), *The Development of Trade Unionism in Great Britain and Germany 1880–1914* (London, Allen and Unwin (for the German Historical Institute), 1984), pp. 185–200

11 'Der New Unionism der Britischen Eisenbahner, 1880–1914' in W.J. Mommsen and H.G. Husing (eds.), *Auf dem Wege zur Massengewerkschaft* (Stuttgart, Klett-Cotta, 1984), pp. 237–55

12 'Sir Francis Henry Dent, 1868–1955, Railway Manager' in D.J. Jeremy (ed.), *Dictionary of Business Biography*, vol. 2 (London, Butterworths, 1984), pp. 66–68.

13 'Lord Claud John Hamilton, 1843–1925, Railway Company Manager' in D.J. Jeremy (ed.), *Dictionary of Business Biography*, vol. 3 (London, Butterworths, 1985), pp. 18–21

14 'Sir Allen Lanyon Sarle, 1828–1903, Railway Company Manager' in D.J. Jeremy (ed.), *Dictionary of Business Biography*, vol. 5 (London, Butterworths, 1986), pp. 65–67

ARTICLES

1 'The Rivalry and Working Union of the South Eastern and London, Chatham and Dover Railways', *Journal of Transport History*, 11, 2 (November 1955)

2 'Early Attempts at National Organisation of the Railwaymen, 1865–67', *Journal of Transport History*, 3, 2 (November 1957)

3 'Union Recognition on the Railways', *Railway Review* (15, 22 and 29 August 1958)

4 'The Railway Interest: Its Organisation and Influence, 1839–1914', *Journal of Transport History*, 7, 2 (November 1965)

5 'The Post Office Steam Packets, 1821–36, and the Development of Shipping on the Irish Sea', *Maritime History*, 1 (April 1971)

6 *The Railway Service Gazette* and *The Railway Review* (in the series: Notes on the Labour Press), *Bulletin of the Society for the Study of Labour History*, 28 (Spring 1974)

7 'Retrospect and Prospect', *Transport Review*, (14 January 1983)

8 'Shunted on to a Branch Line: An Analysis of the Conservative Party's Record on Public Transport Policy', *Times Higher Education Supplement* (30 November 1984)

9 'Why we Need a Political Fund', *Transport Review* (21 December 1984)

10 'Ridley's Take Away Service', *Transport Review* (13 September 1985)

11 'British Railways as They Never Were: A 1919 Prophecy', *Royal Society of Arts Journal* (April and May 1986). Based on a paper read to the History Study Group of the Society in December 1985

12 'Public Transport in Greece', *Transport Review* (24 October 1986)

13 'Coastal Shipping's Relationships with Railways and Canals', *Journal of the Railway and Canal Historical Society*, 29, 5, 139 (July 1988). (Joint author with John Armstrong)

14 'Sources for the History of British Trade Unionism and Industrial Relations', *Business Archives*, 56 (November 1988)

15 'The State of London Underground: Who is to Blame?', *Transport Review*, 25 (November 1988)

16 'Hold-ups on the Underground (The Channel Tunnel)', 'Perspective' article, *Times Higher Education Supplement* (14 April 1989)

17 'The Market Economy Approach to the Provision of Transport Services in the 1980s', *Public Enterprise*, 36 (Spring 1990)

18 'Swedish Interlude', *Transport Review* (12 October 1990)

CONFERENCE PAPERS

1 'Coastal Shipping in Britain in the Eighteenth and Nineteenth Centuries', Transport History Conference 1975. Summarised in Transport History Group *Newsletter*, 6 (November 1980), pp. 11–16

2 'Railway Labour in Britain: The Impact of Technological Change, 1955–1980'. Commonwealth Labour History Conference, September 1981

3 'British Maritime Workers and the Foundation of the International Transport Workers' Federation'. Anglo-Dutch Labour History

Conference, Maastricht, 2 April 1982

BOOK REVIEWS

1 H.G. Lewin, *The Railway Mania and its Aftermath, 1848–52*, David and Charles reprints (1968), *Transport History*, 2, 2 (July 1969)

2 H.J. Dyos and D.H. Aldcroft, *British Transport*, Leicester University Press (1969), *Tribune*, 17 November 1969

3 Arthur Helps, *Life and Labours of Mr Brassey*, Evelyn, Adams and Mackey (1969), *Tribune*, 23 January 1970

4 C. Walker, *Thomas Brassey: Railway Builder*, Muller (1969), *Tribune*, 23 January 1970

5 *Felix J.C. Pole: His Book*, Town and Country Press Ltd., Bracknell (1968), *Transport History*, 3, 1 (March 1970)

6 E. Robinson and A.E. Musson, *James Watt and the Steam Revolution*, Adams and Dart (1969), *Tribune*, 23 January 1970

7 Alfred Williams, *Life in a Railway Factory*, David and Charles reprints (1969), *Transport History*, 3, 1 (March 1970)

8 K. Hudson, *Working to Rule*, Adams and Dart (1970), *Tribune*, 4 September 1970

9 H. Perkin, *The Age of the Railway*, Panther (1970), *Tribune*, 15 January 1971

10 G.R. Hawke, *Railways and Economic Growth in England and Wales, 1830–1914*, Oxford, Clarendon Press (1971), *Tribune*, 8 February 1971

11 D.B. McNeill, *Irish Passenger Steam Ship Services*, vols. 1 and 2, David and Charles (1969 and 1971), *Tribune*, 19 March 1971

12 W. Plowden, *The Motor Car and Politics, 1896–1970*, Bodley Head (1971), *Tribune*, 4 June 1971

13 H. Pollins, *Britain's Railways: An Industrial History*, David and Charles (1971), *Tribune*, 19 November 1971

14 P.W. Kingsford, *Victorian Railwaymen*, Frank Cass (1970), *Journal of Transport History*, new series, 1, 3 (February 1972)

15 J. Stanley and M. Pearton, *The International Trade in Arms*, Chatto and Windus, for the International Institute for Strategic Studies (1972), *Christian Socialist*, 67 (June 1972)

16 F.M. McClain, *Maurice: Man and Moralist, 1805–1872*, SPCK (1972) and O.J. Brose, *Frederick Denison Maurice: Rebellious Conformist, 1805–1872*, Ohio State University Press (1972), *Christian Socialist*, 68 (January 1973)

17 R. Brown, *Waterfront Organisation in Hull, 1870–1900*, University of Hull (1970), *Tribune*, 16 February 1973

18 J. Kieve, *The Electric Telegraph*, David and Charles (1973), *Tribune*, 15 June 1973

19 H.J.M. Johnston, *British Emigration Policy, 1815–1830: Shovelling Out Paupers*, Oxford, Clarendon Press (1972), Society for the Study of Labour History (SSLH) *Bulletin*, 26 (Spring 1973)

20 M. Speirs, *One Hundred Years of a Small Trade Union: Card Setting Machine Tenters Society*, Cleckheaton, Yorks (1972), SSLH *Bulletin*, 26 (Spring 1973)

21 A.E. Grigg, *In Railway Service: The History of the Bletchley Branch of the NUR*, published by the branch (1972), SSLH *Bulletin*, 26 (Spring 1973)

22 R. Terrill, *R.H. Tawney and his Times*, André Deutsch (1972), *Christian Socialist*, 77 (December 1974)

23 A.J. Taylor (ed.), *The Standard of Living in the Industrial Revolution*, Methuen (1975), *Literature and History* (July 1975)

24 A.E. Musson, *Trade Unions and Social History*, Cass (1974), *Literature and History* (October 1975).

25 W. Hamish Fraser, *Trade Unions and Society: The Struggle for Acceptance, 1850–1880*, Allen & Unwin (1974), SSLH *Bulletin*, 33 (Autumn 1976)

26 J. Blackman and K. Neild (eds), *Social History*, 1 (1975), *Literature and History* (Autumn 1976).

27 C. Furniss, *Servants of the North: Adventures on the Coastal Trade with the Northern Steamship Company*, Wellington, A.H. and A.W. Reed Ltd (1977), *Technology and Culture*, Atlanta, Georgia (1977), pp. 804–5

28 *History Workshop*, 1 (1976), *Literature and History* (Spring 1978).

29 J. Simmons, *The Railway in England and Wales 1830–1914*, Leicester University Press (1978), *Economic History Review*, xxxii, 3 (August 1979)

30 D. Marquand, *Ramsay MacDonald*, Cape (1977), *Literature and History* (Autumn 1979).

31 G.L. Turnbull, *Traffic and Transport: an Economic History of Pickfords*, Allen & Unwin (1979), *Economic History Review*, xxxiii, 3 (August 1980)

32 F. McKenna, *The Railway Workers*, Faber (1980), *Journal of Transport History*, third series, 2, 2 (September 1981)

33 T.C. Barker, *The Transport Contractors of Rye*, London, the Athlone Press (1982), *Economic History Review*, xxxvi, 3 (August 1983)

34 T.R. Nicolson, *The Birth of the British Motor Car*, Macmillan (1982), *Economic History Review*, xxxvi, 3 (August 1983)

35 J.H. Ducker, *Men of the Steel Rails*, University of Nebraska Press, SSLH *Bulletin*, 44 (Spring 1984)

36 Sidney Weighell, *On the Rails*, Orbis Publishing (1983), SSLH *Bulletin*, 48 (Spring 1984)

37 E.M. Sigsworth (ed.), *Ports and Resorts in the Regions*, Hull College of Higher Education (1980), *Journal of Transport History*, third series, 5, 1, (March 1984)

38 E. Wistrich, *The Politics of Transport*, Longmans (1984), *Transport Review*, 6 April 1984

39 D. Anderson, *The Kindness that Kills*, University of Nottingham (1984), *Christian Socialist*, 114 (Summer 1984)

40 K. Hamilton and S. Potter, *Losing Track*, Routledge (1985), *Transport Review*, 23 August 1985

41 A. Clinton, *Post Office Workers: A Trade Union and Social History*, Allen & Unwin (1984), *Transport Review*, 24 August 1984

42 B. Bradley, *Amtrak: The US National Railroad Passenger Corporation*, Blandford Press (1985), *Transport Review*, 8 November 1985

43 J. Burnett, D. Vincent and D. Myall (eds.), *The Autobiography of the Working Class: An Annotated Critical Biography*, vol. 1 (1984), *Literature and History*, 12 February 1986

44 K.J. Button and D.E. Pitfield (eds), *International Railway Economics*, Gower (1985), *Transport Review*, 14 February 1986

45 J. Kelly, *Trade Unions and Socialist Politics*, Verso, (1985), *Transport Review*, 11 November 1986

46 J.D. Wolfe, *Workers' Participation and Democracy*, Greenwood Press (1986), *Transport Review*, 19 December 1986

47 T.R. Gourvish, *British Railways, 1948–73: A Business History*, Cambridge University Press (1986), *Transport Review*, 30 January 1987

48 M. Freeman and D.H. Aldcroft, *The Atlas of British Railway History*, Croom Helm (1985), *Journal of Transport History*, third series, 8, 1 (March 1987)

49 R.M. Robbins, *A Public Transport Centenary, UITP 1885–1985*, International Union of Public Transport, Brussels (1985), *Journal of Transport History*, third series, 8, 1 (March 1987)

50 M. Bonavia, *The Nationalisation of British Transport: The Early History of the British Transport Commission 1948–53*, Macmillan (1987), *Times Higher Education Supplement*, 29 June 1987

51 A. Gritten, *Reviving the Railways: A Victorian Future*, Centre for Policy Studies (1988), *Transport Review*, 27 July 1988

52 C.J. Wrigley (ed.), *A History of British Industrial Relations*, vol. 2, *1914–39*, Harvester (1987), *Transport Review*, 28 August 1987

53 J. Rose, *Solidarity Forever: 100 years of King's Cross*, ASLEF (1986), SSLH *Bulletin*, 52, 3 (1987)

54 M.H. Saunders, *Men, Mud and Machines*, Courtney Publications, Luton (1987), *Journal of Transport History*, third series, 9, 2 (September 1988)

55 A. Vaughan, *Signalman's Nightmare*, John Murray (1987), *History*, third series, 9, 2 (September 1988)

56 A. Ferner, *Governments, Managers and Industrial Relations*, Blackwell (1988), *Transport Review*, 25 November 1988

57 J.S. Dodgson and N. Topham, *Bus Deregulation and Privatisation in International Perspective*, Gower (1988), *Transport Review*, 14 April 1989

58 J.A. Eagle, *The Canadian Pacific Railway and the Development of Western Canada, 1896–1914*, McGill-Queen's University Press (1989), *Times Higher Education Supplement*, August 1989

59 Institution of Civil Engineers: Infrastructure Study Group, *Congestion* (1989), *Transport Review*, 11 August 1989

60 CBI, *Trade Routes to the Future*, (1989), *Transport Review*, 8 December 1989

61 P. Parker, *For Starters: The Business of Life*, Cape (1990), *Transport Review*, 12 January 1990

62 C. Mair, *David Angus: The Life and Adventures of a Victorian Railway Engineer.* Royal Society of Arts, *Journal*, cxxxvi, 5405 (April 1990)

63 G. Biddle, *The Railway Surveyors*, Ian Allan (1990), Royal Society of Arts, *Journal* cxxxix, 5414 (January 1991)

64 M. Marmo, *More Profile than Courage: The New York City Transit Strike of 1966*, Albany State University of New York Press, (1990), *Journal of Transport History*, 12, 1 (March 1991)

Notes on Contributors

JOHN ARMSTRONG is currently Professor of Business History at Ealing College, London. He edits *The Journal of Transport History* and his publications include articles and chapters on the economic history of coastal shipping, and company promoters, and a book on *Business Documents*. He was a student of Philip Bagwell's at the Polytechnic of Central London and subsequently research assistant to him for three years.

THEO BARKER is Professor Emeritus of Economic History in the University of London and President of the International Historical Congress. He is joint author (with Michael Robbins) of *A History of London Transport*; (with C.I. Savage) of *An Economic History of Transport*; and editor of *The Economic and Social Effects of the Spread of Motor Vehicles*. His latest books include *The Transport Contractors of Rye* and *Moving Millions: An Illustrated History of London Transport to 1990*.

ASA BRIGGS has been Provost of Worcester College, Oxford since 1976. For the previous ten years he was the Vice-Chancellor of the University of Sussex. He was one of the founders and the first President of the Society for the Study of Labour History. He is currently President of the Social History Society. He is the author of many books, including *The Age of Improvement* (1959); *Victorian People* (1954); *Victorian Cities* (1963); *Victorian Things* (1988); *A Social History of England* (1983); and five volumes on the History of Broadcasting. He is Chancellor of the Open University and was made a Life Peer in 1976.

JOHN HALSTEAD is at Division of Continuing Education of the University of Sheffield. He had a career in government departments before turning to adult education. He has been an editor of *Labour History Review* (better known previously as the *Bulletin* of the Society for the Study of Labour History) since 1971 and has published on a number of adult education and historical topics in British and foreign journals. He was the Jerwood Fellow at Hitotsubashi University, Japan during 1987–88.

ERIC HOBSBAWM is currently teaching for part of the year at the Graduate Faculty of the New School for Social Research, New York. He was previously (1947–82) in the History Department of Birkbeck College, University of London, of which he is Emeritus Professor. Among his books he has published a trilogy on the nineteenth century, *The Age of Revolution, 1789–1848; The Age of Capital, 1848–1875*; and *The Age of Empire, 1875–1914*. A number of his studies on labour history have been collected in *Labouring Men* and *Worlds of Labour*.

DAVID HOWELL teaches Politics and History at the University of Manchester. He has published in the fields of Labour and Socialist politics, trade unionism and Celtic Nationalisms. His publications include *British Workers and the Independent Labour Party; A Lost Left; British Social Democracy*; and *The Politics of the NUM: A Lancashire View*.

JAMES KNAPP is General Secretary of the National Union of Rail, Maritime and Transport Workers. He was born in Ayrshire and joined the railway industry as a signal-box lad in 1955. He held his first union position at eighteen, was elected a full time official of the National Union of Railwaymen in 1972 and its General Secretary in 1983. He is currently a member of the TUC General Council, President of the Railwaymen's Section of the International Transport Workers Federation and President of Unity Trust Ltd. (the trade union bank).

GORDON MINGAY is Emeritus Professor of Agrarian History at the University of Kent at Canterbury. His books include *English Landed Society in the Eighteenth Century* (1963); *Britain and America: A Study of Economic Change 1850–1939* (with P.S. Bagwell, 1970); *The Gentry* (1976); *Rural Life in Victorian England* (1977, new edition 1990); *The Victorian Countryside* (ed.) (1981); *The Agrarian History of England and Wales, vi, 1750–1850* (ed.) (1989); and *A Social History of the English Countryside* (1990).

MARGARET MORRIS is Director of Modular Programmes at the City of London Polytechnic. Her publications include *The General Strike* as well as essays on aspects of labour history and on Sir Austen Chamberlain. Previously she lectured at the Polytechnic of Central London when Philip Bagwell was head of the department.

JOHN SHEPHERD is Principal Lecturer (Staff Development and Research) at Anglia Polytechnic in Cambridge, where he teaches Modern British History and is Research Degrees Adviser for CNAA Postgraduate Research Degrees. He has published journal articles on nineteenth- and ·twentieth- century Political and Labour History and is completing a book on George Lansbury. He manages the College's Staff Development Programme and is a training consultant for a number of organisations.

MARGARET WALSH teaches American Economic and Social History at the University of Birmingham. She has published in the fields of Business, Transport and Women's History and on the History of the American West. Her publications include *The Rise of the Midwestern Meat Packing Industry; The Manufacturing Frontier: Pioneer Industry in Antebellum Wisconsin, 1830–1860;* and *The American Frontier Revisited.* Her most recent work is a series of articles on the long-distance bus industry in the United States.

CHRIS WRIGLEY is Professor of Modern British History at Nottingham University. His books include *David Lloyd George and the British Labour Movement; Lloyd George and the Challenge of Labour; Arthur Henderson;* and two volumes which he edited on the history of British industrial relations. His most recent work has been a short biography of Lloyd George. Like Philip Bagwell he has long been a member of both the Labour History Society and the Christian Socialist Movement.

1

The Transport Revolution from 1770 *in Retrospect*

Theo Barker

Transport history's reputation suffered for long from the attentions of enthusiastic amateurs who derived great personal satisfaction from becoming the greatest authorities in the world on some particular stretch of canal or length of railway line – or worse, carried in their heads such detailed knowledge of railway timetables as to bore their companions with details of when trains were due to pass particular level crossings. There were those, too, very knowledgeable about developments in transport technology, who also lost sight of their purpose: to convey goods and passengers more rapidly and/or at lower cost and, in the process, to earn a reasonable return on the capital invested. Hardly any of these eager enthusiasts or technical experts began to perceive that competition was involved and some knowledge of other transport modes was required.

Economic historians used also to have a similarly blinkered approach. As their subject had, to a large extent, grown out of political history, many of them used to concentrate upon transport by canal and railway, for this could be readily studied from familiar parliamentary sources. River improvements and turnpikes were studied for the same reason. There were also the Great Men of the past, who had gained fame from the widely circulating Sunday School prizes written by Samuel Smiles, more successful as an author than as a railway secretary. Bridgewater and Brindley, McAdam (John Loudon or James) and Stephenson (George or Robert) became the well-remembered names. It is true that some outstanding volumes were available, such as *The Times* correspondent, Edwin A. Pratt's *History of Inland Transport and Communication in England* (1912) and the apparently indefatigable Canadian, W.T. Jackman's two mighty volumes, *The Development of Transportation in Modern England* (1916), and C.E.R. Sherrington's *Hundred Years of Inland Transport, 1830–1933* (1934); but they usually remained, rarely consulted, on library shelves. T.S. Willan's remarkable D. Phil. thesis of 1934 produced not one notable book but two: *River Navigation in England, 1600–1750* (1936) and *The English Coasting Trade, 1600–1750* (1938). Economic history text books paid little or no attention to these important earlier works. Jack Simmons and Michael Robbins, contemporaries at Westminster School who had gone their separate ways, the former into the academic world and the latter into the transport industry, had every reason for claiming, when they launched *The Journal of Transport History* in 1953, that some aspects of the subject had been 'curiously neglected' and its bibliography was 'almost entirely neglected'. The new journal did its best to broaden our field of vision with articles on cable tramways, Imperial Airways, London's airports and the Metropolitan Railway's road services; and it in due course published Philip Bagwell's article on 'The Rivalry and Working Union of the South Eastern and London, Chatham and Dover Railways'. But these were usually articles which came to be consulted much later when the subject had been broadened in topic and extended in time rather than articles which contributed much to the broadening and extending process in the 1950s.

A more significant creation of that decade, dating from about the same time as the *JTH* and publishing its own journal from 1955, was the Railway and Canal Historical Society which, despite a scholarly leadership which included Charles Hadfield and Charles Lee, tended to perpetuate old approaches rather than to encourage new ones. By and large its members' interests were usually limited to either railways or canals, rarely to both and only very exceptionally to any other form of transport. Michael Robbins' lecture to the society in November 1956 on 'What Sort of Railway History do we Want?' was heard in polite silence by even the railway part of the membership and was later published not by the society but in the *JTH*. Not until May 1965 did the, *JTH* draw attention to the importance of freight transport by road by publishing Geoffrey Martin's 'Street Lamps for Kendal: A Note on Inland Transport in the 1770s'.

Ralph Davis's classic, *The Rise of the English Shipping Industry in the Seventeenth and Eighteenth Centuries* (1962) was concerned primarily with overseas trade. So, in the introduction to a new edition of his *English Coasting Trade* in 1967, T.S. Willan, in his diffident way, was able to note with quiet satisfaction that 'the work done by others on this subject during the last 30 years does not seem to have made the picture invalid. Indeed [he added significantly] it is surprising and disturbing to find that so little new work has been published on this subject. It is surprising because the sources are considerable in bulk and interest even if they are not always easy to interpret. It is disturbing because inland trade, of which the coasting trade was a part, needs much fuller interpretation if we are to understand the economy of England in the seventeenth and eighteenth centuries'. This verdict also held true for the nineteenth century. Yet, in the 1960s, the years after 1830 were still being considered almost exclusively as 'The Railway Age', with water transport seen mainly in terms of the rearguard struggle of canals against the new iron roads. Little attempt was made to see water transport as a whole or the continued – indeed growing – importance of horse-drawn road transport during the Railway Age.

Greater attention began to be paid to these neglected aspects at those new universities and polytechnics which decided to give more attention to the teaching of transport history, much encouraged by the great stir caused by R.W. Fogel's *Railroads and American Economic Growth* (1964) and Albert Fishlow's *American Railroads and the Transformation of the Ante-Bellum Economy* (1965). 'The two books approach the question of the importance of the railroad somewhat differently [the words are Fishlow's in the preface to his book]. Fogel's principal interest was in the necessity of the innovation: Could the United States have developed without it? The question I ask, rather, is how much of a stimulus did the railroad afford and by what means? We both may be correct, therefore, when he reaffirms that the railroad was not "important" and I that it was.' Fogel attracted a very large, but not uncritical, audience when he addressed the annual conference of the Economic History Society in Manchester in 1966; and like him, British economic historians were soon taking greater interest in water and road transport; and that enterprising New Zealander, Gary Hawke, came to Nuffield College to investigate the (much fuller) British statistics which resulted in *Railways and Economic Growth in England and Wales, 1840–1870*, published in 1970.

Interest in transport history was growing at such a rate that a promising market was in the making for text books. Christopher Savage had jumped the gun by producing his *Economic History of Transport* in 1959 which went through a revision and two reprintings before his untimely death, aged only forty-four, in 1969. The book dealt entirely with Britain, apart

3

from the final chapter of the original version which dealt hurriedly with the United States in twenty-six pages. He had previously written the excellent volume, *Inland Transport* (1957), in the series of Civil Histories of the Second World War and was also concerned about the neglect of Gilbert Walker's *Rail and Road: An Enquiry into the Economics of Competition and State Control* (1942). Savage's three interwar chapters, which dealt with rail transport after 1918, the growth of road transport, and the state's efforts to regulate it, were splendid; but the four earlier ones were much less satisfactory.

Jim Dyos and Derek Aldcroft were quick to seize the new opportunity and cover the ground more thoroughly. Their *British Transport:An Economic Survey from the Seventeenth Century to the Twentieth*, published in 1969, must, however, be seen in retrospect as academically a little premature, even though it was a sufficient commercial success to go into a Pelican reprint a few years later. Hawke's work was not yet available neither was Michael Thompson's delightful, seminal inaugural lecture 'Victorian England: The Horse-drawn Society', published in the same year, 1970; nor William Albert's *Turnpike Road System in England, 1663–1840* (1972) which successfully challenged the long-held views propounded by the Webbs that turnpikes, because set up locally and piecemeal, did not create an effective system of trunk routes out of London by the mid-eighteenth century; nor Gerard Turnbull's doctoral thesis, available in the same year, which showed how well organised, by the mid-eighteenth century, was freight traffic on one of these routes. Quite an avalanche of new material, in fact, appeared almost immediately after the appearance of Dyos and Aldcroft, including important work by Alan Everitt and Peter Cain and Harold Perkin's *Age of the Railway*, based on a television series, another sign of greater interest in transport history. The new journals *Transport History* and *Maritime History* flourished for a brief period at this time. None of this work could appear in the copious bibliography of Dyos and Aldcroft. Their book noted Fogel's view that 'in the case of America at least the contribution of railroads to economic growth has been somewhat exaggerated' and conceded that this may have been truer in Britain 'which already possessed reasonable transport facilities before the railways arrived' but felt that statistical examination 'would require research on an immense scale, a task clearly outside the scope of this volume'. 'It does not aim at uncovering much new evidence about the history of transport', the authors declared in their preface, 'but seeks particularly to draw into a connected account the many writings that have accumulated on this subject in the last century and more.' These

4

words – indeed the entire text – stood unaltered apart from a few factual corrections, in the Pelican paperback of 1974.

Philip Bagwell's *Transport Revolution from 1770*, which appeared in that year, was at a disadvantage commercially in costing three times as much even in paperback as the Pelican edition of Dyos and Alcroft (£3 instead of £1) and academically in treating by backward glance pre-1770 transport developments which we later came to see were of considerable significance. On the other hand, it did include much original research which the author had undertaken specifically to offset the undue emphasis then being placed on canals and railways. Having just been engaged in the rewriting of Savage for a new edition of that book, I happened to be in a very good – perhaps a unique – position to gauge the measure of Philip's achievement. He had not only combed through the earlier established references but had also tracked down many out-of-the-way contemporary writings and made good use of literary sources. He had indicated what could be discovered about regular transport services from urban directories, a line of investigation to be taken further by Chartres and Turnbull. He must have spent many hours poring over the minutes of evidence, as well as the final reports, of many parliamentary committees. Above all, he had worked among primary manuscript sources among the Public Records, the Post Office Records, at the House of Lords Record Office and in local record offices. Here was enterprise and application beyond the normal call of duty for a text – book writer.

The new book benefited particularly from original work on coastal shipping, especially after steam-powered vessels were used. Having read Philip's article on Post Office packets across the Irish Sea, which had taken pride of place in the first issue of *Maritime History*, the more discriminating readers of the new text book made straight for the third chapter in which he brought out the significance of the new technology when applied to vessels in all Britain's coastal waters. So powerful was this competition that it continued to influence the setting of many railway fares and rates for the rest of the nineteenth century. Only after 1906 did tonnages from overseas shipping entering British ports exceed that of the coasters. For Philip, the pioneer voyage from Glasgow to London via Dublin undertaken by George Dodd in the 75-ton paddle steamer *Thames* in 1815 was an achievement as notable in its context as were the much-publicised Rainhill locomotive trials of 1829.

Because of his 1770 *terminus a quo*, the book hardly does full justice, however, to the importance of coastal shipping, much of it penetrating up estuaries and linking with river traffic farther upstream, before the coming of steam. It does not make enough of Willan and, in particular of the maps showing the growing area of England and Wales already within fifteen miles of navigable water even in the early years of the eighteenth century. These rivers and the long coastline gave the country a considerable transport cost advantage over its European competitors, particularly for the carriage of heavy, bulky goods of low value. If more emphasis is placed upon this efficient water transport system, capable of carrying considerable tonnages per vessel and enabling London to grow and exercise economic domination over the rest of the kingdom, the less important the subsequent canals and narrow boats appear. These deadwater navigations were undoubtedly important, as Philip emphasises, in the opening up of areas unserved by navigable rivers, such as the St Helens area in south-west Lancashire to which the first of the modern canals, the Sankey Brook Navigation, provided waterway access from 1757 and, more obviously, the 'unusually busy Midlands . . . perched on the central Pennine watershed, over 400 feet above sea level'; but otherwise canals usually supplemented a very efficient river and coastal waterway system which, significantly, often survived them. Even more significant, perhaps, is the fact that nearly half a century was to elapse after 1757 before London needed to be linked by canal with the canal system to the north; and even then its river and coastal traffic continued to grow.

The book also underestimates the amount of wheeled traffic by road. Philip, a great admirer of the Webbs' writings on industrial relations, seems to have been too easily persuaded by their *Story of the King's Highway* that piecemeal turnpiking did not provide an effective, through system. Although Albert is mentioned in the bibliography, he is not cited in notes to the chapter on 'Road Transport before the Railway Age', although the Webbs receive several mentions. The Turnbull thesis is neither listed nor cited, though an earlier article on 'Pickford between 1830 and 1850' is included in the bibliography of a subequent chapter on 'Road and Water Transport in the Railway Age'.

This, like the one on nineteenth-century coastal shipping, is another bullseye. Here the continued importance of horse-drawn road, as well as water, transport receives full attention. There were still many roads not paralleled by railway lines; and when more branch railways were built, as well as the last of the main lines, more horse-drawn traffic was created to and from the new railway stations and goods yards. Added to which was the road traffic in the rapidly-growing towns. These points are all stressed. So is the coming of the electric tramcar and the internal combustion engine, though its predecessor, the pedal cycle, receives less than its just deserts. With some of the indigestible statistics made more palatable by helpful diagrams, the chapter manages to foreshadow much subsequent research. So does its successor which deals with motor transport from its hesitant, experimental beginnings before 1900 until 1939, with a graph which continues the series and shows that the Motor Age really dates from only about 1950. Those who have struggled subsequently through the thickets of confusing historical writing on this subject can only stand back and admire the Bagwell treatment. In its earlier stages the industry in Britain was harmed more by financial rogues than the Red Flag Acts and hampered, as elsewhere in Europe, by insufficient social depth of demand. With the growth of road freight transport Philip is much less concerned: a pity, for, from the 1920s, the small-scale, often one-man, road haulier was starting to provide a door-to-door service over medium, as well as short, distances, with which the railways could not compete at any price. The social advantages bestowed by the spread of heavier passenger vehicles – buses and coaches – and the great boost they gave to public transport before the 1950s is well covered. It is only since the rapid rise of car ownership from the 1950s that the internal combustion engine has failed to provide more and more travel for the majority.

In the final chapter covering 1939–1970 nearly 100 pages in length, Philip's commitment to railways and railwaymen, about whom he has written impressively elsewhere, emerges most clearly. If the main lines had been electrified during the 1930s when money was cheap, he argues British Railways 'would have been in an exceptionally strong position to provide fast, reliable and inexpensive freight and passenger services . . . The present nonsensical situation of an under-utilised railway system existing alongside a grossly overcrowded road network need not have arisen'. He begs the question of lack of door-to-door goods service and the continued technical improvement and greater size and efficiency of road freight vehicles; but his arguments are widely held and forcefully expressed. Motorway competition, built up with considerable sums of public money, provided no long-term solution. And here enters Philip's basic, caring philosophy: 'For those who consider that the quality of life is more important than the maximisation of individual wealth and the Gross National Product, the transformation of Britain's roads is regarded as a menace rather than a blessing. Motorways do not merely transfer traffic from over-congested inferior roads; they generate new traffic . . . The crucial question, of course, is what happens to this greatly increased volume of traffic before it entered and after it left the motorway? . . . Flows of traffic between major conurbations were speeded up; but only at the expense of greater congestion and slower traffic flows within the urban areas'. 'In the densely populated Britain of the 1970s', he concludes,' 'it was every bit as important that welfare and amenity considerations should influence transport policy. Whether or not life in Britain in the year 2000 will be pleasanter than it was in 1970 will depend very much on the wisdom of transport planners in the years which lie between'.

This conclusion remained unaltered in the 1988 edition of the book. The new final chapter there, a well-documented lament about the continued relative decline of public transport by train and its absolute decline by bus and coach, reads like an appendix to the original work. Philip's main concern is for the young, the old and and those who do not own, or have ready access to, private transport. Their lives are made less agreeable because more of the better-off run their own cars. But even the privileged are now perceiving that private transport is posing greater problems for them, too. Travel in towns at certain hours is increasingly unsatisfactory. Even motorways are becoming overloaded at times. For all the environment is being damaged by noise and atmospheric pollution.

The Transport Revolution From 1770 marked a great stride forward as a general survey of Britain's transport history. It is still very well worth reading as such and remains now, as in 1974, a valuable tract for the times. As Wray Vamplew put it in his review (*Economic History Review*, May 1975): 'It may not be the type of work one is reluctant to put down but it certainly deserves to be taken up'.

2

Professor Symonds' Tour, 1790

Gordon Mingay

Arthur Young's agricultural tours of the later eighteenth century have long been a major source for our knowledge of the farming of the period, and indeed more than the farming, for Young commented in passing on the state of the roads and the quality of the inns in which he stayed. Young's tours are justly famous, but what is less generally known is that Young had a longstanding friend whose own interest in agriculture led him not only to undertake the editing of much of Young's work and its preparation for the press, but also a major tour of his own. This friend was the Rev. John Symonds (1729–1807), Professor of Modern History at Cambridge, whose residence was situated close to Bury St Edmunds and thus within a very few miles of Young's home at Bradfield Combust.

Symonds was a keen amateur agriculturist, who like Young consorted with leading figures in the farming world, entertaining in his home the celebrated Robert Bakewell on at least one occasion. Both Symonds and Young were members of a select group of intellectuals who in 1782 dined every Thursday at Ickworth, some three miles from Bury, with Frederick Hervey, fourth earl of Bristol and bishop of Derry. In consequence the Cambridge professor came to be Young's closest friend, and they met frequently not only at Ickworth but also at Symonds' beautiful new house at St Edmund's Hill, about a mile from Bury.

From his correspondence and other sources Symonds appears a typical eighteenth-century clergyman and academic; friendly, easy-going, but perhaps something of a bore.[1] We get some intimate glimpses of him from the journal of François de la Rochefoucauld, a young French visitor to England, who in 1784 spent the best part of a year in Bury St Edmunds, together with his younger brother and his friend and tutor, M. de Lazowski. Symonds was one of the first people in the neighbourhood to notice and entertain the visitors. Subsequently they moved from their lodgings in the town to stay with him in his home as paying guests. Symonds went to endless trouble to please the Frenchmen, made them free of his excellent library and took the time every day to correct their translations and compositions. The visitors, however, found life at St Edmund's Hill somewhat restricting. The meal hours were rigid – nine o'clock for breakfast, three for dinner and nine for supper – and at nine the house was locked up for the night so they could not take a walk after that hour. Further, the tea-time receptions given by Symonds every Tuesday were such formal occasions as to prove tedious for the Frenchmen – few young people came – although Arthur Young's version of these occasions is rather different: he recounted that Symonds was in the habit of giving a 'weekly ball when the Frenchmen were with him, and these parties were uncommonly agreeable'.[2]

Not unlike some academics of the present day, the professor was not well-informed on the regulations of his university; to answer the Frenchmen's questions about these he was 'obliged to have recourse to old books, read up the origins of the university, etc.' The visitors went to Cambridge in the hope of finding 'someone there better informed' on the syllabus of studies, 'the most interesting subject'. They found life in the Symonds household excellent for improving their English, but rather unfortunate in some other respects. They were 'obliged to listen daily, and sometimes twice a day' to their host's recollections of a long journey he had made in Italy some twenty years earlier, a narrative that he was preparing for publication. 'One may imagine the vanity of a man who falls half-asleep after dinner and has everyone yawning with sitting so long at table.'[3]

Symonds' interest in agriculture was such that he contributed no fewer than nine articles to the first six volumes of Young's *Annals of Agriculture*.

---

[1] John G. Gazley, *The Life of Arthur Young, 1741–1820* (Philadelphia, 1973), pp. 147–8.

[2] Ibid., pp. 176–7; Norman Scarfe, ed., *A Frenchman's Year in Suffolk, 1784* (Woodbridge, Suffolk), 1988, p. 100.

[3] Scarfe, op. cit., pp. 94–95, 99–100.

One of these was a satirical discussion of turnip cultivation in France, while a second dealt briefly with some experiments with different fertilizers carried out by Symonds on his own lawn. The remainder harked back to the Italian tour he had made in the 1760s, discussing at considerable length the irrigation systems, soils, chief crops and climate of that country.[4]

Symonds was fond of travel, as his journeys to Italy and France reveal, and it was in the summer and autumn of 1790, at the advanced age of sixty-one, that he resolved to make a long tour through eastern England to southern Scotland, returning by the western side of England and the midlands. His tour began in East Anglia, proceeded through Yorkshire and Northumberland to Edinburgh and Glasgow, and then turned southwards again via the Lake District, Liverpool, Manchester, Cheshire, the Peak District, Leicestershire and Nottinghamshire. Subsequently he made a separate tour through Wales and western England. Symonds' journal of the northern England and the Scottish tour (as of his Welsh one) took the form of a series of lengthy letters addressed to Arthur Young, and these letters have survived among the Young papers in the British Library.[5] So far as this writer is aware, none of these letters has yet appeared in printed form, either in full or in part. They were not in fact highly circumscribed, for Symonds' observations were by no means entirely concerned with agricultural matters, but included a large variety of interesting comments on the considerable number of towns and districts through which he travelled, throwing a good deal of light on the conditions of the time.

Perhaps the best way to convey within a brief compass the flavour of this little-known journey, is to select a number of brief representative quotations, in the hope that the reader will find them as instructive and entertaining as this writer has done.

The Diary

8 July: Cambridge to Huntingdon

White-faced sheep made their appearance soon after we passed through the turn-pike gate – fallows in bad condition for the most part to

---

[4] Gazley, op. cit., pp. 158–59.
[5] B.L. Add. MS 35, 127.

Huntingdon: wheat good, and barley better than yesterday, but the whole bean-crop a prey to weeds – Saw at Fenstanton a pigeon-house, like a Campanile, erected lately by the parson, who, with his parishioners, looks upon it as a wonderful flight of architecture – Huntingdon has the appearance of a new town, having been lately paved – Slept at the Wheatsheaf at Alconbury, and had the good fortune to have a parlour opposite to the great road, which gave me an opportunity of seeing all the waggons, carts, coaches, chaises, whiskies, gigs, and buggies that stopped at the inn; and I can hardly determine, whether mine eye was most delighted, or mine understanding most improved by the conversation which I heard.

12 July: Folkingham, Lincolnshire

The little market-town of Folkingham stands on a great ascent. The trustees of Sir Gilbert Heathcote, a minor, have lately purchased the Lordship, and are determined to make the town considerable, if possible. They have removed the Town-hall and many other nuisances; almost entirely rebuilt the chief inn, which is now the best on this road; repaired many other houses, rebuilt several, and are now preparing new shambles; and they go so far as to engage to contribute to the expense, if any other proprietor will slate or tile his house, and take off the thatch. Such spirited exertions are very uncommon; and, what is still more singular, the leading man among the trustees is Sir Gilbert's steward.

14 July: To Leeds and Wakefield, Yorkshire

A stranger must needs be terribly disappointed in viewing the interior of Lincoln, which enjoys so proud a situation; the lower town being full of filth, and broken causeways; and the great street, which leads into the upper, and is not above 12 feet wide, being so steep and dangerous, that scarcely any carriage ever is seen in it.

Here is a better kind of irrigation; for a connoisseur has just gravely informed me, that Great Tom [the famous bell of Lincoln cathedral] is capable of holding 420 gallons of *Ale-measure*. Besides, the musical tones are enchanting; and it is a wonderful advantage to conversation, that you can hardly hear your neighbour speak, when Tom proclaims the hour of the day.

Hitherto in Yorkshire 2 horses only ploughing, and no oxen – Boys and men employed in picking up the dung on the road in little wheelbarrows and baskets – most of the country inclosed, and no part of it ugly – dined at the vast town of Leeds, full of wealth, population, and filth, having been not in the least improved, since I was here 28 years ago – Between Leeds and Wakefield saw a very fine field of cabbages, which however seemed improper for so light a soil. Much teazle for their manufactures, but too often choken by weeds – Wakefield is greatly improved by its new pavement; 2 or 3 spacious streets, with many large new-built houses, but no *totalité*, without which a town is nothing. When we see the quantity of coal-pits and inland navigations in this part of Yorkshire, we cannot wonder that the manufacturers removed hither out of Suffolk.

29 July: Morpeth, Northumberland

Morpeth receives no advantage in point of beauty from its river, but receives much from the pretty hills by which it is encircled. There is a very considerable fair here every week for sheep and black cattle brought from both sides of the Tweed. These are chiefly sent to Newcastle by the butchers of Morpeth, who are supposed to be one-half of the town, and who go to Newcastle to kill these animals. This intercourse enables Morpeth to support 2 post-coaches which set out every day for Newcastle.

31 July: Berwick upon Tweed, Berwickshire

I have now made 402 miles without the least pain or even difficulty to my horse; sixty-three of which I have made in Northumberland, where I have not seen a scrap of flax, hemp, or cabbages; and tares in one parish only, not far from Belford; those were spring-ones; for they told me, that winter-tares had been given up some years, because they never proved so forward as clover – no expense spared in liming for wheat, especially when the collieries and lime-kilns are near each other – potatoes in great abundance, but not half so well-managed as in Yorkshire – the country almost entirely denuded of trees (to use a Johnsonian phrase) except recent plantations intended chiefly for ornament; nor do I remember to have seen what ought to be dignified with the name of a wood, since I left the neighbourhood of Leeds. Churches and chapels of ease seem to be as rare as trees, so that I should suspect many of the peasants to be pagan.

1 August: Press Inn, Coldingham, Berwickshire

My landlord pleased me much by his inn, which is as neat & decent, & as well served, as any in England; but he did not please me less by taking a walk with me, & showing me his own farm of about 200 acres, which he hires of Mr Hume. His course of crops is as follows: 1. Fallow 2. Wheat 3. Turnips 4. Barley with clover & Rye-grass 5. Clover 6. Dᵒ. 7. Oats. As an Antifallowist, I could not help remonstrating with him; but he assured me, that he and all the neighbouring farmers had tried wheat after clover, which did not succeed; and that they found liming answered best for it, though the lime was brought 14 miles distant. I saw very fine oats upon what had been moors, & stout barley & clover upon what had been heaths – Turnips are sowed in drills; hoed twice at the expense of 5, 6, or 7s. an acre, & the horse-hoeing is solely at the expense of the farmer, who hath it done immediately after they have been hoed by hand – They give labourers from 10d. to 1s. in winter, & from 15d. to 18d. in summer. Harvest-work however is cheap, a shilling a day with breakfast & dinner, & a moderate allowance of beer. From this inn we see nothing else than a stable hired by the owners of the mail-coach, & a small hut which is distinguished by the honourable title of a Post-house; but for 5 miles together we had in view a great number of detached farm-houses singularly neat, & not unhandsome kirks.

3 August: 18 August: Edinburgh

In approaching to the city, we meet with more gentlemen's carriages, more stage-coaches, more carts, & men on horseback, than near Paris; but the road is much inferior. All the tolls from Berwick to Edinburgh ought to be doubled.

I had heard much of the new city of Edinburgh, as it is called; but it has much surpassed my expectations, as other things have fallen short of them. Figure to yourself three streets in breadth from a half to a third of a mile, running parallel to one another, built of a good-coloured stone. One of the outer streets is on the banks of the Forth, & the other commands the old town, castle, etc. than which nothing can appear more romantic. The middle, or George street, is 100ft broad from house to house, & 60ft if we allow 10f. for the palisades, & 10 more for the *trottoir*. I have not seen such a street in any city whatever. The whole is terminated E. & W. by 2 squares, one of which called St Andrew's, about as large as

Cavendish square, is completed, & the other is just begun. Many very fine houses, with good architecture, in three streets, & not one, tho' designed for tradesmen, is unhandsome. Detached parts in London, or other cities, might possibly be put together to equal them; but such a *continued* mass of excellent buildings I never beheld. You will naturally ask, whence could this expense be supplied? It could not arise from the increase of wealth in the inhabitants, for though Edinburgh hath about 100,000, taking in Leith & its other suburbs, & though it has some manufactures of woollen cloths, stuffs, & satins, yet it cannot justly be called a trading city; nor can it be ascribed to the flourishing state of the university; for £40,000 a year, which the students & their friends are supposed to spend, could not afford a sufficient fund. The truth is, it is the consequence of Oriental wealth. Numberless petty nabobs, whose names we never hear of, have brought home from £40 to £70, or £80,000 during these last 30 years. Their younger sons having had no house or property of their own, sought for a residence in the capital, which could not be furnished by the ordinary buildings.

16 August: Linlithgow, W. Lothian

We returned by the same road to see the Carron works, which it would be useless and idle to attempt to describe; for, besides that they are well known, an account of them would employ a long letter. Let it suffice to say, that when I was there in 1762, 2 years after the establishment of them, they were confined within a very narrow compass; whereas they are now in a precinct of above three-fourths of a mile, inclosed by a wall from 30 to 40ft in height; and there are so many houses & even streets about them, that they have the appearance of no small town – that the chief vent of the goods is in the N. of Europe – that there is a cut made from the Carron into the precinct, whither the lighters come up to carry them to the Forth – that every thing is made there without commission, except cannons and shot – that they buy all the old Dutch cannons, & break them into pieces, to work over again; and that they never fail to work their own manufactures over again, if they happen to discover the least flaw in them – that they cannot succeed in casting without using 3 different sorts of iron stone of their own in equal quantities, and without using a fourth part of Lancashire Ore, for they cannot find the same sort of Ore in Scotland – in fine, that on an average 100 tons of coal are consumed every day.

On the Move

25 August: Dumfries, Dumfriesshire

Near Kilpatrick was a small piece of turnips, the first which I had seen for the last hundred miles. They had been sown broadcast, were close to one another, & choked with weeds; and the farmer, to obviate these difficulties, had ploughed furrows among them, that they might have had the same advantage as those sown in drills; but the rows left in this manner had not been thinned. When I was near Perth, I stepped out of my chaise to talk with a farmer, who was practising this curious mode of husbandry; and he very gravely assured me, that the English knew not how to manage turnips.

1 September: Longtown, Cumberland

To Gretna Green the plain is chiefly inclosed with hedges of white thorn, but, like the former, in bad condition, as are the turnips & potatoes – The view of the Solway Firth cannot make this country appear tolerably agreeable – Gretna Green is distinguishable at a great distance, both in England & Scotland, by the trees that surround it, which ought to be called 'The Italian grove'. The chief house in the village is an inn, in which marriages are often both solemnised, & consummated. Yesterday a gentle pair was here imparadised on one another's arms. The priest has been unjustly represented to be a blacksmith, which he complains of; whereas he is a tallow-chandler, and is said to be something inebriated, when he performs the ceremony. He is called here *the Bishop*, not only on account of his reverend aspect, but that he may be distinguished from a cobbler in the village, who has presumed to break in on his clerical emoluments, by tying also the sacred knot.

18–21 September: Kendal, Westmorland

Kendal is certainly well built & well paved, but cannot be called a handsome town – No street, except the high street, which deserves to be mentioned; and even that in the middle is interrupted by a row of shops & houses. The manufacture of knit stockings, for which it was once so famous, is much on the decline; but those of cotton, & linsey-woolsey are very flourishing; and tanneries in great abundance – A few years ago they obtained an act of Parlmt. to inclose their common, which was far from being productive;

16

this is now let for £170 pr ann: and the money thrown into the poor's rate towards the aid of those only, who have landed property. These persons are still much more materially assisted by the mode of assessment; for all are rated for their stock in trade, generally about a fifth of the supposed value. I saw the four last quarterly assessments for Mr Wilson's house; and all of them together amounted but to fourteen pence halfpenny in the pound – Though there are about 7,500 inhabitants, there are not more on an average than 100 in the workhouse, because the children are early sent to the cotton mills. Whether this be a good plan of education, is matter of dispute; for it renders them unfit for any other employment, & their promiscuous way of living together often provokes love-adventures.

26–29 September: Liverpool

Liverpool has been so much enlarged & improved, since I was there in 1762, that it had the appearance of a new town. The Corporation have demolished entire streets, in order to open a free communication to the exchange; and a regular & handsome mode of building is adopted in the outskirts, as well as in the central parts – As the fort built under the directions of the D. of Richmond is ridiculous, and does the nation great discredit, so the Workhouse reflects an honour upon the town. This vast fabric is seated upon an eminence, which commands a prospect not much inferior to that from M. Edgecumbe – about 1,000 paupers in summer, & 1,200 in winter, supported at the expense of 18d. to 20d. a week – meat 4 times a week – the beer made partly of malt liquor, & partly of treacle, which, they say, is better, & goes farther – I saw the bread-account, whence it appeared, that during the last 8 months, they had consumed 11,078 loaves weighing 28lb. each, made of an equal mixture of barley and wheat – As soon as children can spin well, they quit the house, being sure of finding employment in the neighbourhood of Manchester. Every one, who is able to work, is obliged to follow his respective trade, if it be compatible with the house: whence there are not only weavers, & persons of a similar denomination, but also coopers, carpenters, blacksmiths &c. so that it is a little republic within itself – The poor's rates are extremely moderate, not more than 2s. in the pound upon an average. They raised this year half a crown, that produced the enormous sum of £16,000; but this extraordinary assessment was made to liquidate the remaining part of the debt incurred for this building; it having cost not less than £14,000. It is usual to rate no one higher for stock in trade than for £500, nor lower than for £50. 4s.

8d. in the pound discharge the poor's-rates, church-rates, & surveyor's, & Easter offerings, and all parliamentary duties whatever, which is not, I believe, the case with many towns or villages in England.

1–5 October: Manchester

From Warrington I went to Manchester in the Duke of Bridgewater's pacquet-boat. There are two passing every day between these towns, and are supposed to yield together a clear profit of £2,000 a year. During the greatest part of the way we were in Cheshire, where the inclosures are small, & fringed with trees – passed by the little village of Lymm, which is a Matlock in miniature; by Dunham, the seat of L. Stamford, where the Duke was put to an enormous expense, being obliged to pay for ever £9 yearly for every acre of land, and to raise it 27 feet that the water might be kept on a level; and by Altrincham, where are some cotton-looms – May I be permitted to anticipate the order of my Journal, by mentioning, that I did not neglect to visit Worsley? But I found there no considerable additions, yet enough to convince me, that he is the greatest dealer in coal, & timber that I know.

What has been done at Liverpool by the Corporation, has been effected at Manchester by voluntary donations. A few years ago £11,000 were subscribed & immediately paid for the embellishment of the town; and as that sum was found to be inadequate £7,000 were soon afterwards added. Hence the openings to the exchange, King's street, & Moseley street, which is to be terminated by a beautiful little church designed by Wyatt, & half finished – Dr Percival informed me, that, according to a census very lately taken, the number of inhabitants amounted to 53,000; so wonderfully has the population increased since the publication of the Northern Tour! Yet there is a complaint of a want of hands, which strongly marks out their flourishing state. Wisely despising the absurd law of settlements, they receive whoever will work; but give 10s. to anyone who apprehends a vagrant, & £40 if the person who lodged him is convicted. You may imagine that some attention is paid to the police, since there are not more than 230 inns in this vast extent of ground – The poor's rates, however, are twice as much as at Liverpool. Stock in trade is rated very little, houses & ware-houses being the great object, & assessed at two-thirds of their value. Dr Percival told me, that he paid £180 p.a.: for the rent of his house, and was rated at £120. Are there many instances of country-physicians paying so much rent?

As to the extent of the trade & manufactures at Manchester, I find myself at a loss what to say; yet as I had the good fortune to be recommended to cool & sensible men, who carry on a great deal of business, I may speak with less diffidence. Mr Samuel Taylor assured me in the presence of Dr Percival, who agreed to it, that the goods at Manchester ready for sale, were in general worth 6 millions sterling. They have scarce any vent in Portugal; little in Spain; a very good one in Italy; but the great & most beneficial export is by Hull to Germany, where they force their way in spite of all the regulations & prohibitions of the different states; whence it is, that it is become an established custom for every house of credit to send a son or nephew into Germany, to learn the language of that country – The African trade is likewise very considerable. They have factors on the coast of Africa merely to know from the natives the patterns which they like best, that are worked accordingly at Manchester – I saw Mr Drinkwater's patterns of fustians, which were wonderfully beautiful. His father was a yeoman, & left him about £300, which is now converted into £70,000, though he is scarcely more than 40 years old. Mr T. told me, that it cost some manufacturers from £300 to £400 p.a.: purely for patterns which they sent abroad; and I can easily credit it, as Mr Drinkwater's roll of patterns could not fall much short of 20 feet in length – There are some houses whose riders cost them £1,000 a year.

Upon the whole, Manchester appears to be as thriving as possible. The language of the manufacturers is, 'we want no encouragement, from government; we desire no other favour, than to be let alone'.

18 October: Cromford, Derbyshire

The road to Kedleston leads us near Sir R. Arkwright's three cotton-mills in Matlock & Cromford; one of which is so large as to have 200 windows. The sapient knight thought he had the same skill in building a private house, and therefore ventured to plan for himself. The situation is truly romantic, as it stands upon the Derwent; but in order to leave his lawn undiminished, his genius prompted him to cut away part of a rock at an immense expense, and to insert his house into its place, by which means the back front is almost totally devoid of light. The principal façade is eminently ridiculous; designed to be built castle-wise but all modern, except the battlement & four towers, which are so small, that they actually look like cannons painted white. Another proof of his taste appeared in the useless walls which he erected; so numerous, that if extended in a straight line, they would be more than half a mile in length. When he sent for Eames, the faint emulator of Browne, to embellish his grounds (which by the by are not above 12 acres) this artist refused to work, unless the walls were demolished. Impossible! said the knight, I shall be laughed at by all the world. Very true, Sir; but is it not better to be laughed at once, than to be derided every moment of your life, which must infallibly happen, if my advice be not followed? This reproof had its effect, and the walls are falling by degrees.

20 October: Dishley, Leicestershire at Robert Bakewell's farm

The tup-trade brings into Dishley & its neighbourhood about £10,000 a year; and B. who had just examined his accounts, said, that the year 1790 had been more profitable to him than any preceding year. What do you think of a Tup-Society? So many have of late favoured this employment, that they talk of establishing one: The fair sex will probably be not averse from entering into it.

B. will not suffer himself to be considered as a farmer, but only as a breeder of cattle; yet the amazing number of stacks in his yard does not less show the produce of his farm, than a cursory look will convince one of the good management of it. The stubbles as clean as possible – the turnips excellent – & the N. American cabbages, or drum-headed, as called in Leicestershire, at the rate of 40 tons pr acre – But what pleased me most, were the advantages derived from flooding the lands. B. hath a brook of his own, by which he waters about 150 acres; & would water a hundred more, if the brook were sufficient; but at different times of the year it serves the use of the public, by feeding the Loughborough canal. There are three fields called in the old writings Hassock close, Rush close, & Rough meadow, which have now entirely changed their natures. These & others which were not worth more than 13s. an acre, are now worth from 35 to 50 – B. shewed me a meadow of his neighbour, which he advised him to flood, & offered him the use of his water; but the sagacious farmer declined it, alleging, that his sheep would have nothing to eat in winter. What a melancholy reflection on this island, that I should travel 1,100 miles, and not see a single instance of irrigations before my arrival at Dishley?

22 October: Bunny, Nottinghamshire

Slept at Bunny, the dirtiest village in England, if not in Europe; but rendered illustrious by being the residence of the late Sir T. Parkyns, who immortalised himself by his epitaph, not caring to trust his name to ordinary scriblers. He records of himself 'that he studied Physic Galenic & Paracelsic for the benefit of his neighbours; and that he had a competent knowledge of most parts of the Mathematics, especially Architecture & Hydraulics, and drawing all his plans without an architect.' Had he no better success in Physic than in architecture, it may reasonably be supposed that he killed most of his parishioners, for the additions which he made to his house abound with the grossest absurdities.

29 October: Newark, Nottinghamshire

1211 miles without the least accident, and all well – Two years ago a knowing friend advised me to get new wheels for my carriage; but behold! They have stood this journey admirably well.

The Voice of The West Riding: Promoters and Supporters of a Provincial Unstamped Newspaper, 1833–34

John Halstead

The history of the cheap popular radical press before Chartism tends to be dominated by the history of the London unstamped. This is as it should be. London, as the major metropolis and the seat of power and government, produced the vast majority of such newspapers, whether in the first post-war wave launched by William Cobbett's *Address to Journeymen and Labourers* (1816) or in the second illegal newspaper wave following the appearance of William Carpenter's *Political Letters* and Henry Hetherington's *Penny Papers for the People* (October, 1830). London also produced the most important newspapers; perhaps most notably, Thomas Wooler's *Black Dwarf* (1817) and Hetherington's *Poor Man's Guardian* (July, 1831). It is not surprising therefore that of the two standard histories, Hollis's is a study of the London unstamped press; and though there is a wider range of reference to provincial newspapers in the other major work by Wiener, London people, papers and associations appear to feature most strongly.[1]

Yet, the role of the provinces was not negligible. The judgement that the first wave of unstamped journalism was sustained by the provincial

---

[1] Patricia Hollis, *The Pauper Press: A Study in Working-Class Radicalism of the 1830s* (Oxford, 1970); Joel H. Wiener, *The War of the Unstamped: The Movement to Repeal the British Newspaper Tax, 1830–1836* (Ithaca, 1969).

radicalism of the the Hampden Clubs, the Political Protestants and the Great Northern Union, whereas the radical mainspring of the second was the London National Union of the Working Classes, is certainly sound,[2] but this large motif has its small coda. The flow of radical political intelligence from the metropolis to the provinces was started and organised in 1830 by James Watson, a Yorkshireman. Carpenter was prompted to produce his *Political Letters* in 1830 by anger at the government's 'selective repression' of John Doherty's Lancashire-based *United Trades Co-operative Journal*.[3] And among the provincial unstamped newspapers of the post-1830 wave, at least one, Huddersfield's *Voice of the West Riding*, has attracted quite a lot of attention.

In this essay, the character of the paper and aspects of the career and radicalism of its publisher are re-examined. Some apparent misconceptions may be corrected and some new light is cast on Hobson's career. The main main purpose of the essay, however, is to reduce the hitherto almost complete emphasis on the association between Hobson and the *Voice* by drawing attention to previously unused sources about the newspaper's supporters and promoters.

Weiner was impressed by the tone of many passages in the *Voice* which displayed 'extreme class animosity' and 'class bitterness'; its interesting character as 'one of the liveliest and most controversial of the illicit provincial journals' was complemented by its 'factory journal' function. Under Hobson's 'editorship' the *Voice* forged a similar link between 'the factory and newspaper issues' in Huddersfield as that provided for the south Lancashire factory hours movement by John Doherty's *Poor Man's Advocate*.[4] Weiner's text exudes an enthusiasm which is absent from that of Hollis. She chooses to note, correctly, that the 'sickly' paper was of limited importance. It only circulated in and around Huddersfield, and the neighbouring Yorkshire towns of Bradford, Leeds, Halifax and Barnsley. The prosecution of the publisher almost certainly

---

[2] Hollis, *Pauper Press*, p. 99.

[3] Ibid., pp. 110 and 103–4. Cf. J.R. Sanders, 'Working-class Movements in the West Riding Textile District 1829 to 1839, with Emphasis upon Local Leadership and Organization' (Manchester University Ph.D thesis, 1984), p. 435, on Watson. Cf. Joel H. Wiener, *Radicalism and Freethought in Nineteenth-Century Britain: The Life of Richard Carlile* (Westport, Conn., 1983), pp. 86–88, on Carlile's northern shopmen. Some new circumstantial evidence in support of early northern interest in a free press is presented below.

[4] Weiner, *War of the Unstamped*, pp. 189–90 and 216–17. The reference to Hobson's 'editorship' is on p. 216, but see the discussion below.

saved the newspaper from failure, for as it noted itself, 'Our bitter enemies, in the excess of their hostility, have not only lent us crutches but stilts'.[5]

Yet, from all the prosecutions against the promoters of the unstamped, the speech of Joshua Hobson, the publisher of the *Voice*, to the gentlemen of the bench of magistrates at Huddersfield on 6 August 1833, was among the most widely circulated.[6] Hollis reprints the speech, as reported in *Man* on 18 August 1833.[7] It provides a fitting preface to the main section of her book's treatment of the unstamped press, for Hobson was a fine writer as well as an impressive political organiser. The speech bears repetition.

Hobson explained to the bench, with fine sarcasm, why he had taken it upon himself to break what they were 'pleased to call the law':

> I was induced to publish . . . because a paper was wanted to support the rights and interests of the order and class to which it is my pride to belong, it being notorious that their just privileges were not only left unadvocated, but absolutely denied.

The object of the paper was to:

> . . . teach the productive classes the means by which they might extricate themselves from their degraded state of thraldom, and place society upon a basis where every individual member of the social brotherhood should enjoy his just rights and no more.

Its further object, and its distinctive function with respect to much of the rest of the unstamped, was, 'the exposure and reformation of local as well

---

[5] Hollis, *Pauper Press*, p. 117; *Voice of the West Riding* (hereafter *VWR*) 17 August 1833.

[6] Reports of the speech appeared in *VWR*, 10 August 1833; the *Halifax Express* (copy in the Place newspaper collection, set. 70, f. 304, cited in Wiener, *The War of the Unstamped*, p. 126n.); the *True Sun*, 8 August 1833; *Leeds Intelligencer*, 10 August 1833; and the *Leeds Mercury*, 10 August 1833; as well as in *Man*, 18 August 1833.

[7] Hollis, *Pauper Press*, p. 94. Also in P. Hollis, *Class and Class Conflict in Nineteenth-Century England, 1815–50* (London, 1973), p. 147.

as national abuse'. The local emphasis continued as he went on with the recital of objects:

> To drag the tyrant and the hypocrite from their den of infamy, and to show up the hideous monsters to the gaze and virtuous indignation of every good man in the community – to teach the sanctified knaves they could not with impunity practise those vices which they affect so loudly to condemn – to learn the oppressors of the poor that though they might for a time pass unnoticed, and be allowed to practise their unholy deeds unmolested, yet there was a point which they could not pass, when the Argus eyes of the great moral corrector should be directed upon them, and every movement and action of their lives watched and noted for adoption by others if virtuous, or rejection if vicious.

The passage has a fine rhetorical ring and the classical reference to the hundred eyes of Argus, in the service of the 'great moral corrector', seems well-calculated to strike terror. Argus is the People: they have a multitude of eyes and it is their sense of moral outrage and their actions, such as the exclusive dealing which Hobson supported, that should provide the correction. The image works at the religious and secular levels. The 'great' moral corrector would surely remind his listeners of the Great Jehovah of the Old Testament and much fire and brimstone preaching, while the classical allusion would conjure up a republican *virtù* that is more directly hinted at in the concluding justification of a press:

> I contend . . . that the printing and publishing of such a paper, is not a violation of any moral principle, but, on the contrary, one of the most virtuous actions that man can do, that of doing good to his species.

The suggestion of a classical republican sense of the duties of citizenship was surely deliberate and not an accidental consequence of similarity between the English word and its Latin root. We know almost nothing of Hobson's reading, but bearing in mind that his prosecution was prompted by an attack upon a 'drunken parson' and the educative moral purpose of his paper's war on all forms of corruption, one wonders whether something of Francis Hutcheson's *System of Moral Philosophy*, or of other writings from the classical republican strain of English political thought, had reached him.[8] Whatever the case on this point, it is difficult to resist the conclusion that there was much in Hobson's character which served to lift his prosecution and imprisonment above the level of the ordinary.

Certainly Hobson's incarceration in the gaol for common criminals at Wakefield attracted national and parliamentary attention.[9] And as Sanders has been perhaps the first to note, his treatment made him a leading figure – 'ensured him a special martyr's place' – in West Riding radicalism.[10] It is here perhaps, rather than in the short life and limited circulation of the paper, that the significance of the *Voice* truly resides.

Yorkshire of course, as the most populous and largest county of England, had had a prominent place in the plethora of reform movements from the late eighteenth century onwards. The placing of Hobson at the centre of Yorkshire radicalism after his release from prison has to be seen in the context of the political importance of the county.

After the failure of the *Voice*, Hobson first attempted, from his Huddersfield base, to continue flying the drooping flag of the West Riding's radical journalism. He took responsibility for the Leeds *'Demagogue'*, conducting it, in a clear echo of his speech before the Huddersfield magistrates, under the new title of the *Argus and 'Demagogue'*. This new venture also was a failure.[11] He then moved to Leeds and successfully established an important radical publishing house.

There is some uncertainty concerning the precise circumstances of the move. Hobson undoubtedly was well connected throughout West Riding radical circles by this time, and connections may have had something to do with his decision, but the traditional account of the matter is open to

[8] Cf. Caroline Robbins, *The Eighteenth-Century Commonwealthman: Studies in the Transmission, Development and Circumstance of English Liberal Thought from the Restoration of Charles II until the War with the Thirteen Colonies* (Cambridge, Mass., 1959), pp. 185–96; J.G.A. Pocock, 'Virtues, Rights, and Manners: A Model for Historians of Political Thought', *Political Theory*, 9, no. 3, 1981, reprinted in Pocock, *Virtue, Commerce, and History: Essays on Political Thought and History, Chiefly in the Eighteenth Century* (Cambridge, 1985), pp. 37–50; Donald Winch, *Adam Smith's Politics: An Essay in Historiographic Revision* (Cambridge, 1978), pp. 30 and 106–7.

[9] *British Parliamentary Papers*, 3rd. series, 20, July–August 1833, col. 582; *VWR*, 17 August 1833.

[10] J.R. Sanders, 'Working-class Movements', p. 18.

[11] *'Demagogue'*, as Sanders observes, 'Working-class Movements', p. 41., was William Rider's nom-de-plume, as well as the title of the paper which appeared for the first time on 28 June 1834. There were at least four issues of the *Argus and 'Demagogue'*. The last known issue appeared on 23 August 1834.

question. This version has held that he went to Leeds in partnership with Alice Mann and revived the family's radical bookselling business, which had been ailing since her husband James's death in 1832.[12] The most recent researcher has found no evidence for the partnership; and points out that the only known publications of Mrs Mann's printing press for the period 1833–34 – a series of almanacs – do not credit Hobson. Moreover, when Hobson was convicted for a second time for selling unstamped newspapers in Leeds, in January 1836, he appeared in court on the same day, but separately from Mrs Mann, who was also found guilty of selling an unstamped newspaper.[13] Until direct evidence can be cited it seems safer to infer the absence of a partnership. This question does not detract from the fact that Hobson's printing business at Market Street, Briggate, became an important one in the history of radical, especially Owenite and Chartist, publishing.

The most important consequence of Hobson's record of activity, stemming originally from experience with the *Voice* but rooted in the general vigour of West Riding radicalism, was his role in the establishment of the *Northern Star and Leeds General Advertiser*, that 'essential medium of national communication and organization for the Chartist movement'.[14] As is well known, Feargus O'Connor first broached to Hobson the subject of establishing the paper, when attending the great anti-Poor Law meeting at Hartshead Moor in May 1837.[15] O'Connor was the prime mover here, but Hobson suggested William Hill as editor, and as publisher played an important role in the practical business arrangements. So much is uncontroversial. I think it should be possible to demonstrate that Hobson's role in the foundation and conduct of the *Star* was rather more important than these bare bones and Epstein's detailed treatment of the matter – quite clearly the best currently available – would allow;[16] but this is not the place to enter the lists. It is sufficient to note that no account can deny Hobson a significant role.

[12] J.F.C. Harrison, *Robert Owen and the Owenites in Britain and America* (London, 1969), p. 266, n. 2.

[13] S[imon] C[harles] E[dward] Cordery, 'Voice of the West Riding: Joshua Hobson in Huddersfield and Leeds, 1831–1845' (York University M.A., 1984), p. 42.

[14] James Epstein, *The Lion of Freedom: Feargus O'Connor and the Chartist Movement, 1832–1842* (London, 1982), p. 60.

[15] Ibid., p. 61.

[16] Ibid., pp. 61–68; also 'Feargus O'Connor and the *Northern Star*', *International Review of Social History*, 21, (1976), pp. 51–97.

To return to the earlier part of his career however, discussion of responsibility for the creation of the *Voice* must commence with Hobson's hitherto unremarked upon point that he was 'induced' to publish. That he needed any inducement is perhaps a surprise. His first reported public speaking appearance, as Sanders has noted, was at a Liberty of the Press meeting in 1831.[17] Despite his relative youth, being but twenty-one years old at the time, it is said that he 'headed' the Huddersfield General Committee of the Political Union and Operatives, which took the initiative calling for a delegate meeting at Manchester 'to arrange a plan and frame general resolutions for a grand meeting all over Britain and Ireland, on the same day and hour'.[18] His speech to the magistrates two years later, at the age of twenty-three, certainly demonstrates the intelligence and leadership quality which would have justified such a role. Earlier details in his biography, which have him leaving home when 'scarcely in his teens', possibly at the age of fourteen, and 'unbeknown to his mother', in response to straitened circumstances caused by the early death of his father,[19] confirm Hobson's early independence of character. He worked as a hand-loom weaver at Oldham and wrote for publication in the Lancashire press, 'revolutionary effusions' – which, regrettably, have not yet been traced – under the pseudonym, 'The Whistler at the Loom'.[20] His return to Huddersfield, possibly in or about 1828 at the age of eighteen, since he was unlikely to have commenced his apprenticeship with the Huddersfield joiner Thomas Flockton when older, apparently deepened rather than diminished his involvement in radical politics.[21] This evidence of early energy and activity in politics is quite consistent with a supposition that

[17] Sanders, 'Working-class Movements', p. 436; *Poor Man's Guardian*, 17 September 1831.

[18] John Belchem, *'Orator' Hunt: Henry Hunt and English Working-Class Radicalism* (Oxford, 1985), p. 250, citing, inter alia, *PMG*, 5 November 1831 and HO 52/13 ff. 272–73.

[19] Simon [C.E.] Cordery, Joshua Hobson entry in J.M. Bellamy and J. Saville [eds.], *Dictionary of Labour Biography*, VIII (London, 1987), pp. 113–19; Hobson's obituary, *Huddersfield Weekly News*, 13 and 20 May 1876; J.R. Sanders, 'Joshua Hobson: "One of Freedom's Boys", 1829–37' (Manchester University BA dissertation, 1973), p. 7, n. 29.

[20] The reference to 'revolutionary effusions' is most familiar from D.F.E. Sykes, *The History of Huddersfield and its Vicinity* (Huddersfield, 1898), pp. 301–2. Cordery, 'Voice of the West Riding', p. 21; Hobson's obituary in the *Huddersfield Examiner*, 13 May 1876.

[21] Cf. Sanders, 'Joshua Hobson', p. 9. The *HWN* obituary notice, 13 and 20 May 1876, indicates an involvement not later than 1829. The first contemporary newspaper reference is somewhat later: *Leeds Patriot*, 22 January 1831.

the idea, and much of the drive to establish the newspaper, may have come from Hobson. If the reports of early journalistic activity are correct, the common assumption that he was the editor of the *Voice* gains credence, though Cordery has noted that direct evidence is lacking.[22] What we know for certain is that he was the printer and publisher of the paper, and used his skills as a carpenter to build the wooden press because there was a shortage of funds.[23] Hobson's own reference to his 'inducement' alerts us to the fact that others were involved.[24] The *Voice* was certainly not Hobson's personal venture.

At the proceedings before the magistrates, Hobson read from a prospectus issued prior to publication of the *Voice*. Addressed to 'Friends and Advocates of the Rights of Man', it asserted:

> We have long been compelled to submit to the capricious and dictatorial monopolists of the Press, who have hitherto abetted the claims of Wealth against Poverty, of Power in preference to Right, of Institutions rather than Persons; by whom Faction and Legitimacy have been eulogized at the expence of Liberty and Justice.

It had not been possible to publish anything 'emanating from the Working Classes, setting forth their wrongs and vindicating their rights'. The choice had been either to undergo 'petty and arbitrary censorship', or engage a printer at Manchester or some other place, incurring expense, trouble and risk. Now, however, they had their own press, 'to vindicate the Working Classes from the calumnies and misrepresentations of our parasitical scribes who figure in the Provincial Newspapers', and would welcome donations and shares of five shillings to match the already pledged assistance of 'many friends in all the principal towns in the West Riding'. The promoters of the paper were careful to explain to prospective shareholders, however, 'we are not influenced by pecuniary motives, but by the good which we are sure will arise out of truth and moral rectitude'; and concluded with a rousing appeal:

> UP then fellow operatives rally round the standard of Union. Swell the pahalanx of your own ORDER, let us reject the

22 Cordery in Bellamy and Saville, *DLB*, p. 114; Cordery, 'Voice of the West Riding', p. 35.

23 *HWN* obituary, 13 and 20 May 1876.

24 *VWR*, 10 August 1833.

livery of sycophancy, and win (or at least deserve) the 'Patriots' Wreath'. [25]

It is clear from all this that the launching of the *Voice* had been widely discussed and support solicited from key radicals throughout the West Riding before the publication of the newspaper. Cordery and Sanders have demonstrated that Hobson was operating a 'Union Free Press' from Swan Yard, printing handbills, broadsides and posters for the Huddersfield Short Time Committee and the Huddersfield Political Union, before it was turned on to newspaper production. What may be the press's first product, *The Woodites 'Forget-me-not'*, appeared in January 1833. [26] It is not clear whether this press, which, in Cordery's view, was second-hand and had been 'purchased', [27] had also been paid for by the time of the issue of the prospectus. One suspects that credit may have been allowed on the type, possibly obtained from the firm of Bower at Sheffield, [28] and that the public subscription was solicited because the private pledges were insufficient to cover repayment of debt, as well as to meet a need for working capital to cover forward expenses. Unfortunately neither a copy of the printed prospectus, which presumably included the names of a number of the principal promoters of the *Voice*, nor a shareholders' book or list, which was presumably drawn up, appear to have survived. We are denied direct evidence as to the names of the promoters and the subscribers to the paper. Yet indirect evidence is available, which stems from a controversy between Hobson and O'Connor over the Chartist Land Plan. [29]

William Rider entered the controversy, taking the side of O'Connor. He referred to the decision to solicit five-shilling subscriptions or shares in the *Voice*, and alleged that Hobson cheated those working men who responded by devoting the money to:

> . . . ballads and the publication of last words and dying speeches. Well it all came to its end . . . Joshua *took all the type, the presses*

---

[25] *VWR*, 10 August 1833.

[26] Sanders, 'Working-class Movements', p. 438; Cordery, 'Voice of the West Riding', p. 35.

[27] *DLB*, p. 114.

[28] Hobson went to Bower for type when setting up the *Northern Star* press. Hobson from Huddersfield, 2 November 1847. *Manchester Examiner*, 17 November 1847.

[29] The arguments were aired in public in *ME*, November–December 1847. The reference in n. 28 above forms part of the series.

and the printing materials, and I believe sold one of the presses to O'Connor [Rider's italics].[30]

This accusation produced a response, revealing for the historian the existence of a managing committee of the *Voice of the West Riding*.[31] The members of the committee confirmed that Hobson had done 'his duty faithfully and satisfactorily', and when the establishment closed 'bought from the shareholders the whole of the printing materials *at a price fixed by the committee*' [italics in the original].[32]

We should note, incidentally, an apparent and potentially significant difference in the statements of Rider and the managing committee. The latter refer only to 'the whole of the *printing materials*' [my italics], apparently excluding the type and presses which Rider listed seperately. However, I believe the first part of the expression indicates the type and press, as well as stocks of paper and ink. The *Argus*, which succeeded the *Voice*, apparently was not a joint-stock venture,[33] presumably because Hobson had now purchased the press out of his own pocket.

The letter from the managing committee was signed by four Huddersfield residents: John Wood; R. Halliday; George Brook; and William Wilson; men of considerable interest. Wood was described as a master currier and leather cutter; it was he who, on behalf of the committee, had received payment from Hobson. Halliday was described as, 'a manufacturing chemist in a most extensive way of business, having establishments at Huddersfield, Bradford, Sheffield and in the immediate neighbourhood of Manchester'. Brook appeared as 'a master dyer, with considerable property'; and Wilson as a 'master boot and shoemaker' of five years standing.[34]

As Wood is and was a common surname in the Huddersfield district, and the first name of the managing committee member was ubiquitous, there are difficulties in linking this appearance in Hobson's defence to other historical records. Perhaps he was the John Wood, currier and leather cutter, who was located in Upperhead Row in 1830;[35] and the person of the

[30] Quoted in Hobson from Huddersfield, 10 November 1847: *ME*, 17 November 1847.

[31] Letter from the managing committee, 6 November 1847, cited by Hobson, *ME*, 17 November 1847.

[32] This statement contradicts Cordery's suggestion that: 'The *Voice* was owned by a group of radicals who *rented* [my italics] the Union Free Press from the Political Union . . .', *DLB*, p. 114.

[33] Cf. Cordery, 'Voice of the West Riding', p. 41.

[34] *ME*, 17 November 1847.

[35] Parson and White, *Directory*, 1830, p. 313.

same occupation who voted, from premises in the High Street, for Captain Wood, the Radical candidate, at the Huddersfield by-election of January 1834.[36] More speculatively, one might note that a John Wood was signatory to a handbill calling a Huddersfield Chartist meeting of 10 August 1839.[37]

Read (or Reid) Halliday, or Holliday, as became the convention in the spelling of the family name, was born at Bradford in 1809, son of a wool spinner. He moved to Huddersfield in 1830 at the age of twenty-one, and began the distillation of liquid ammonia from gas works ammoniacal liquor in premises rented at Tanfield, Leeds Road. At this time ammonia was a novel chemical in the woolscouring trade. When his premises were moved a short distance to Turnbridge in 1839, he allowed the gasworks to dump tar on his land, mixed it with ashes and fired his ammonia stills. Among his earliest patents was a naphtha lamp, which developed a large business until the perfection of the paraffin lamp. Coal tar was distilled for naphtha and creosote oils were sold for the treatment of railway sleepers.[38] Holliday went to Paris in 1850, saw work being done on benzol or benzine dyes, recruited a French chemist and became one of the most important dyestuffs manufacturers in the country.[39] But his political sympathies appear to have been Owenite, for he employed Robert Cooper when the latter was lecturing in Huddersfield for a time in 1847.[40] The apparent contradiction between Holliday's political radicalism and his position as a not inconsiderable employer in 1847, disappears however when one considers the terms in which Cooper reported his employment:

> I am engaged as a clerk to Messrs Holliday and Co, Manufacturing Chemists of this town, but the salary is so low, and the firm is so wanting in respectability that it would be sheer madness to remain longer than could be avoided. The people, too, are so very illiterate that there is little society either for Mrs Cooper or myself. I exist here in a mental wilderness.[41]

[36] *VWR*, 11 January 1834.

[37] HO 40/51.

[38] *Huddersfield Weekly Examiner*, 1 March 1919, and the *HWE Jubilee Supplement*.

[39] L. F. Haber, *The Chemical Industry during the Nineteenth Century* (Clarendon Press, Oxford, 1958); Roy Brook, *The Story of Huddersfield* (London, 1968), pp. 144–45 and 211–12; W.J. Reader, *Imperial Chemical Industries: A History, I, The Forerunners, 1870–1926* (London, 1970), p. 273.

[40] Edward Royle, *Victorian Infidels: The Origins of the British Secularist Movement, 1791–1866 (Manchester*, 1974), p. 94.

[41] Robert Cooper to Robert Owen, 10 July 1847, *Owen Coll.* 1480, Cooperative Union, Manchester. I am grateful to Dr Edward Royle, who drew my attention to this reference.

Perhaps it was the dirtiness and smelliness of the manufacture that left Messrs Holliday so wanting in respectability. At any rate, Holliday had acquired sufficient respectability by 1857 to start appearing in the surviving pollbooks, when he consistently voted Liberal.[42]

The third member of the managing committee was George Brook (1803–80). He had been dismissed from his position as foreman dyer at the Starkey brothers dyeworks in Huddersfield for being an Owenite. He had a very successful career as a dyer, however, and was able to retire in 1856, at the age of fifty-three, leaving the business to his son.[43]

Little is known of William Wilson, the fourth member of the managing committee. He was probably the same William Wilson, boot and shoemaker of Manchester Street, who was recorded as having voted for Wood in 1834;[44] and there is a possibility that he was the person who appeared in the Carlile victim lists three times during the 1820s.[45]

What is known of the members of the managing committee of *Voice* shareholders suggests that they were elected or appointed because they possessed energy and integrity in business matters, as well as a commitment to radical politics. We can infer that they would have been shareholders. They appear to be identifiable among the lists of Hobson victim fund subscribers.

The published record of Hobson victim fund contributions was an incomplete account. The complete list of subscriptions is annexed to this essay.[46] The last published total of £29 19s 5½d may approximate quite well to the final amount received, but the report requested agents and subscribers to bring money into C. Tinker's before Monday next. The intention plainly was to wind up the fund, since the same issue of the *Voice* reported Hobson's return from prison. His journey from Wakefield to the outskirts of Huddersfield had concluded at Moldgreen, where he had been met 'by a great number of his fellow workmen . . . bearing

---

[42] Holliday voted for Cobden in 1857; and Leatham in 1865 and 1868. *Pollbooks*, Huddersfield Public Library.

[43] *Secular Review*, 22 January 1881, p. 57; *SR*, 5 March 1881, pp. 149–50; *HE*, 15 January 1881. My thanks to Dr Edward Royle, who generously provided these references.

[44] *VWR*, 11 January 1834. A William Wilson, boot and shoemaker, was at Upperhead Row four years earlier: Parson and White's *Directory*, 1830.

[45] *Republican*, 4 October 1822 and 14 February 1823; *The Lion*, 17 July 1829.

[46] In the following commentary on the personalities appearing in the victim fund subscription list I avoid references to the sources for information about their various contributions. They appear as part of the list in the appendix.

torches and a flag inscribed "The Press shall be Free'".[47] The published record is incomplete in another sense. Identifiable individual subscriptions only amounted to £18 1s. 11¾d., or 60.38 per cent of the total recorded amount. Also, a number of reports of subscriptions received failed to state any amount; and subscribers on a 'list of weekly subscribers' had only one, or two, or three, contributions listed.

Nonetheless, the published data are of considerable interest. It can be calculated from the 'already published' lists that contributions ran at a rate of approximately £1 0s. 11d. per week from 6 August 1833 through to 24 August; then at £1 14s. 4d. per week to 19 October; at £0 16s. 2d. per week to 30 November; and £1 2s. 5d per week to the last report on 25 January 1834. In other words, though there was a fall in the level of contributions during late October and November, support appeared at its highest level towards the end of Hobson's imprisonment. If the victim fund subscribers were at all characteristic of those who took out shares in the *Voice*, the size distribution of their contributions would appear to bear out Hobson's contention that the paper, 'started by a few operatives and their friends', appeared only by extraordinary exertion 'for a great outlay of capital (or at least great for working men) was necessary, and they in . . . days of grinding and low wages . . . [had] . . . not much superfluous cash at their command'.[48] Of an estimated 311 separate identifiable subscriptions, 73.7 per cent fell into the 'not more than 6d.' category, and 40.6 per cent into the 'not more than 3d.' category; the largest element in the 'more than 6d.' category comprised subscriptions of 12d., constituting 19.6 per cent of the total.[49] Larger amounts are usually identifiable as collections, therefore representing an undefinable number of smaller contributions.

A core of regular subscribers apparently contributed on a weekly basis. Interpretation of the data on 'weekly subscribers' is uncertain, but the number of regular contributors would appear to have comprised about twenty-four people, accounting for not less than 40 per cent and not more than 54 per cent of total contributions. Four of the twenty-four were listed as 'a friend', or under some other uninformative sobriquet. Seven appeared merely with initials, but we have full names for the thirteen remaining. The lists contained a 'W. Wilson' and a 'John Wood'; 'R.H.' could be Read Halliday, and there is a 'G.B.' among the regular subscribers. In any case,

[47] *VWR*, 25 January 1834.
[48] *VWR*, 25 January 1834.
[49] These calculations are based on the lists in the appendix.

a 'George Brook' was among those not identified as a weekly contributor. It is not possible to demonstrate conclusively that these were the members of the shareholders' managing committee, but the probability must be high.

The weekly subscribers included prominent Huddersfield radicals who are well known to historians. There was John Leech (1803–71), who had been part of the Huddersfield Short Time Committee deputation to Richard Oastler on the lawn at Fixby on Sunday, 19 June 1831.[50] He was to be described, four years after Hobson's imprisonment, as 'one of the honestest and best patriots of our town', in the course of a reference to his taking the chair at a public meeting for delegates of the Glasgow Cotton Spinners.[51] His Chartist activity came to the notice of the Home Office,[52] and he was one of the secretaries to the Huddersfield branch of the Northern Union formed on 26 September 1838.[53]

Another weekly subscriber to the Hobson fund was 'L. Pitkethly' (Lawrence Pitkeithley, 1801–58). Pitkethly was one of the most indefatigable of West Riding radical organisers; never a great orator, but an assiduous correspondent who laboured and travelled extensively in the cause – to Rotherhithe, Manchester, Glasgow, Edinburgh, and America, and elsewhere no doubt, as well as around the West Riding.[54] In his own town Pitkethley regularly attended Vestry meetings and was to be found on juries; committees to agree the duties of the deputy constable or to inquire into tyranny at the workhouse, and much more;[55] moving motions and chairing meetings.[56] In the local context, and of particular significance for the line of argument being developed here, he was chairman of the Huddersfield Political Union.[57] In the West Riding the orchestration of the great radical meetings, as at the Peep Green Chartist meeting in 1839,[58]

---

[50] Cecil Driver, *Tory Radical: The Life of Richard Oastler* (New York, 1946), p. 87.

[51] *Northern Star*, 17 March 1838.

[52] Chartist handbill calling for the Huddersfield meeting of 10 August 1839, in HO 40/51.

[53] *NS*, 29 September 1838; obituary in *Huddersfield Observer*, 7 January 1871.

[54] Mark Hovell, *The Chartist Movement* (Manchester, 1918), p. 144; *NS*, 14 April 1838; Pitkethly to Robert Owen, 3 December 1833, *Owen Coll* 607; Ray Boston, *British Chartists in America, 1839–1900* (Manchester, 1971), pp. 39–40; Harrison, *Robert Owen and the Owenites*, p. 227, n. 1.

[55] *VWR*, 15 June 1833; *VWR*, 31 August 1833; *Vestry Minutes*, HPL, 22 October 1835 and 30 March 1837; *VWR*, 2 November 1833.

[56] *PMG*, 17 September 1831; *VWR*, 15 June 1833. *LI*, 30 August 1832; *PMG*, 29 June 1833; *Working Man's Friend*, 29 June 1833.

[57] *PMG*, 16 March 1833.

[58] John Brown to Jno. Sutcliffe, 22 May 1839. HO 40/51.

usually involved his hand: he was often placed in a prominent position at the head of a procession, as when he rode on horseback with Oastler from Knavesmire to York during the county meeting on Sadler's Ten Hour Bill, 24 April 1832;[59] on the platform at county meetings, as at the Hartshead Moor anti-Poor Law meeting of 15 May 1837, and when called to the chair at Feargus O'Connor's Queenshead, Bradford, dinner;[60] or in an important office within a county-wide organisation, such as his secretaryship to the West Riding District meeting of the Association of All Classes of All Nations,[61] despite the lack of charisma reported by his contemporaries. Robert Gammage wrote that he, 'was a man of a benevolent turn of mind . . .; a speaker whose earnestness rather than his oratory, made him popular';[62] while Lloyd Jones commented that his platform contributions were always short because he had a high voice and was not a good public speaker.[63] Nonetheless, his connections were such that we find him writing letters of introduction for no less than Robert Owen.[64] Mott, at the Home Office, singled him out among the delegates to the National Chartist Convention, as one who 'doubtless write[s] home the particulars of their proceedings and views', in the course of advocating seizure of papers and the arrest of leaders of 'thousands . . . armed and ready for any mischief'.[65] O'Connor was undoubtedly correct to stress the impact of the establishment of the *Star* in projecting radical leaders and their politics beyond local confines, but his suggestion that 'PITKEITHLEY . . . could see at one glance the limits of his influence'[66] owed more to his talent for hyperbole than exactitude of expression. Lloyd Jones recalled how, on reaching Huddersfield:

> . . . the first place I used to make for was Lawrence Pitkeithley's and there in his first floor room over the shop, he was sure to be met with . . . surrounded by a small group of the most thorough radicals, and

[59] *Poor Man's Advocate*, 5 May 1832.

[60] J.T. Ward, *The Factory Movement, 1830–1855* (London, 1962), p. 179; *NS*, 19 January 1839.

[61] Royle, *Victorian Infidels*, p. 50.

[62] R.C. Gammage, *History of the Chartist Movement, 1837–1854* (1854; revised edition, 1894; reprinted London, 1969), p. 64.

[63] *Newcastle Weekly Chronicle*, 16 August 1879.

[64] A letter to John Clarke requested that Owen, 'on a tour of Regeneration', be introduced to Messrs Woodcock and Travis. Pitkethly to R. Owen from Manchester, 19 December 1833. *Owen Coll* 600.

[65] Mott to the Poor Law Commissioners, 22 March 1839. HO 73/55.

[66] *NS*, 27 April 1839.

when business permitted, John Leech, his manager, was one of the company.[67]

We see already, in other words, that among the victim fund subscribers there was a close-knit band of local radicals which had extensive regional and national connections.

A third weekly subscriber of some prominence was Christopher Tinker (1797–1844). We noted at the start of this essay some influence of the north on the London unstamped. Tinker points to the possibility of an earlier and apparently so far unsuspected connection between the north and south on the question of the freedom of the press. His son, Thomas C. Tinker, recorded that: 'He was a printer by trade; a Liberal [sic] in politics; a member of "The Band of Freemen" so called – that fought the good fight for full *Freedom of the Press* in England'. He also mentions that his father 'had made the acquaintance and formed a friendship with Leigh Hunt'; and established his book and periodical shop in Huddersfield in 1822.[68] There is an intriguing question here. How did Tinker make Hunt's acquaintance? There does not appear to be any record of Hunt having visited Huddersfield and it is more likely that Tinker visited London. It is interesting that Thomas mentions his father's acquaintance with Hunt before going on to refer to the decision to leave the printing trade and establish 'the book and periodical shop – with a circulating library attached'. Thomas may have retailed his facts in this sequence because Hunt's was a name to drop and came to mind first; but if his account was constructed to conform to the real chronology of events we have the possibility that the provincial printer went to London to see the famous editor at the height of his notoriety: that is, following the appearance of the leader on 'Princely Qualities' in the *Examiner* of 22 March 1812. Hunt was incarcerated from 3 February 1813, when he was tried for criminal libel, until 2 February 1815, but received a procession of visitors. All were not necessarily of the same quality as Lord Byron.[69] If Tinker did indeed visit Hunt in gaol he would have been between sixteen and eighteen years of age, but it is clear from Hobson's example that this relative youthfulness should not rule out the possibility. In any case, should age rule out this suggestion, it could be that

[67] *NWC*, 16 August 1879, quoted in Sanders, 'Working-class Movements', p. 30.

[68] Letter of 31 March 1914, in the Thomas C. Tinker MSS, Wisconsin State Historical Society.

[69] Edmund Blunden, *Leigh Hunt: A Biography* (London, 1930), pp. 69, 73, 75–80 and 88.

Tinker made Hunt's acquaintance during the Queen Caroline affair, which rekindled something of the latter's first political strength. [70]

Whatever the facts concerning this matter, it is clear that from 1822 Tinker:

> . . . *handled* all the 'Liberal' publications of the time, received by *Mail Coach* from London, Leeds, Manchester and other places of publication within the realm. Publications under 'Ban' of Church and State came to him by 'Special Carrier' (so called then).

The accuracy of this account and the importance of Tinker's premises as a radical centre is well confirmed by other sources. His recorded agencies include sale of the *Poor Man's Guardian, Destructive, Man, People's Hue and Cry* and the *Voice*, as well as *An Address to the Members of Trades Unions (and to the Working Classes Generally)* by a Journeyman Bootmaker. [71] Tinker's son explained the success of the business in the following terms:

> It should be borne in mind that the working class of England – had they a *Vote* or otherwise – were strongly inclined towards the Liberalism of the time in Politics and Religion also, for the old aggressive overbearing attitude of the 'State Church' with its bunch of *Beadles* and *Church Wardens* in Uniform, was not of the kind to promote *hearty* friendly feeling. To these people my Father's Circulating Library was a 'God-send' and abundantly patronized and there was a constant demand for books of *Liberal* tendency and teaching.

When Tinker emigrated to America early in 1842, urged on by Robert Owen, the Huddersfield socialists took over the shop and business at a fair valuation but had trouble finding the cash to meet the first payment. Mrs Tinker remained to 'settle the business' and sailed from Liverpool to New York during August 1842, having sold it to Joshua Hobson. [72]

Tinker was imprisoned three times for selling the unstamped, almost as many times as Hobson. As his son put it:

[70] Blunden, *Leigh Hunt*, pp. 155–56.

[71] *PMG*, 21 September, 12 October, 9 November 1833; *Man*, 24 November 1833 and *People's Hue and Cry*, 10 August 1834 in HO 64/15; *VWR*, 10 August 1833.

[72] Tinker MSS; *HWN*, 13 and 20 May 1876.

Oh! he got 'His Medecine' – *three doses* therefore, – and took it like 'A Little Man'. The *dose par excellence* was a fine of £250 sterling and twelve months imprisonment in York Castle (Clifford's Tower) . . .[73]

His tendency to intransigent radicalism was in evidence on other occasions. When Alfred Power visited Huddersfield on 10 January 1837, to have his first meeting with the local Poor Law Overseers at the George Inn, Tinker capped the heckling and turned the meeting into uproar by shouting:

If all the labourers were of his mind, they would mark their names on a bit of lead, put it into a rifle, and send it through the first man that attempted to put the law into force.[74]

As a Chartist he was a committee member of the Huddersfield branch of the Northern Union formed on 26 September 1838; sold tickets for Chartist meetings; signed bills calling for meetings; and, most menacingly of all, displayed a dagger in his shop window.[75] The central function of Tinker's business, situated in the town's Market Walk, can be illustrated in other ways. He was named as the Huddersfield recipient of subscriptions to the unstamped victim fund in the 'Appeal from the London Union of Vendors of Useful Knowledge, Male and Female'; as recipient of subscriptions for the Derby turnouts, forwarding via Hetherington on one occasion, the sum of £3 8s. Od.[76] Tinker was 'nominated' to receive Hobson's correspondence after his incarceration.[77]

It is almost certain that these three committed radicals – Leech, Pitkethly and Tinker – who were victim fund subscribers, also were *Voice* shareholders; as well as the four members – Wood, Holliday, Brook and Wilson – of the paper's managing committee.

Other relatively well-known people appeared in the victim fund lists without being identified as 'weekly subscribers'. One of the most important figures was a 'W. Vevers': certainly William Vevers. Vevers was, after Christopher Tinker, the most important of a group of collectors for the Hobson victim fund. Like Tinker, he maintained a 'book' for subscriptions. There was not merely a similarity but a direct connection between Vevers

---

[73] Tinker MSS; *Leeds Times*, 20 February 1836.

[74] Driver, *Tory Radical*, pp. 336–37.

[75] *NS*, 29 September 1838; handbills in HO 40/51; deposition of William Duke: Laycock to the Home Office, 5 March 1839 in HO 40/51.

[76] *Pioneer*, 17 May and 1 March 1834 in HO 64/19.

[77] *VWR*, 10 August 1833.

and Tinker. Just as Hobson purchased from Tinker, as we have seen, the latter established his unstamped newspaper selling, bookbinding and printing business at Market Walk in premises taken over from William Vevers.[78] Under Vevers beer, as well as political intelligence, was almost certainly dispensed. He was described as a beer retailer only six months later at the time of the Huddersfield by-election. His move was virtually next door since his new premises were also in Market Walk. Perhaps he was moving up in the world at this stage. Certainly he qualified for the vote in his new situation, supporting the Radical parliamentary candidate, Captain Wood.[79] He was a 'publican' at the same address when he voted for Richard Oastler at the 1837 general election.[80] He was still in business in 1853, now the licensee at the Globe Inn, 49 King Street, but had apparently retired by the 1857 General Election when he was recorded as 'Neutral'.[81] At that time his address was Market Street. The supposition that he had retired by 1857 is an inference from the voting registration details for 1864, which recorded his property as a dwelling-house rather than an inn.[82] By the time of the 1865 election he was dead.[83]

Another Vevers who appeared in the Hobson victim fund subscription lists was Thomas Vevers, a prominent Huddersfield district radical. He first appeared in the sources as a Huddersfield subscriber to Richard Carlile's victim fund list of 1822.[84] He was one of the main speakers at the Huddersfield unstamped press meeting of 9 August 1831.[85] A number of reports in the historical record omit to provide a first name, but it appears to have been Thomas rather than William who took the chair at the meeting of the Huddersfield Political Union addressed by Cleave on 10 June 1833;[86] and at the public meeting held in the Union Room on 17 September.[87] We get a glimpse of the man from sources relating to the Chartist period. He was described early in 1839 as 'an intelligent looking old man' who had been among the people for forty years and was well known.[88] He was reported as

[78] *VWR*, 6 July 1833.
[79] *VWR*, 11 January 1834.
[80] *Pollbook*, 1837, HPL.
[81] White's *Directory*, 1853, p. 622; *Pollbook*, 1857, HPL.
[82] *Canvass Book*, 1864, HPL.
[83] *Pollbook*, 1865, HPL.
[84] *Republican*, 4 October 1822.
[85] *PMG*, 17 September 1831.
[86] *VWR*, 15 June 1833.
[87] *VWR*, 14 September 1833.
[88] *NS*, 9 February 1839.

saying, in a speech to the Peep Green Chartist meeting of 21 May 1839, that:

> . . . he had been tutored under Major Cartwright and . . . was for nothing but universal suffrage . . . the middle and higher class had got arms to defend themselves against night robbers – now he wanted the working class to defend themselves against daylight robbers. [89]

It is an interesting fact that Hobson delivered the funeral oration at Vevers' death in 1843. Sanders has acutely drawn attention to a similarity between Vevers and Hobson, who seem to have shared characteristics which made them into archetypes of the lonely leader. Vevers may have combined as, according to his closest friend, did Hobson, a 'strange mixture of sweetness and bitterness, of tenderness and harshness'. [90] It is interesting also that Hobson's homage to Vevers was only one of three marks of respect for the departed which can almost certainly be attributed to him. Taken together, and considered alongside other sources, the three cast considerable light on Hobson and the circle in which he moved.

Ten years before Vevers' death, the *Voice* had published a memoir of the late Godfrey Higgins Esq, FSA, FRAS, of Skellow Grange, and JP for the West Riding. [91] The memoir was not signed, but it has the characteristics of Hobson's pen. It noted, as in the informer's statement on Thomas Vevers, that Higgins' politics were of the Cartwright school. The politics of the 'Cartwright school' had a great appeal to Hobson and his confrères in the Huddersfield Political Union. The memoir noted that Higgins shared these politics with Captain Wood, who was to be the Huddersfield Radical candidate at the parliamentary by-election about four months later; and though the members of the Political Union thought their principles were, as it was stated to Higgins, 'somewhat more radical perhaps than those of Major Cartwright', they admitted him to their membership 'with great enthusiasm'. The memoir hints at that mixture of 'tenderness and harshness' noted in Hobson's character, for while it contains evident admiration for Higgins' political and scholarly record there is a clear indication of independence and readiness to reject him.

[89] Statement of John Brown to Jno. Sutcliffe, 22 May 1839 in HO 40/51.

[90] Sanders, 'Working-class Movements', p. 49. Hobson's closest friend, from sometime after their acquaintance at the end of 1848, was the solicitor Nehemiah Learoyd, of the firm of Cookson and Floyd. *The Late Mr Joshua Hobson, with a Tribute to his Memory by N. Learoyd* (Huddersfield, 1876), reprinted from *HWN*, 13 and 20 May 1876.

[91] *VWR*, 31 August 1833.

The third mark of respect relates to Hobson's grandfather, Joshua Hobson (1729–1833). We appreciate more clearly here the importance of what I take to be Hobson's historical sense. This historical sense was central to his politics and, I believe, to his conception of himself as a man. Hobson's grandfather attained the great age of 104. His health was good: he worked in the field until the last two years. He neither took fermented liquors nor 'that noxious weed tobacco', though he was remarkably fond of coffee. He had come to the Huddersfield district in 1755 at the age of twenty-six, apparently via Leeds, having been born in the village of Clifton on the borders of Knaresborough Forest. He was admitted to a Deighton farming family as a carpenter, eventually marrying the only daughter. In due course, Joshua inherited the farm and stock in trade, which was on land rented from the Thornhill Estate. Joshua senior appears to have been a person of some substance and accomplishment: he was a 'standing overseer' for four years, and sang at St John's Church, Leeds, in his younger days, before continuing the practice at Huddersfield Parish Church.[92]

The fact that his grandfather was resident on the Thornhill Estate, which had a reputation for harmonious relations between landlord and tenant, almost certainly has some bearing on the close relationship which the grandson was already developing with Richard Oastler, the estate steward. The grandson, like the grandfather, appears to have been abstemious and among those who would have gathered at Thornton's Temperance Hotel from 1851 onwards. The atmosphere at Thornton's was intellectual: it was the place where gathered 'all the local intellectuals – real and would be . . .' It was freethinking: a favourite topic in the discussions which Thornton good-humouredly chaired from a chair on a raised platform at one end of the large room was Joseph Barker's latest change of faith. The atmosphere also was cultured. Thornton was musical and had been instrumental in forming a drum and fife band in Huddersfield; he was a 'keen follower of the immortal Shakespeare'; and a small room was provided for chess and draughts. Under Thornton's auspices all kinds of radicalism thrived and his hotel 'was thought by the more timorous townsmen to be the resort of wicked conspirators and schemers plotting against religion and the throne'.[93]

Joshua Hobson of the *Voice* was free-thinking and cultured. His recital of his grandfather's record as a chorister suggests a respect for musical

[92] *VWR*, 30 November 1833.

[93] Royle, *Victorian Infidels*, p. 227, citing *Parkin's Almanac*, 1925 for 'Closing of Thornton's', HPL Press Cuttings book, p. 86, and miscellaneous press cuttings in HPL; also HPL Obituary Cuttings Book, obituary 4 October 1887.

accomplishment; and his reference to Godfrey Higgins' labours on his 'almost completed work on the origins of nations, languages and religions' suggests a respect for learning.[94] In Hobson's three obituaries and through the pride with which he appears to record his grandfather's yeoman stock,[95] we surely discern a sense of belonging to a great tradition – a great radical tradition, into which fits Major Cartwright, Godfrey Higgins and Thomas Vevers.

Thomas Vevers was resident at Dalton, Kirkheaton, in 1839,[96] not far from Hobson's grandfather's late home at Deighton. A number of other places in the Huddersfield district provided victim fund subscribers: villages and hamlets within the Huddersfield district such as Honley, Holthead, Longley and Lowerhouses, Newsome, Milnsbridge and Meltham Mills. It is possible in some cases to identify a collector or a key supporter, such as Thomas Ledger – a woolsorter who died later in the year aged thirty-eight, 'a kind husband, a good father, and a well wisher to the human race'[97] – at Honley, or a supporting organisation, such as the village political union at Holthead.

The prospectus for the *Voice*, as we have seen, referred to pledges received from 'many friends in all the principal towns of the West Riding', and a certain, if indeterminate amount of support for the paper, from Bradford, Dewsbury, Leeds and Wakefield, can be detected in the victim fund subscription lists. There was too, a contribution from a friend at Manchester and another at Glasgow. Seven Leeds victim fund subscribers were identified out of a total of eleven contributors: James Helliwell, the treasurer for Leeds collections; William Rider, the Leeds fund committee secretary; and Alfred Mann, son of Alice and James; and others. Bradford appears to have provided the largest number – ninety-one – of identifiable contributions from outside the Huddersfield district; and those from Wakefield, where Joshua Hobson's grandfather

---

[94] *VWR* 31 August 1833.

[95] I use the term 'yeoman' in the loose sense of a farmer or countryman of respectable standing, rather than that of a freeholder, since this is what fits the circumstances. Freeholders were relatively numerous in Yorkshire; and even tenant farmers on estates such as Thornhill's, or those of the neighbouring Ramsden family, where a customary tenure apparently allowed inheritance and the enjoyment of property in perpetuity, were not without that sense of independence commonly associated with freeholder status.

[96] Petition for a county meeting on universal suffrage in HO 40/51.

[97] *VWR*, 2 November 1833.

attended the market for nearly fifty years,[98] appears to have exceeded those of Leeds. Commercial connections between Leeds and Huddersfield were strong: around 1830 the Leeds merchants were the chief buyers in the Huddersfield market for woollens;[99] and close ties were evident politically and journalistically. It has been suggested that replacement editors or publishers, in the persons of John Francis Bray and William Rider, were supplied from Leeds when Hobson was imprisoned.[100] There is some uncertainty whether Bray worked on the paper as more than a printer, and whether Rider was more than a contributor,[101] but whatever the precise form of their connection the cooperation between the towns was close. Rider had contributed to the founding of the *Voice* by selling its shares in Leeds.[102]

In addition to the regular collectors for the victim fund, whether at Leeds or in the Huddersfield district, there were a number of less important, anonymous or obscure collectors. The appearance of twenty-one subscriptions from Lowerhouses and Longley suggests the presence of some indefatigable individual. It is clear from the survey of Almondbury township conducted by Brook eleven years later, that the two hamlets still only contained about as many houses as victim fund subscribers.[103] Even in the absence of the precise calculation that easy access to 1831 and 1841 census data would permit, it is obvious that the ratio of identifiable contributions to population at these places was unusually high. Collectors sometimes worked spontaneously, as may have been the case with the efforts of Mary Ann Tinker and Jane Bradley 'in the [union?] room'. Certainly the collection at the Court House, which was obviously on the day of Hobson's appearance before the magistrates, falls into this category. Twenty-six women can be identified among the subcribers, and more may be hidden beneath some initial, as well as the sobriquet 'a few ladies'. There appear to be some family connections. There is no known family relationship between Thomas and William Vevers, but Elizabeth Vevers may have been related – perhaps to the latter. A little

[98] *VWR*, 30 November 1833.

[99] W.B. Crump and Gertrude Ghorbal, *History of the Huddersfield Woollen Industry* (Huddersfield, 1935), p. 110.

[100] H.J. Carr, 'John Francis Bray', *Economica*, 7, (1940), p. 399; Epstein, 'Feargus O'Connor', *IRSH*, 21, (1976), p. 82.

[101] See the discussion in Cordery, 'Voice of the West Riding', pp. 38–40.

[102] Ibid., p. 37.

[103] *Map Coll.*, HPL; *Huddersfield Maps from 1634* (Huddersfield, 1971).

nest of seven Sykeses at Lowerhouses and Longley probably contained some family relationships and the list contains other possibilities.

Subscriptions came from Longroyd Bridge on one occasion, and these could have been associated with workers at the Starkey Brothers' large and successful mill which, in 1834, employed three twenty-eight-horsepower engines and 521 workers. [104] William Hirst, who claimed to have been the first to introduce mechanical shearing to the Leeds cloth manufacture, utilizing an improved eight-blade Lewis cutter, [105] also suggested that he had converted the Starkey brothers to his method of making fine broadcloth and was aggrieved by their lack of generosity. [106] His sense of grievance was undoubtedly fuelled by his one-time prosperity and subsequent misfortune, but its basis seems real. [107] In 1833 the Starkey brothers were among those firms resolved 'not to take into our employment any fresh Workman, who does not bring in a good character, from his previous master'; an action calculated to 'break down the [trade] Union . . . and put down all radicals into the bargain'. [108] They were opposed to factory hours legislation. [109] It is not surprising that the ire of the *Voice* was aroused, it having, 'a particular aversion to back of the Counter men, they having been some years ago sadly tired of their call at Croppers Row and Common Side next door to the Poor House'. [110] The meaning of this skit is not clear. Perhaps the reference to Croppers Row draws attention to strains in the Starkeys' relationship with their finishers.

Whatever the case concerning the finishers at Longroyd Bridge, which was the location of John Wood's cropping shops where the Luddite leader George Mellor had been employed, [111] it is interesting that the only occupational group identified among the subscription lists was the

---

[104] The workmen at Starkey, Buckley and Co, as the firm was then known, subscribed, seven years previous and at the time of commercial crisis, £25 to the Huddersfield Relief Committee: *Leeds Mercury*, 13 May 1826. D.T. Jenkins, *The West Riding Wool Textile Industry: A Study of Fixed Capital Formation* (Edington, 1975), p. 66.

[105] Jenkins, *West Riding Wool Textile Industry*, pp. 130–31; William Hirst, *History of the Woollen Trade during the Last Sixty Years* (Leeds, 1844), pp. 20–22; Edward Baines, *History, Directory and Gazetteer of the County of York*, I (Leeds, 1822), p. 30.

[106] Hirst, *History of the Woollen Trade*, pp. 34–35.

[107] Ibid., p. 16. John Mayall, *Annals of Yorkshire*, I (1870), pp. 443–44.

[108] *VWR*, 27 July 1833; *VWR*, 26 October 1833; *PMG*, 17 September 1831.

[109] Ward, *Factory Movement*, p. 355.

[110] *VWR*, 23 November 1833.

[111] Crump and Ghorbal, *Huddersfield Woollen Industry*, pp. 96-97, which includes a lithographic illustration of Wood's cropping shop; Robert Reid, *Land of Lost Content: The Luddite Revolt, 1812* (London, 1986).

'[cloth] dressers at Joe Atkinson's'. The dressers, twenty years on from the Luddite episode, were still a relatively well-paid group. The particular group here found subscribing to the victim fund were probably employed at Bradley Mills since, in the *Voice*'s skit on those attending a dinner at the George Inn from which we have already quoted, Joe, or Joseph Atkinson, was described as the 'son of a bankrupt 2× and a family most notorious for *chastity and piety*' [italic in the original].[112]

Another set of subscriptions which may be associated with a particular employer's workers was that coming from Meltham Mills. Here the firm of Jonas Brook and Brothers had established a large cotton-spinning establishment. The three storey fireproof mill, constructed in 1828, had a floor area of 800 square yards and was insured for £1,200; at thirty shillings per square yard compared with the typical figure of fifteen to twenty shillings for a similar sized mill of the same period.[113] The firm of Jonas Brook and Brothers were signatories three years later to the Huddersfield district manufacturers petition against Hobhouse's Factory Employment Bill.[114] By 1834 the firm was manufacturing sewing cotton and throwing silk.[115]

The victim fund lists and the information about the managing committee, when read with other sources, would appear to provide our best insight into the shadowy group of *Voice* shareholders. The key people discussed above were almost certainly shareholders. Their radical careers may also help us to produce a more accurate characterisation of the paper.

The first issue is the relation between the paper and the factory movement. As we have already noted, one historian referred to the paper as a 'factory journal' and another averred that the paper was originally intended as the organ of the Huddersfield Short Time Committee.[116] Direct evidence is not available on the last point, however, and the *Voice* was not produced from a factory by a group of factory workers.

Of course the paper reported frequently on events and issues related to the factory question. Hobson was a leading member of the Huddersfield

[112] *VWR*, 23 November 1833; *Tomlinson Diaries*, HPL, p. 80; *LM*, 2 December 1826, 31 May, 7 June and 16 August 1828.

[113] Jenkins, *Wool Textile Industry*, p. 61.

[114] *PMG*, 17 September 1831.

[115] Edward Parsons, *The Civil, Ecclesiastical, Literary, Commercial and Miscellaneous History of Leeds, Halifax, Huddersfield, Bradford, Wakefield, Dewsbury and Otley and the Manufacturing District of Yorkshire* (Leeds, 1834), p. 60.

[116] N. 4, above; J.F.C. Harrison, 'Leeds Chartism' in Asa Briggs (ed.), *Chartist Studies* (London, 1958), p. 67.

Short Time Committee. And the 'Union Free Press' printed broadsides for the Short Time Committee, as we have already seen. Cole referred to the *British Labourer's Protector and Factory Child's Friend*, the chief organ of the West Riding Short Time Committees, as 'the forefather of the *Voice*'.[117]

Nonetheless, it would not be safe to assume more than informal connections between the paper and the factory movement. It is not clear what weight Cole's remark was intended to bear, but Cordery has correctly noted that the two papers had little in common beyond the chronological coincidence of the termination of one and the beginning of the other.[118] Some strain developed between Oastler and the conductors of the *Voice* at the time of the Huddersfield by-election in January 1834, and, as Cordery has pointed out, the *Voice* was not consistently a supporter of Oastler's schemes.[119] It is not clear whether, and to what extent, this strain extended to the working-class members of the Short Time Committee, but it probably found some echo. If Hobson was a most influential member of the Short Time Committee, there is no evidence that he occupied any leading office. The committee's chairman during 1833-34 was Samuel Glendinning. There was some overlap of local support for the factory movement and for the paper, but a content analysis of the first sixteen issues shows that only 15.7 per cent of its space was devoted to the factory question; 37.4 per cent was devoted to general political matters and topics of interest to radicals; 11.1 per cent to local non-factory questions; and a considerable amount, 16.2 per cent, to reporting Hobson's trial and matters connected with the press. Most of the factory question material in the paper actually appeared in the first sixteen issues, so an extension of content analysis to the entire production would reduce rather than increase its weight. Any classification of newspaper subject matter has about it an element of arbitrariness since any particular report may be justifiably allocated to more than one category, but I doubt that a fresh eye would produce figures so radically different as to disturb the central line of argument being presented here.

There is little doubt that Sanders' judgement on the paper - in 'content and tone it was above all radical' is correct. Indeed the circumstantial evidence points towards Sanders' further conclusion: that it was also radical in origin.[120] The Political Union was the most likely progenitor, in the sense of being the forum within which the *Voice* was conceived. Cordery

---

[117] G.D.H. Cole, *Attempts at General Union*, (London, 1953), pp. 77-78.

[118] Cordery, 'Voice of the West Riding', pp. 30-31.

[119] Ibid., pp. 31-33.

[120] Sanders, 'Joshua Hobson', p. 46; 'Working-class Movements', p. 438.

apparently agrees, commenting that the *Voice* was 'ostensibly' a private enterprise, although it exhibited 'close ties' with the Political Union.[121] This new view rests on several observations. Firstly, that the paper was started as 'a conscious act of political defiance'; and that the project may have been conceived as a consequence of 'difficulties experienced during the 1832 midwinter election'.[122] Secondly, the programme of four points which the *Voice* adopted in its first issue appears to have been the programme of the Political Union.[123] Thirdly, and more significantly, the paper's first eight issues were published from Swan Yard, the location of the Political Union's meeting room.[124] Fourthly, the close involvement of Huddersfield's leading radicals in support of the publisher and the paper, which emerges from study of the victim subscription lists, supports a quite literal interpretation of Cleave's address to the Huddersfield Political Union on 10 June 1833, in which he congratulated the union on at last having its own press.[125] When Hobson's release from prison was expected and announced, the plan was to meet him at Green Cross, Moldgreen, and move in procession to the Union Room, Swan Yard.[126] In the event, so great were the numbers 'of his fellow workmen . . . bearing torches and a flag inscribed "The Press shall be Free" ', with music and bands, that the Union Room could not hold the people; Hobson, after an introduction by Pitkethly, addressed the crowd from a window of the White Hart Inn.[127]

The history of the *Voice* is rather more than just an episode in the history of political radicalism. In any case, that political radicalism was central rather than marginal to the life of communities in the West Riding, as in many places elsewhere. Huddersfield was one of the important category of industrial revolution growth towns that even now have been inadequately studied as a genus.[128] Its population growth between the 1801 and 1831 decennial censuses was fast, particularly during the first and third decades.[129] By 1833, despite this growth, the town was still

[121] Cordery, 'Voice of the West Riding', p. 26.

[122] Sanders, 'Joshua Hobson', p. 46.

[123] Cordery, 'Voice of the West Riding', p. 26.

[124] Sanders, 'Working-class Movements', p. 439; Cordery, 'Voice of the West Riding', p. 26.

[125] *VWR*, 15 June 1833; Sanders, 'Working-class Movements', p. 439.

[126] *VWR*, 18 January 1834.

[127] Ibid., 25 January 1834.

[128] Cf. Richard Dennis, *English Industrial Cities of the Nineteenth Century: A Social Geography* (Cambridge, 1984), especially pp. 293-96.

[129] B.R. Mitchell (with the collaboration of Phyllis Deane), *Abstract of British Historical Statistics* (Cambridge, 1962), Population and Vital Statistics Table 8, pp. 24-27.

primarily a market town and had more of an eighteenth-century character than a recognizably nineteenth-century one, not yet having received a railway connection.[130] Yet it was, through its experience, in the course of stamping a spirit on the age. This point is evident in the columns of the *Voice* and the career of its publisher. There is much of the parish pump in the paper. What appear to be Hobson's contributions are often highly personal. The characters are assumed to be known to the readers and the comment appears to draw on a stock of local intelligence and incident in a way rather reminiscent of the eighteenth century. Yet the paper is recognisably a newspaper and it deserves recognition as Huddersfield's first local newspaper; more than the political squib which the town's other unstamped publication appears to have been.[131] In this it is of the nineteenth century. Hobson later played a major part in the development of the town's journalism, editing two newspapers from 1855 to 1876 and indirectly stimulating surreptitious financial assistance to another.[132] He was, in fact, himself a curious amalgam of the eighteenth and nineteenth centuries. His radicalism looked back, in many respects, to the eighteenth century: to a set of democratic ideals developed or elaborated then; paradoxically, through friendships and Tory Radical political associations, to a paternalism associated with land and owners who recognized their social duties; to a 'golden age', in which a just society was ruled by the actions of a humane and representative parliament rather than by the legislation of an unjust and unrepresentative ruling class;[133] to an artisanate and small-propertied social class of producers, rather than a factory proletariat; and to the mobilization of a moral majority. The close relationship with Oastler and his move into Conservative, rather than Liberal politics, after the demise of Chartism, sums it up. The local 'establishment' and 'millocracy' in these later years was still predominantly 'Whig'. Hobson, as a man true to himself, his friends and his enemies, merely extended the politics of the Radical-Tory alliance into the second half of the century-a period in which most working men, and some of those who had been successful like

[130] Huddersfield's first railway connection was made on 2 August 1847.

[131] The *Witness*, 'a defunct farrago of cant, hypocrisy, bigotry and intolerance, and truckling to the powers that be', *VWR*, 10 August 1833. Unfortunately no copies appear to have survived.

[132] The *Huddersfield Chronicle*, 1855-71, and the *Huddersfield Weekly News*, 1871-76; for financial assistance to the *Huddersfield Examiner* see J.W. Ramsden to Wright Mellor, 7 and 12 May 1864.

[133] Cf. Cordery, 'Voice of the West Riding', p. 24.

himself and were no longer working men, largely attached themselves to Liberalism. Yet he was forward-looking too, and in that sense profoundly of the nineteenth century. He was everywhere on the side of reform, from factory legislation, the franchise and the press, to drains, parks and model lodging houses. Municipal reform and public property presented no more of a difficulty for Hobson than it did for Chamberlain. As he was to remark in the course of his last great campaign:

> Now if [the property] is to be given up, why not to the nation? The nation has as much right to it as Sir John; and in every sense affecting the community, the usufruct arising from the giving up to the nation would be far more beneficial than any that could possibly arise from the gift to the individual. [134]

Appendix
The Hobson Victim Fund Subscriptions

The dates of the *Voice* issue numbers were: no. 10, 10 August 1833; no. 12, 24 August 1833; no. 14, 7 September 1833; no. 16, 21 September 1833; no. 17, 28 September 1833 no. 20, 19 October 1833; no. 26, 30 November 1833; no. 29, 21 December 1833; no. 31, 4 January 1834 no. 34, 25 January 1834.

Name	*Amount* [*d.*]	*Voice* Issue No
Agar, Benj. (Lowerhouses and Longley)	6	14
Armitage, Ann	8	10
Armitage, Joseph	3	20
Balmforth, R.	6	12
Battey, B. (Honley)	6	12
Bentley, James	3	20
Bentley, Nathan	3	20
Berry, J. (From W. Vevers book)	2	26
Best, [Henry?]	3	20
Binns, [D.?]	3	20
Birkhead, Henry	3	20
Blagburn, George (Lowerhouses and Longley)	6	14
Bothroyd, C. (Honley)	6	12
Boothroyd, Elizabeth	2	10
Boothroyd, John (Lowerhouses and Longley)	6	14
Boothroyd, Joseph	6	10
Boothroyd, Lucy	2	10
Boothroyd, Thomas (Honley)	6	12
Bottomley, John (Honley)	6	14

[134] *Huddersfield Chronicle*, 6 October 1860.

Bottomley, T.	2	*20*
Bottomley, W.	2	*20*
Bradley, Jane	6	*10*
Bradley, William (C. Tinker's list)	6	*14*
Broadley, Robert	3	*20*
Brook, George	12	*10*
Brook, Joshua	3	*20*
Brook, S. (List of weekly subscribers)	2	*26*
Brook, Sarah	1	*10*
Broom, Joseph	3	*20*
Buckley, Ann	6	*10*
Buckley, Matthew (Honley)	3	*12*
Bury, James	6	*12*
Calkshaw, T.	3	*20*
Carter, Geo.	3	*20*
Castle, Elizabeth (Honley)	1	*12*
Castle, Joseph (Honley)	6	*12*
Chadwick, E.	12	*12*
Charlesworth, D.	3	*20*
Charlesworth, Sarah (Honley)	2	*14*
Cleworth, D.	6	*10*
Cochrane, W. (C. Tinker's list)	6	*20*
Collingwood, Eliza	3	*12*
Collins, J.	6	*12*
Crossland, James	3	*20*
Crossland, John	12	*20*
Crow, Arlam	3	*20*
Crow, J.	6	*12*
Danaley, T.	2	*12*
Dearnley, J (From W. Vevers book)	6	*26*
Denton, John (Lowerhouses and Longley)	3	*14*
Dickinson, Mary	15	*10*
Dickinson, Joshua (C. Tinker's list)	12	*20*
Downing, Charles (Honley)	6	*14*
Dyson, Joseph (C. Tinker's list)	12	*20*
Eastwood, Joseph (carpenter, Meltham)	2	*31*
Ellis, Henry	1	*20*
Field, Mary	1	*10*
Firth, George (Honley)	6	*14*
Firth, John	3	*12*
Firth, John and friends	9	*12*
Firth, John (C. Tinker's list)	6	*20*
(C. Tinker's book)	12	*34*
Fox, [W.?]	2	*20*
France, James	3	*20*
France, John	3	*20*
Franklin, B.	6	*12*
Fumpled, James (C. Tinker's list)	6	*14*
Garside, James	3	*20*
Garside, John	3	*20*
Gledhill, James (Lowerhouses and Longley)	6	*14*
Gledthill [Gledhill?], J.	12	*12*

	Amount	Voice
Greenhalgh, James (Lowerhouses and Longley)	12	14
Grieg, Charles (Leeds)		14
Haigh, G.	6	20
Haigh, H. (C. Tinker's book)	6	34
Haigh, J. (C. Tinker's list)	6	14
Haigh, James	3	20
Haigh, Joseph	2	20
Haigh, W. (Holthead)	12	16
Hairling [Harling?], J.R. (C. Tinker's book)	6	34
Haley, A.	6	12
	3	12
(2 from W. Vever's book)	3	26
	3	26
Hanson, Harriet	6	10
Harling, J.R. (C. Tinker's list)	6	20
Harrison, Hannah	6	10
Haynes, W.	2	12
Heblethwaite, T. (List of weekly subscribers)	2	26
Helliwell, James (Leeds. Victim Fund Treasurer)		14
Helliwell, Mary (Leeds)		14
Heppenstall, S.	3	12
Hetherington, Mary	3	16
Hirst, Henry	6	20
Hirst, J. (Holthead)	6	16
Hirst, Joseph (Honely)	3	12
Hirst, Joseph	3	20
Hirst, M.	3	20
Hirst, W. (Honley)	1	14
Holt, William	12	14
Hooper, Mrs (C. Tinker's list)	3	14
Horsfall, John	2	20
Horsfall, John (Honley)	6	12
Horsfall, [M.?]	3	20
Hoyle, Edmond	3	20
Johnson, T.	6	20
Jones, T. (2nd) (From W. Vever's book)	6	26
Jones, Tom	6	12
	6	12
(2 from C. Tinker's list)	6	20
	6	14
(1 from W. Vever's book)	6	26
Kinder, Jonathan	3	20
Ledger, Elizabeth (Honley)	1	12
Ledger, R (Honley)	6	12
Ledger, T(homas) (Honley) (named as a collector)	9	12
	2	14
Lee, Dick (Honley)	3	14
Lee, Thomas	3	20
Leech, John (list of weekly subscribers)	6	26
Lister, Thos.	6	34
Littlewood, Daniel (list of weekly subscribers)	3	26

Littlewood, John (list of weekly subscribers)	3	*26*
Liversedge, D.	2	*20*
Liversedge, Elick (C. Tinker's list)	6	*14*
Liversedge, Robt. (Lowerhouses and Longley)		*14*
Lockwood, B. (list of weekly subscribers)	6	*26*
Lodge, Thomas (C. Tinker's list)	5	*20*
Lord, Charles	3	*20*
Lumb, [W.?]	3	*20*
Lunn, W.	2	*20*
Mann, Alfred (Leeds)		*14*
Mason, G.	3	*20*
Matthewman, J.	3	*20*
Matthewman, L.	2	*20*
Mauvire, M.	3	*14*
May, James	3	*20*
Michel, M.	12	*14*
Mitchel, Abel	3	*20*
Mitchell, Michael	12	*10*
Mellor, Joseph	2	*20*
Mellor, Levi	6	*10*
Moore, James (Lowerhouses and Longley)	6	*14*
Mowbery, S.	3	*20*
Neil, John	3	*20*
North, Joseph (Lowerhouses and Longley)	12	*14*
Oldfield, Godfrey (Honley)	6	*14*
Oldfield, J. (list of weekly subscribers)	3	*26*
Oldfield, W.	3	*20*
Osborn, Hannah (Honley)	6	*14*
Parkin, J. (Holthead)	6	*16*
Pilling, Sarah (Leeds)		*14*
Pitkethly, L. (list of weekly subscribers)	6	*26*
Priestley, William	6	*20*
Rawson, T. (2) (list of weekly subscribers)	12	*20*
	6	*26*
Rider, William (Leeds Victim Fund Secretary)		*14*
Roberts, Geo. (Honley)	12	*14*
Robinson, C.	6	*12*
Rollett, W. (Holthead)	12	*16*
Scott, W. (Honley)	3	*14*
Senior, Fanny (Honley)	3	*12*
Senior, Jonas	6	*12*
Senior, Ruben (Honley)	6	*12*
Senior, W. (Emley. C. Tinker's list)	6	*14*
Senior, William (C. Tinker's list)	6	*20*
Sharp, John (Lowerhouses and Longley)	6	*14*
Sharp, Nancy (Lowerhouses and Longley)	1	*14*
Shaw, James	3	*20*
Shaw, Jonathan	2	*20*
Shaw, Joseph (C. Tinker's list)	12	*14*
Shaw, Ralph	3	*20*
Skain, James (Honley)	6	*12*
Slater, John	3	*20*

	Amount	Voice
Smith, Thomas	3	20
Spencer, John	12	10
Stead, Sarah (C. Tinker's book)	12	34
	6	34
Swift, B.	3	20
Swift, John (Honley)	6	12
Sykes, Abraham (Lowerhouses and Longley)	6	14
Sykes, Alfred (Lowerhouses and Longley)	3	14
Sykes, David (Lowerhouses and Longley)	12	14
Sykes, Edward (Lowerhouses and Longley)	6	14
Sykes, J. (Holthead)	6	16
Sykes, James (Lowerhouses and Longley)	6	14
Sykes, Rebecca (Lowerhouses and Longley)	2	14
Sykes, Samuel (Lowerhouses and Longley)	12	14
Sykes, Titus	2	20
Taylor, Abraham (Honley)	6	14
Taylor, B. (Honley)	6	12
Taylor, C.	3	20
Thorne, Mr	30	10
Thornton, Jos. (Honley)	2	14
Thornton, Peter	3	20
Tinker, Christopher (list of weekly subscribers)	12	10
	6	26
Tinker, John	3	20
Tinker, Mary	24	10
Tinker, Mary Ann	12	10
Todd, John	12	20
Townend, W. (list of weekly subscribers)	3	26
Turner, John	6	10
Vartrey, Joseph (Honley)	3	14
Vetch, Thomas	6	29
Vevers, Elizabeth	12	10
Vevers, Thomas	12	10
Vevers, W. (2 from W. Vevers book)	12	26
	12	26
Walker, Thomas (Leeds)		14
Walker, Martha (Lowerhouses and Longley)	1	14
Walker, Oliver	3	20
Walker, W.	3	20
Walker, William (Lowerhouses and Longley)	3	14
Walshaw, John (C. Tinker's list)		20
Warburton, S.	2	20
Webb, G.	3	20
Webster, Geo. (C. Tinker's book)	12	34
Whitikar, Joseph (Honley)	12	12
Whitwam, Jos. (Honley)	2	14
Wilkinson, John	3	20
Wilkinson, Joseph (C. Tinker's list)	12	14
Wilson, W. (list of weekly subscribers)	6	26
Winterbottom, C.	3	20
Wood, A.	6	20

Wood, John (Lowerhouses and Longley)	6	*14*
Wood, John (list of weekly subscribers)	6	*26*
Wood, Joseph (Honley)	6	*14*
Wood, Saml.	6	*34*
Woodhouse, John (C. Tinker's list)	30	*20*
Wrigley, W.	6	*20*
T.A. (list of weekly subscribers)	1	*26*
G.B. (list of weekly subscribers)	6	*26*
J.B.	3	*20*
(list of weekly subscribers)	1	*26*
N.B.	3	*12*
E.C. (collection by)	44	*12*
N.C. (list of weekly subscribers)	6	*26*
Wm. C (by J.O.)	12	*34*
B.D. (C. Tinker's list)	2	*14*
J.D.	2	*12*
W.D.	12	*10*
W.E. (collection by)	26	*12*
D.G.	12	*10*
D.G. (list of weekly subscribers)	6	*26*
T.G.	12	*12*
G.H.	2	*12*
R.H. (list of weekly subscribers)	6	*26*
W.H.	2	*16*
W.H. (C. Tinker's list)	5	*20*
B.J. (list of weekly subscribers)	1	*26*
F.K.	2	*20*
G.L.	12	*10*
J.M. A Friend to fair play	12	*10*
G.N.	2	*12*
J.O. (by J.O.)	6	*34*
J. Pan, an enemy to false Justice and Government	12	*12*
J.T.	3	*12*
W.T.	12	*10*
H.R.	12	*10*
G.S. An enemy to drunken parsons	2	*16*
J.S. A friend to the free press	6	*12*
M.V. (C. Tinker's list) (2)	3	*20*
	6	*20*
J.W. (C. Tinker's list)	6	*14*
J.W. A Republican	2	*16*
P.W.	3	*12*
S.W.	6	*12*
An enemy of drunken parsons	12	*10*
An enemy to informers, particularly		
at the instigation of a Parson	12	*10*
An enemy to stamps	12	*14*
An enemy to the Stamp Act	12	*12*
A Female Friend (2)	6	*10*
	6	*10*
A few ladies	12	*34*
A Friend (9)	8½	*34*

	Amount	Voice
	12	*20*
	2	
	1	
	12	*12*
	12	*10*
	24	
	13	
A Friend (C. Tinker's book) (5)	3	*34*
	3	
	24	
	12	
	2½	
A Friend (C. Tinker's list)	12	*14*
A friend (C. Tinker's list) (5)	12	*20*
	12	
	3	
	27	
	12	
A friend 2nd. sub. (C. Tinker's list)	12	*20*
A friend 3rd. sub. (C. Tinker's list)	12	*20*
A friend at C. Tinker's (list of weekly subscribers)	12	*26*
A friend (list of weekly subscribers)	240	*26*
A friend (list of weekly subscribers)	6	*26*
A friend (Honley) (3)	3	*14*
	6	
	3	
A friend (from Honley)	6	*12*
	24	
A friend from Glasgow	30	*14*
A friend from Manchester	12	*14*
From a few friends at Mill Bridge	30	*29*
A friend that can feel for another (C. Tinker's list)	12	*20*
A Friend to Freedom	6	*10*
A friend to freedom (C. Tinker's list)	12	*14*
A Friend of Liberty (C. Tinker's Book)	6	*34*
A friend to liberty (C. Tinker's list)	3	*20*
A friend to liberty of the press (C. Tinker's list)	24	*14*
A friend to the cause	30	*12*
A Hater of Priestcraft (from Meltham)	3	*31*
A lover of Freedom (from Meltham)	6	*31*
A real Radical (C. Tinker's list)	2	*14*
A republican	12	*34*
A Republican (C. Tinker's list)	12	*14*
A Republican (Honley)	4	*14*
A weekly subscriber (C. Tinker's list)	2	*14*
By a friend – collection	25	*12*
Collected by a friend	39	*12*
Collected at Court House	4	*10*
Collected by C. Tinker	141	*12*
Collected at Longroyd Bridge	79	*10*
Collected at Union Room	45	*10*

Collected in room by Mary Ann Tinker	18	*10*
Collected in room by Jane Bradley	12½	*10*
C. Tinker's box	80¾	*34*
D.	6	*10*
Hater of Tyranny (C. Tinker's list)	3	*20*
Holthead	104	*14*
Joe Atkinson's dressers (from W. Vevers book)	78	*26*
L. Pitkethly's box	78½	*34*
Mr M. (2) (1 by J.O.)	30	*34*
	6	*29*
Small sums	10	*10*
Subscriptions from Bradford (91)		*16*
Subscriptions from Dewsbury (10)		*20*
Subscriptions from Halifax (1)		*17*
Subscriptions from Leeds		
(11, including 7 identified and listed above)		
Subscriptions from Meltham Mill (C. Tinker's list)	20	*20*
	78	*26*
Subscriptions from Newsome (C. Tinker's list)	45	*20*
Subscriptions from Wakefield (28)		*12*
Subscriptions from Wakefield (25) (includes weekly		
subs. of a few friends at Huddersfield for one		
month)	341	*17*
The martyr's friend (C. Tinker's list)	30	*14*
Was rather Whiggish (2)	6½	*29*
	134	*28*
Weekly sub. for 2nd. month (C. Tinker's list)	291	*20*
W. Vevers box	234	*34*
The 'already published' lists	644½	*12*
	3881	*20*
	5046	*26*
	383	*26*
	7193½	*34*

4

The Imaginative Response of the Victorians to New Technology: The Case of the Railways

Asa Briggs

The Victorians, early, middle and late, had no doubt that theirs was 'an age of invention', a phrase that they themselves invented. Their responses to particular inventions, however, were various and often ambivalent, as they were in relation to urbanisation, to industrialisation and, indeed, to change itself. Pride was most obvious, but with it came both hope and fear, and above all, threat. After this there could come routine. The novelty associated with invention was lost. So also were the shock – and the fun.

The imaginative response to invention of the early Victorians, like that of their parents and grandparents, began with steam which, like machines for Thomas Carlyle, both attracted and repelled many of them:

> Whence, self-impulsive being, hadst thou birth?
> Heaven's living sun begat, as sages tell,
> The food by which thou livest deep in earth,
> Long ages hidden, and there spiced full well.
> O spirit-king! when thou with mighty mirth,
> Freshed with deep draughts of wine from nature's cell,
> And flushed with sun-born food and fiery hearth
> Dost rouse thee from thy lair at battle's smell –
> Forth from thy forehead float live plumes of snow,
> Aye dying and aye leaping forth to life . . .

The rich imagery of this poem by Charles Fox, published in 1864, could be found in prose too, as in the voluminous, encyclopedic writings of the Rev Dionysius Lardner, author of one of the best-known nineteenth-century treatises on the steam engine, *The Steam Engine Familiarly Explained and Illustrated* (1827). It seemed significant, as William Cooke Taylor put it in 1844, that 'the steam engine had no precedent' and that the spinning jenny was 'without ancestry': it had 'sprung into sudden existence like Minerva from the brains of Jupiter.'

One of the most fascinating examples of the imaginative response to the steam engine comes from Charlotte Brontë, who lived in a place where moors and mills met. In her novel of the industrial West Riding, *Shirley*, published in 1849, the proud and innovative millowner Robert Moore, when emotionally distressed, is asked by the most Yorkshire of Yorkshiremen, Mr Yorke, what has gone wrong. 'The machinery of all my nature,' he replies, 'the whole enginery of this human mill: the boiler, which I take to be heart, is fit to burst.' 'That should be put into print', Mr Yorke tells him, not without a touch of irony. 'It's striking. It's almost blank verse.' You'll soon be 'jiggling into poetry.'

'Jiggling into poetry' might have produced verse of the stuffed owl variety, and there was plenty of this in the nineteenth century, not least about steam engines – and railways. Yet the Industrial Muse, if significantly less active than the Pastoral Muse or even the Religious Muse, was seldom silent; and railways more than any other subject were often capable of evoking her. For the Victorians themselves, everything began with steam and the railway. The great mid-Victorians set the perspectives. 'We who lived before railways and survive out of the ancient world', wrote the novelist Thackeray in 1860, 'are like Father Noah and his family out of the Ark . . . Your railroad starts the new era, and we of a certain age belong to the new time and the old one.'

The early history of steam power had not been associated with locomotion, however, nor with mechanisation, but with mining, mining both of coal and of iron, the master materials of what Lewis Mumford was to call 'carboniferous capitalism'. Both had their 'romance'. For some, indeed for most people, coal seemed a 'miracle' product. You might start thinking about it with a cheerful fire burning in your grate or as you watched the last dying embers of a fire and moved back dreamily to prehistoric forests, the remains of which were fortuitously buried deep below English earth.

For such dreamers, geology was not a remote subject. Yet William Morris, who preferred history to pre-history and the history of the middle ages to the history of modern times, wished that coal had never been discovered. For good measure, John Ruskin added in iron also. He had an almost ideological objection to its comprehensive use as a material, a comprehensiveness which most Victorians favoured in what they thought of as a new 'iron age'. Once mainly considered as a metal of war, iron now could be extolled by Francis Horner, political economist, politician, and Member of Parliament, as 'not only the soul of every other manufacture, but the mainspring of civilised society'.

As soon as steam was applied not to pumping but the movement of machinery, the imaginative response to it became more ambivalent than it had been before, as I tried to show in my book *The Power of Steam* (1982). The work of civil engineers, particularly bridge builders, stimulated friendly responses; the work of mechanical engineers, widely diffused as it was through mechanics' institutes, provoked both enthusiastic and hostile reactions. Ebenezer Elliott, the Sheffield anti-corn law rhymer, in 'Steam of Sheffield' (1835) might salute 'Engines of Watt' as symbols of peace and might find 'glorious harmony' in 'the tempestuous music of the giant, steam', but the Chartist leader – and poet – Ernest Jones thought about steam power in terms not of harmony but of conflict:

> There, amid the wheel's dull droning
> And the heavy, choking air
> Strength's repining, labour's groaning
> And the throttling of despair.

And if not conflict, there was monotony. 'While the engine runs,' James Kay had written in 1832, 'the people must work: men, women and children are yoked together with iron and steam. The animal machine . . . is chained fast to the iron machine which knows no suffering and no weariness.'

Charles Dickens seized on such passages, adding his own poetry to them, when he wrote in *Hard Times* (1854), rightly regarded as the outstanding Victorian novel about factory industry – and there were not many of them – of the piston of a steam engine working 'monotonously up and down like the head of an elephant in a state of melancholy madness'. For Dickens, the rhythms of Coketown's working day, hot or cold, wet or fine, depended not on people, but on 'all of the melancholy mad elephants polished and oiled up for the single day's monotony'.

Not only for Dickens, but for other writers steam power applied to machines generated general responses both about environment – 'black country' – and about human relations – the 'exploitation' by employers of those whom they regarded as their 'hands'. Ruskin dwelt on both. So did Morris:

> Forget six counties overhung with smoke,
> Forget the snorting steam and piston stroke,
> Forget the spreading of the hideous town;
> Think rather of the packhorse on the down,
> And dream of London, small and white and clean.

These lines were written long before Morris, a Londoner himself, became a socialist.

Dickens, also a Londoner, had stage coaches, not pack horses, in mind, as he contemplated journeys north from London towards the industrial midlands, as in *Dombey and Son* (1848), with its unforgettable writing about railways, 'the greatest power in nature and art combined'; and in one of his 'Christmas Stories' he described inimitably how on a journey north 'the pastoral country darkened, became coaly, became smoky, became infernal, got better, got worse . . . miserable back dwellings, a black canal, and sick black towers of chimneys . . . The temperature changed, the dialect changed, faces got sharper, manner got shorter, eyes got shrewder and harder: yet all so quickly'.

It was easy to write of the railway simply, as did a Leeds engineer, Colonel Kitson Clark, engineering forebear of a distinguished twentieth-century historian of Victorian England, when he observed that 'there is nothing so serviceable or so valuable to mankind as the steam locomotive . . . a machine easy to make, easy to run, easy to replace, never weary from its birth in mint condition to the days that saw it worn, dirty and old, wasteful as nature and as inefficient as man, very human in characteristic'.

Such human metaphor, which started with the sense of a blueprint and ended with the sense of an engraving, was usually supplemented or replaced by animal metaphor, as basic notions of the utility or the serviceability of what Walt Whitman called 'the strong and quick locomotive' were enriched, not least for Whitman himself, by fantasy. 'Thee for my recitative', Whitman wrote in his poem 'To a locomotive in Winter':

> Thee in thy panoply, thy measur'd dual throbbing and thy beat convulsive,
> Thy black cylindric body, golden brass and silvery steel,
> Thy panderers side-bars, parallel and connecting rods, gyrating, shuttling at
>   thy sides . . .
> The dense and murky clouds out-belching from thy smoke-stack . . .

> Law of thyself complete, thine own track firmly holding
> (No sweetness debonair of tearful harp or glib piano thine).
> Thy trills of shrieks by rocks and hills return'd.

The 'music' of railways, caught in the twentieth century on records and discs, has never been simply an enthusiasm of vintage railway lovers.

For Whitman, who saw 'fierce-throated beauty' in the locomotive, which he called 'type of the modern – emblem of motion and power – pulse of the continent' – it was natural that 'the Muse' should summon him to recite about it:

> For once come serve the Muse and merge in verse, even as I here see thee.

Whitman was not alone on either side of the Atlantic in invoking the Muse. For Charles Mackay, poet and journalist – he was editor of the *Illustrated London News* from 1852 to 1859 – the locomotive, 'triumph of mind', 'fire-bowell'd, iron ribb'd, of giant strength' was also 'snake-like,' while for Alexander Anderson, writing a generation later, the locomotive had 'a heart of fire and a soul of steel and a Samson in every limb'. Other writers spoke of dragons and crocodiles. Anderson had worked as a railway linesman before becoming in later life a librarian at Edinburgh University.

Long after railways had lost their novelty, two modern poets, W.H. Auden and Stephen Spender, like the documentary film makers of the 1930s, expressed the same feelings as Mackay in their poems 'Night Mail' and 'The Empress'. Auden thought of the 'disciplined love' that alone could have produced great engines, while Spender described the locomotive moving 'entranced', 'like a comet through flame':

> Wrapt in her music no bird song nor bough
> Breaking with honey buds, shall ever equal.

Interestingly, Rudyard Kipling had anticipated Auden's thought in 'M'Andrew's Hymn' (1893), as illuminating a poem as his famous poem of empire, 'Recessional'. In it he makes M'Andrew say;

> Lord, Thou hast made this world below the shadow of a dream
> An', taught by time, I tak' it so – exceptin' always Steam.
> From coupler-flange to spindle-guide I see Thy hand, O God,

Predestination in the stride o'yon connecting rod.
John Calvin might ha' forged the same – enormous, certain, slow,
Ay, wrought it in the furnace-flame – my *Institutio*.

Inspired by a liner's engines, that was Scots poetic imagination, without the benefit of Max Weber or Tawney! 'Religion and the Rise of Machinery'.

A year later, Kipling wrote his poem 'The Nine-fifteen', in which he dismissed those of his readers who saw no 'romance' on a railway. Yet it was not only his more conventional readers who missed the romance. And even while Kipling was writing, there were other poetic reactions. John Davidson, born in 1857, saw the railways as 'inadequate', and in his poem of 1909, 'The Testament of Sir Simon Simplex concerning Automobilism', a wonderful title, he turned the railway into a symbol of a dying nineteenth century:

> . . . The future sage
> Will blame sententiously the railway age,
> Preachers upon its obvious vices pounce,
> And poets, wits and journalists pronounce
> The nineteenth century in prose and rhyme
> The most unhappy period of time.

Sir Simon was right. In a poem called 'The Nineteenth Century', Roy Fuller born in 1912, saw the locomotive as 'an anachronistic god' who had 'lasted beyond his final period'.

Fuller, too, however, could not leave the music out when he turned back to the first railway age, although this time it was not the music of the railway that he seized upon, but rather great parallel music:

> Stockton to Darlington, 1825:
> Stephenson on the sparkling iron road –
> Chimney-hatted and frock-coated – drives
> His locomotive, while the Lydian mode
> Of Opus 132 may actually be
> In the course of making.

Beethoven triumphed.

At the beginning of the railway age Carlyle had led the way with railway imagery. In his *Signs of the Times* (1829) he explained that 'there is no end to machinery. Even the horse is stripped of his harness, and finds a fleet fire-horse yoked in his stead'. Fantasies about the iron horse were as compulsive during the 1830s and 1840s as facts concerning the amount of coal consumed by locomotives, the mileage of track, 'the iron way', or a little later, after Bradshaw (1839) the first detailed railway timetables. Tennyson was to muse about the track in 'Locksley Hall' (1842) without understanding its mechanics. Wordsworth in his sonnet 'Steamboats, Viaducts and Railways' had invoked the Muse, as Tennyson did after him, to gain 'prophetic sense of future change', and he was still as optimistic as he had been in 'The Excursion' (1814)

> . . . Time,
> Pleased with your triumph o'er his brother Space,
> Accept from your [Nature's] bold hands the proffered crown
> Of hope.

Arthur Hugh Clough saw no hope. In his 'Dipsychus', first published in 1865 but written around fifteen years earlier – before Tennyson's *In Memoriam* - he had described 'the age of instruct' as gone.

> . . . the modern Hotspur
> Shrills not his trumpet of 'To Horse, To Horse!'
> But consults columns in a railway guide;
> A Demigod of figures; our Achilles
> Of computation.

'Fiddling with a piston or a valve' had nothing exciting about it for Clough.

Dickens was always aware, however, of what Wordsworth in 'The Excursion' had called 'the darker side', and in *Hard Times* he brought back real, if magical, horses – circus horses – to set against the facts of the machine and of the locomotive. In *Dombey and Son* (1847) the railway train had become not a 'symbol of modernity' but of 'Death'. 'The power that forced itself upon the iron way – its own – defiant of all paths and road, piercing through the heart of every obstacle, and dragging living creatures of all classes, ages and degrees behind it, was a type of the triumphant master Death.' A generation later, Thomas Cooper, the ex-Chartist leader, nostalgically recalled a time when;

> There was no Rail whereon the steam-steed sped
> With snort, and puff, and haste to turn men pale
> With fear, and fill their hearts with instant dread
> of death . . .

Victorians and New Technology: The Railways

In an age of horses, their last great age, as Michael Thompson has shown, it is not surprising that much of the language of locomotion was related to the language of the horse. Without any sense of symbolism, the controversial power of steam had been measured in terms of horse power; and before the locomotive had been described as 'the iron horse' pre-Victorian bicycles had been called 'hobby horses'. At the end of the century, the automobile was to be first known as a 'horseless carriage', a description that inspired one enthusiast publicly to express the hope in 1897 that 'the horse would soon be abolished and found only in the hunting field and parks'. The response of his audience to that was laughter, always, like curiosity, one imaginative response to any invention.

It is a response that can easily be ignored, particularly in the case of railways, because of the death motif. All invention has usually had a fun element, starting with the work of the inventors themselves, many of whom have been fully aware that discovery involves play as well as work, and the first customers, too, have often been attracted to new products as much by delight in novelty as by trust in their merits. 'Novelty' was one of the first names of a railway locomotive, and Fanny Kemble in her famous and much quoted letter to Harriet St Leger, written on 26 August 1830, dwelt on the novelty when she travelled on a trial run on the Liverpool and Manchester railway with George Stephenson himself in command.

Fanny Kemble was as inspired by Stephenson himself, an unequivocal enthusiast, as she was by his locomotive: he told her 'he would soon make a famous engineer of me, which, considering the wonderful things he *has* achieved, I dare say is not impossible'. As for the locomotive he was driving:

> . . . she (for they make these curious little fire horses all mares) consisted of a boiler, a stove, a small platform, a bench, and behind it a barrel containing enough water to prevent her being thirsty for fifteen miles. She goes upon wheels, which are her feet and are moved by bright steel legs called pistons; these are propelled by steam, and in proportion as more steam is applied to the upper extremities (the hip-joints, I suppose) of these pistons, the faster they move the wheels; and when it is desirable to diminish the speed, the steam, which unless suffered to escape would burst the boiler, evaporates through a safety valve into the air. The reins, bit and bridle of this wonderful beast is a small steel handle, which applies or withdraws

the steam from its legs or pistons, so that a child might manage it.
The coals, which are its oats, are under the bench.

Given the spell of such writing, it mattered little that four years later
R. Cast could produce a pamphlet called 'Rail-Road imposters detected; or
facts and arguments to prove that the Manchester and Birmingham Railway
has not paid one per cent nett profit; and that the Birmingham, Bristol,
Southampton, Windsor and other railways, are, and must for ever be, only
bubbly speculation'. It had mattered, however, that the official opening of
the Liverpool and Manchester line was associated not only with technical
triumph but the terrible accident of Huskisson's death.

Thereafter much of the poetry and the prose of the railway – and
much of the poetry was anonymous – was focused on accidents. William
McGonagall's 'The Tay Bridge Disaster' was one of the best-known
examples, though McGonagall was a stuffed owl poet:

> So the train mov'd slowly along the Bridge of Tay,
> Until it was about midway,
> Then the centre girder with a crash gave way
> And down went the train and passengers into the Tay!
> The storm fiend did loudly bray,
> Because ninety lives had been taken away,
> On the last Sabbath day of 1879,

Which will be remember'd for a very long time.

McGonagall found a moral, however, in the sad story:

> . . . Your central girders would not have given way
> At least many sensible men do say,
> Had they been supported on each side with buttresses,
> At least many sensible men confesses,
> For the stronger we our houses do build
> The less chance we have of being killed.

The Tay Bridge had needed a civil engineer as firm and forthright as
Kipling's mechanical engineer M'Andrew.

In Dicken's periodical *All the Year Round* the role not of the railway
builder or the locomotive driver, but of the signalman had been stressed
in a short anonymous poem published in 1862 which begins:

> The dry tense cords against the signal post
> and Rattle, like rigging of a wind-tossed ship.

One of Dickens's own 'Christmas Stories', 'No 1 Branch Line: The Signalman', catches a genuine sense not only of strain but of horror. If the signals went wrong either as a result of human error or any other cause, terrifying accidents might happen.

It is remarkable, however, that although Dickens himself was involved in a railway accident in Kent in 1865, the Staplehurst crash, which affected him profoundly for the rest of his life, it was with cool detachment that he described what had happened in a postscript to *Our Mutual Friend* (1865), the manuscript of which he was carrying with him. In the postscript he wrote simply:

> On Friday 9th June in the present year, Mr and Mrs Boffin . . .
> were on the South Eastern Railway with me in a terribly destructive
> accident. When I had done what I could to help others, I climbed back
> into my carriage – nearly turned over a viaduct, and caught aslant upon
> the turn – to extricate the worthy couple. They were much soiled,
> but otherwise unhurt!

In retrospect, Dickens was so much affected by the accident that when memories of it returned he would even leave a train before he had completed his journey.

The imagery of the journey is often striking, though seldom as profound as it is in Chapter 20 of *Dombey and Son*, 'Mr Dombey goes upon a Journey'. Thomas Hardy hints at profundities, however, in his 'Midnight on the Great Western', where his 'journeying boy', with a railway ticket stuck in the band of his hat, goes out into the night:

> What past can be yours, O journeying boy
> Towards a world unknown,
> Who calmly, as if incurious quite
> On all at stake, can undertaken
> Thus plunge alone?

There had been many earlier attempts to conceive of the railway journey as a 'type' of a spiritual journey not into the unknown but towards a named destination. Indeed, there was more than one version of 'A Spiritual Railway', one of which, commemorating two victims of a railway accident in 1845, was inscribed on a tombstone in the cloister in Ely cathedral. It began

> The line to heaven by Christ was made
> With heavenly truth the Rails are laid,
> From Earth to Heaven the line extends
> To life eternal where it ends.

'Repentance' was the name of the station where passengers were taken in, and on this railway there was no reason to fear either the driver or the signalman. 'God's Word' was the first engineer:

> God's Love the Fire, his Truth the Steam,
> Which drives the Engine and the Train.

There was, however, a first, second and third class on the train. Which 'poor sinners' were in which class of carriage was not stated.

W.E. Henley, born in 1849, put trust in himself rather than in God, and as he 'flashed across the level', 'thundered through the bridges' and 'swayed along the ridges', he thought in 1876 of the girl waiting at his destination:

> I think of her waiting, waiting
> And long for a common hansom.

Whom you would meet at the end of the journey was as common a theme as whom you would meet in the carriage.

There seem to have been few changes of train on Henley's or on other imaginative journeys. Yet railway junctions, where everyone changed, figured prominently in many reflections on the railway, including the reflections of Dickens; he compared them to a 'congress of iron vipers'. In 'The Lazy Tour of two Idle Apprentices', published in *Household Words* in 1857, he contrasted day and night: the station was 'either totally unconscious or wildly raving'. At times it looked 'as if the last train for ever had gone without issuing any railway tickets'. It was Trollope, however, who made the most of the junction theme in his novel *The Prime Minister* (1876). It was at the Tenway Junction, 'a marvellous place, quite unintelligible to the uninitiated', that Ferdinand Lopez met his death. There was no music here, only 'pandemoniac noises'. Some trains crashed through, like 'flashes of substantial lightning', while others stopped, 'disgorging and taking up passengers by the hundreds'. Shocking though his theme was, there was nothing shocking about Trollope's images. One of them was designed to appeal to a large section of his readers who had never even been to a railway junction: 'the space occupied by the convergent rails seems to be sufficient for a large farm.'

Trollope himself was at home on railways in a way that Dickens was not. He wrote elsewhere of writing and reading in trains. He found it possible, employing a pencil, 'to write as quickly in a railway-carriage as [he] could at [his] desk'. The 'greater part' of *Barchester Towers* (1857) was composed in this way. Many Victorians, too, must have read it on a train. The term 'railway novel' was first used during the late 1840s, and one publisher, Routledge, introduced a shilling series of reprinted fiction called 'The Railway Library' in 1849. Two years later, W.H. Smith secured a monopoly of bookstalls on the London and North-Western Railway and by the time *Barchester Towers* appeared his business had a dominating position on many other lines also.

By then, talk of railway junctions was as familiar to mid-Victorian readers as new railway embankments, symbols of a great divide, had become to their parents; and there is at least one poem – by Arthur Hugh Clough which describes a junction. *Sic Itur* begins:

> As at a railway junction, men
> Who come together, taking then
> One the train up, one down again,
> Meet never! . . .

and goes on to suggest that there can, after all, be a new meeting. The poem is taut, like much else by Clough, and the 'brief encounter' theme is missing from it.

There was less mystery, if more magic, about speed than there was about either journeys or junctions, and Fanny Kemble's letter, already quoted, is mainly cited because of its references to speed. For her, travelling by rail was 'almost like flying'. The speed of travel increased, but did not increase dramatically during the last years of the century, when Robert Louis Stevenson wrote his lines 'From a Railway Carriage' in *A Child's Garden of Verses* (1885):

> Faster than trains, faster than witches,
> Bridges and houses, hedges and ditches . . .
> And ever again in the wink of an eye,
> Painted stations whistle by.

The thrill of railways for the child produced new generations of 'railway children', a theme that was to be developed not only in words but on the cinema screen (1970) in the twentieth century.

Poets were more interested in express trains than in parliamentary trains that chugged slowly on local lines, and they preferred to describe them roaring through the night rather than in the daytime. Edmund Blunden, born in 1896, when the branch lines were complete, was one of the few poets to salute the small train on the branch line in a poem published in 1904:

> The small train went from view behind the plantation,
> Monotonous – but there's grace in monotony.

It was a rural train, however, and the monotony was very different from the monotony of Coketown.

Railways had introduced the concept of speed as well as the concept of power – the latter concept was already there in the late eighteenth century with Erasmus Darwin and Matthew Boulton – into the literature of the imagination inspired by technology. Locomotives, even branch-line locomotives, were not only more powerful than horses; they were faster. They were faster too than the last magnificent stagecoaches which had set out to be both faster and more magnificent than any vehicles that had gone before. Stagecoaches were already being were treated as symbols of the past by the late 1830s. Even by then it had become clear that the speed of the railway was not merely physical speed. For one of George Eliot's characters, Mr Deane in *The Mill on the Floss* (1860), steam drove 'every wheel double-pace [a gross under-statement] and the wheel of fortune along with 'em'. Mr Deane did not complain, however: 'I don't find fault with the changes as some people do. Trade, Sir, opens a man's eyes; and if the population is to get thicker on the ground, as it's doing, the world must use its wits at inventions of one sort or another.'

There were to be many inventions 'of one sort or another' during the nineteenth century, and in some ways the railway set the pattern for most subsequent reactions to new technology, just as railway legislation set the pattern of legislation for telegraphy and wireless. Indeed, railway metaphors and railway analogies were taken up later in the history of apparently quite different forms of invention. Thus, Isaac Pitman's Victorian version of shorthand, so-called 'stenographic soundhand', introduced in 1837, the year that Queen Victoria ascended the throne, would only succeed, according to Pitman, if it 'rolled upon its own wheel'; and when Pitman's first biographer looked back over the first fifty years of progress in 1887, he compared the inventor's first system with the first locomotives, the Rocket and Puffing Billy. In fact, of course, as I showed in *Victorian Things* (1988), shorthand had not rolled upon its own wheel. It had benefited, if belatedly, from the invention of the typewriter, another great invention which caused a few writers of articles and short stories to express the regret that it had not been available to the blind John Milton in the seventeenth century: it would have saved him, they claimed, from dependence on his daughters.

From a modern perspective, the railway, shorthand and the typewriter belong to what we now call 'communications', so that the images and comparisons conjured up by Pitman's reverential biographer do not seem unduly out of the ordinary. It required the telegraph, however, following in the wake of the postage stamp, another Victorian invention, to focus attention on systems of communication which did not require actual physical transportation. And after the telegraph came the telephone and radio and in the new century, after the typewriter, the computer and the word-processor.

Significantly, however, by the end of the nineteenth century, much of the relevant imagery was no longer that of arteries and flows, imagery associated with railway systems, but of nerves and circuits. As Sir Gabriel Stokes put it in 1889 in a speech at the Institution of Electrical Engineers – he was replying to the Prime Minister, Lord Salisbury: 'nowadays the whole earth resembles, in a measure, one of our own bodies. The electrical wires represent the nerves, and the messages are conveyed from the most distant regions to the central place of government, just as in our bodies where sensations are conveyed to the sensorium'.

The telegraph was the link between two phases of response, providing as it did, in the words of *The Times*, 'a vast enlargement . . . given to the sphere of human activity'. Its users were in no doubt about 'the miracle'. Nor was Dickens. In a highly rhetorical article in *Household Words* in 1850, called 'Wings of Wire', he displayed none of the ambivalence that he displayed towards the railway. 'In an age of express trains, painless operations, crystal palace [it had not yet been built], revolutions and republics, Mormons and Puseyites and a hundred curiosities, such as our grandfathers and grandmothers never dreamed about,' Dickens began:

there is yet little difficulty in saying which of our modern wonders is really the most wonderful. In our fast days, we have one thing above

71

all others, the fastest; in our generation of marvels, we have one thing of all others the most marvellous . . . Among all the useful things which human ingenuity has of late completed, it would not be difficult to show that the Electrical Telegraph is one of the most useful.

Yet Dickens soon turned, as he had always promised that he would do since the time of the first issue of *Household Words*, from utility to romance. 'The old heroes of the racecourse – the fleet-footed descendants of Arabian desert', he went on, back to the horses again, 'have been outdone.' Writing long before the automobile enthusiast drew laughter from his audience when he talked of the abolition of the horse, Dickens must have drawn applause from his readers when he wrote that:

> . . . horseflesh in its finest forms may henceforth aid our sports, grace
> our vehicles [here he was up-to-date, not prophetic], give vitality to
> our green pastures, but may not longer typify haste. We have caught
> and can control another steed. We have bitted and bridled and broken
> in another wonder which for ages sported in elemental freedom round
> about us . . . [We have outdone] even delicate Ariel, the tricksy spirit
> who could 'put a girdle round about the earth in forty minutes'.

That such a passage, which in retrospect points to the age of broadcasting – the BBC's house journal is called *Ariel* – comes so early in Queen Victoria's reign qualifies in my view some of the points about the newness of responses to time and space that have been made by Stephen Kern in his interesting book, *The Culture of Time and Space* (1983), in which he argued that between 1880 and 1918 'sweeping changes in technology and culture created distinctive new modes of thinking about experiencing time and space'. There was little that the Victorians said of an imaginative kind about the telephone, indeed, that they had not already said about the telegraph, just as they and their successors had little of an imaginative kind to say about wireless that had not already been said about the telephone.

There were, in fact, continuing patterns of response to the different 'novelties' in the sequence that we now call a continuing 'communications revolution' – with an undoubtedly forward-looking orientation throughout, as one invention gave way to another and with many inventions being foreseen even before they became technically feasible. As the *Popular Science Magazine*, one of many such magazines launched during the 1880s and 1890s, put it after wireless had become the latest 'miracle of science':

Wireless telegraphy [and that was all that there then was] is the nearest approach to telepathy that has been vouched to our intelligence, and it serves to stimulate our imagination and to make us think that things greatly hoped for can always be reached, though not exactly in the way expected.

This is the other side of the coin to those statements from famous men, not least scientists, insisting that after the railway it would never be possible ever to invent things like aeroplanes and television which we now take for granted. Indeed, it was before Marconi arrived in London in 1896 with his bag of primitive wireless apparatus that the future world of television was forecast in the magazines. Air travel, if not necessarily by aeroplane, was a familiar theme during the 1890s when Bell was actually experimenting with kites to study lift and drag, an example of his own technological progression that is as striking as Edison's. Yet a decade or more earlier, the imagination of the first cyclists, like those of the first railway travellers, had often turned to flying, and in Washington in 1897 Professor S.P. Langley, Secretary of the Smithsonian Institute, struck an acceptable note of confidence when he proclaimed that 'the great universal highway overhead is soon to be opened'. A year earlier he had invented a steam-driven flying machine that flew 4,200 feet over the Patromac river without a pilot.

By then, of course, there was a new form of power, electricity, the marvel of which stimulated an immediate imaginative response in pictures – as steam had done earlier – as well as in words. A memorable *Punch* cartoon of 1881 showed King Steam and King Coal anxiously watching the young infant Electricity and asking 'What will he grow up to?' This was not the only time that *Punch*, appealing, as it always did, to comfortable middle-class opinion, found invention a matter of anxious concern rather than, as was more often the case in its pages, a topic of fun.

No one in Britain seems to have been quite as deeply stirred by electricity, symbol of light as well as of power, as Henry Adams on the further side of the Atlantic in his disturbing comparison of the roles of the Virgin in the thirteenth century and the Dynamo in the nineteenth century, or Nikola Tesla, whose imagination sometimes outran his science, or Park Benjamin, whose breathless book *The Age of Electricity*, published in 1887, is a kind of electrical rhapsody. Electricity for Benjamin could 'impel the locomotive and control the brake which stopped its motion. It could ring the chimes in the steeple or the bells in the kitchen'. It could record the votes which 'will change the destiny of a great nation or set down the music of the last popular melody'. Benjamin left the most profound of his contrasts, however, to the last. Electricity could serve the purposes both of peace and of war, of defence and attack. It could operate either as 'a vigilant and sleepless sentinel', guarding signals, or as a most treacherous foe', exploding 'the deadly torpedo' and 'firing the hidden mine'.

A study of such material before and after the invention of the railway reinforces the view that for the historian there are quite different ways of approaching the history of technology. Narrowly technological historians approach it in terms of materials and processes, including replication and standardisation, and some of them have become industrial archaeologists in the process. There can be nostalgia in this, the nostalgia not of the gospel of steam but of vintage steam, and not only of steam but of the vintage locomotive, the vintage automobile and the vintage aeroplane.

Economic historians, like economists, approach technological history in terms of the geography of resource distribution; the choice of available technological options; cost ratios and profit expectations; the diffusion of technologies; the lags between discovery and application; and the relationship between innovation and development. They leave many questions unanswered, however, including some of the most strategic questions concerning timing and policy,

Social and cultural historians drawn to the subject increasingly – and for a variety of reasons – are interested primarily in human reactions at different levels, above all, perhaps, in the impact of invention on the attitudes of established and new interest groups and on the ways of life of different types of workers, some of them displaced by machines, some of them mastering new skills, as locomotive drivers and signalmen, not to speak of construction engineers, undoubtedly did. They can move on easily to popular culture, which can seldom be separated off from technology. The most adventurous of them – and in the United States Daniel Boorstin has led the way – have set out to integrate technological and general history, narrative and analysis. A few cultural historians have interested themselves in the cultures surrounding specific technologies – railways provide only one example – and have compared one culture with another. Few, however, have yet dared to try to explain why the same technologies have been set in different frames in different places.

I should add, of course, that cultural historians must concern themselves with responses in the visual arts and in music with at least the same degree of scholarly attention as responses in words. It was in 1844 that Turner in his seventieth year exhibited his much discussed painting *Rain, Steam and Speed*, in which a hare vainly tries to outdistance a train. A point was made

74

with complete economy, although there were other points that are still being argued about. Later Victorian paintings focused more on the railway station than on the track itself or on the locomotive.

For yet another response, that of the social as distinct from the financial accountant, it is interesting to turn to the biologist A.R. Wallace, who, in his book *The Wonderful Century*, which appeared in 1898, attempted to present a kind of balance sheet of nineteenth-century gains and losses. As far as invention was concerned, Wallace claimed, the nineteenth century had been superior to any others that had gone before it. Indeed, any accountant would be driven to compare it with 'the whole preceding historical period' since time began. There had been only seven 'inventions of the first rank' – his phrase – before 1800 – alphabetical writing, Arabic numerals, the printing press (he left out gunpowder which Francis Bacon, endowed with a very special technological imagination, had put in at the beginning of the seventeenth century), the mariner's compass, the telescope, the barometer and the steam engine. During the nineteenth century there had been thirteen. And it was the railway, above all else, that carried the Victorians into the future.

5

Railways and Coastal Shipping in Britain in the Later Nineteenth Century: Cooperation and Competition

John Armstrong

Among Philip Bagwell's many publications, one of his earliest was on the Railway Clearing House (RCH).[1] This was the first definitive history of the establishment, functions, and mechanisms of the RCH. One of the functions which Philip highlighted was its role as an impartial administrator of the various pooling agreements, conferences and grouping arrangements that the independent railway companies concluded to ensure through working and to reduce inter-company competition especially on long distance hauls. This work predated Philip's interest in coastal shipping and, as befits a book on a railway institution, there is relatively little about competing modes of transport. The railway companies did not confine their attempts to regulate long distance traffic to their own transport mode. For long hauls their chief rival was the coastal steamboat and this remained surprisingly competitive until the Great War. Hence many railway conferences were only too keen to bring their sea-borne rivals into an agreement in order to restrict competition, raise freight rates and allocate traffic on a 'reasonable' basis. Philip Bagwell noted that the Dundee, Perth and London Shipping Company was brought into the English and Scotch Traffic Agreement in

---

[1] P.S. Bagwell, *The Railway Clearing House in the British Economy, 1842–1922* (London, 1968).

1856, as did Channon in his thesis,[2] and that in 1867 'a similar kind of agreement' was concluded on the Clyde-Mersey route by railways and steamboat firms,[3] but neither he nor Channon pursued the analysis to show what these agreements implied about coaster-railway competition.

The purpose of this essay is to demonstrate that there were a range of methods of restricting inter-modal competition which have previously been ignored. The use of pools and conferences by the railway companies is now well known, as is the adoption, in the later nineteenth century, of conferences among shipping companies in some foreign liner trades.[4] Recently it has been shown that agreements, analogous to conferences in all but name, existed from a much earlier date among firms plying the coastal trade using steam liners and that these were widespread geographically and continued in existence at least until the First World War.[5] In other words, the coastal liner companies endeavoured to minimise competition and regulate trade among themselves just as the railways did. This essay will show that there was also inter-modal collaboration over freight rates and levels of service, both formally through written agreements between railway conferences and coastal liner companies and by more informal understandings.

In that it draws heavily on the records of the RCH it follows in Philip Bagwell's footsteps, but inasmuch as he did not pursue the steamboat theme it builds on that work in trying to elucidate the nature of railway-steamboat competition and collaboration, drawing essentially on railway-generated sources because of the paucity of coastal shipping records that have survived.

It has been established elsewhere that an east coast steamboat pool came into existence in 1839, was undoubtedly in operation in 1845 and was probably still active in the 1860s.[6] One of the lines which made up this pool

---

[2] Ibid., p. 254; G. Channon, *Pooling Agreements between the Railway Companies Involved in Anglo-Scottish Traffic, 1851–69,* unpub. Ph.D. thesis, University of London (1975) pp. 363–64.

[3] Ibid., p. 255.

[4] See for instance, G. Channon, 'Railway Pooling in Britain before 1900: The Anglo-Scottish Traffic' in *Business History Review,* Vol. 62 (1988), and J.H. Dyos and D.H. Aldcroft, *British Transport: An Economic Survey from the Seventeenth Century to the Twentieth* (Leicester, 1969) pp. 269–72.

[5] J. Armstrong, 'Conferences in British Nineteenth-Century Coastal Shipping', in *Mariner's Mirror,* 77 (1991).

[6] Ibid., pp. 58–59.

was the Aberdeen Steam Navigation Company (ASN). It is clear that as well as cooperating with other steam coaster firms, this company was also collaborating with the long distance railways at least from the later 1850s. In March 1856 the goods managers of the railway companies which made up the English and Scotch Traffic Committee worked out with the Aberdeen shipping company revised rates for goods traffic between London and Aberdeen.[7] This deal was then put to the Octuple Agreement for its approval.[8] Although two of the railways – the Aberdeen and the Scottish Midland Junction – were unhappy with the details, the Octuple insisted on the increases as the previous rates were not remunerative.

The terms of the agreement with the shipping company can be pieced together. Freight and passenger rates were set mutually and there was a differential in favour of the steamboat company of roughly 10s. per ton. Cattle traffic was to be divided proportionately between the two modes, with the railways taking two thirds and the steamers one third. There is no detail of the workings of this agreement in its early years but in the 1860s the ASN was in frequent correspondence with Mr H. Ormond, the Liverpool cattle traffic manager of the London North Western Railway Company (LNWR) about alterations in freight rates. For instance on 26 September 1861 Ormond wrote requesting that 'the Steam Packet companies . . . agree to advance the present ruinously low rate [on cattle] from 15s. to 20s. per head, as in that case the Railway companies will be spared the necessity of making the reduction proposed'.[9] This suggests continuity in preferring mutually beneficial pricing policies rather than cut-throat competition. At the time of this request the ASN felt unable to agree to the rise because it was facing severe competition from another shipping company, the Northern Steam Company, whose cattle rates had been reduced below 15s. However, once the two competing steamboat companies agreed to amalgamate they wasted little time in writing to Ormond, on 25 October, to assure him they 'were in a position to give effect to' his proposed increase in cattle rates,[10] and on 19 November the

---

[7] Public Record Office (henceforth PRO) RAIL 1080/508, minute 18.

[8] The Octuple Agreement commenced in 1851. It derived its name from the fact that eight railway companies were involved, whose lines made through routes from London to Edinburgh and to Glasgow. Effectively the Octuple controlled all Anglo-Scottish long distance traffic. See Bagwell, *The Railway Clearing House* pp. 251–53.

[9] Aberdeen University Library (henceforth AUL) Ms 2479/8, minute of 26 September 1861.

[10] AUL, Ms 2479/8, minute of 25 October 1861.

secretary of the ASN confirmed that the rate on cattle was being advanced to 20s. per head 'after Saturday next'. [11]

That this sort of collaboration was not unusual but rather part of the normal methods adopted to regulate competition is shown by a further incident in the mid 1860s. In the spring of 1864 a deputation from the English and Scotch Traffic Sub Committee called upon the ASN to try to agree rates for livestock carriage between Aberdeen and London and possibly north of Aberdeen as well. [12] The railway companies hoped to conclude an agreement binding for five years which would cover not merely the freight rates to be charged but also how the total traffic was to be divided between the two modes of transport. [13] Although there was some disagreement between the various railway companies who were parties to the conference as to the best course of action, there was no fuss about the principle of talking with the steam packet companies. This suggests that it was perceived as a normal course of action which had been used before to prevent 'ruinous' competition.

This view is supported by evidence of events two years later when the railway companies decided to increase their rates on cattle and meat traffic from Aberdeen to London. For they wrote to the ASN, *inter alia*, informing the coastal company of the new rates and subsequently called upon its manager 'with a view to induce that company to advance their rates for meat and cattle from Aberdeen to London'. [14] Initially they met with little success, for the steam packet company replied that 'while not averse to entertain the consideration of an increase in the rates on cattle from Aberdeen, [we] cannot in the meantime and without further information on the effects of the through rates proposed by the railway companies, agree to the terms of rates stated in their letters'. [15] What is evident from the tone of this letter is that the coastal firm was not surprised to be approached in such a manner by the railway companies. Quite the opposite, it was obviously a normal part of business. The only question was whether to accede to the request, or how much resistance to put up.

The reason for the railway companies repeated approaches to the shipping company is straightforward. In the eyes of the railway firms the steamers were proving annoyingly effective in retaining a significant

---

[11] Ibid., minute of 19 November 1861.
[12] PRO, RAIL 1080/509, minute 1108.
[13] Ibid., minute 1210.
[14] Ibid., minute 1498 and appendix.
[15] AUL, Ms 2479/10, minute of 20 November 1866.

share of the trade in cattle and meat. This is surprising, for it is in just such perishable or damageable high value commodities that the railway should have had a significant advantage over the coaster and hence have been able to charge a premium price to compensate for their rapid speed of transit. Yet throughout the 1860s and 1870s there were complaints voiced in the railway conference of the coasters carrying too large a share of cattle or meat. For instance in 1861 the railways needed to reduce their rate on both cattle and sheep 'with the view of getting back the Traffic at present diverted to the sea route'. [16] In 1868 it was suggested that for the railways to compete with the steamers the cattle rate needed to be the same on both modes. [17] This implied the railway service was perceived as comparable to the steamer. An investigation held in 1869 revealed that while in 1867 the railways carried 64 per cent of total cattle, their share of the extensive sheep traffic was only 3.5 per cent and they carried no pigs. In 1868 their market share was even worse, being only 43 per cent of cattle and the same low shares for sheep and pigs as the previous year. [18]

In September 1872 the railway companies again approached the coastal firm to inform it of a contemplated rise in freight rates. The steamboat company raised its rates in sympathy. [19] Not content with this rise, in March 1873 the railways were keen to raise their rates yet again believing that the coastal company would agree to an advance of about 8 per cent. So a railway delegation called upon the coastal company. [20] The directors of the ASN then agreed to consider it at their next board meeting in April 1873. [21] In April 1875 the railways were horrified to learn that the steamers were charging only 50s., delivered in London, for meat from Aberdeen, whereas the equivalent charge by railway was 79s. 2d., a premium of nearly 60 per cent. [22] Not surprisingly much of the trade was now going by sea. So much so that in March 1876 the railway companies considered reducing their rates because their current charges 'had the effect of causing a larger proportion of meat to be sent by sea'. [23] As it

[16] PRO, RAIL 1080/509, minute 857.

[17] PRO, RAIL 727/1, minute 508.

[18]PRO, RAIL 1080/510, minute 1905. The trade in sheep and pigs was extensive, amounting to nearly 28,000 sheep and 4,500 pigs in 1867 compared to 7,200 cattle.

[19] PRO, RAIL 1080/511, minute 2634.5.

[20] Ibid., minute 2725.

[21] Ibid., minute 2749.

[22] PRO, RAIL 727/1, minute 1379.

[23] Ibid., minute 1420.

transpired, no reduction was made because the railway companies thought a lower rate unremunerative.

As a result the coaster continued to carry a 'large proportion' of meat traffic, so that in May 1878 the goods managers were again considering a reduction in rates 'to secure a better share of the traffic'.[24] By February 1879 they had decided against any such cut, as the return on the traffic did not justify any reduction.[25] As late as July 1889 the railways were still concerned over 'the decreased tonnage (of dead meat traffic) carried by rail and the large weight taken by sea' and were considering 'a more convenient and accelerated train service for dead meat and other perishable traffic from Aberdeen to London'.[26] They had obviously abandoned any idea of trying to compete merely on price, because they could not bring their costs close to those of the coaster, and instead were considering competition via the quality of their service to justify their premium price. In October 1887 the railways expressed concern over the 'large number of passengers travelling by sea' between Aberdeen and London, and contemplated running excursion trains at special low fares.[27] Given the railway's superior speed of travel for passenger traffic it is surprising to find the steamers competing successfully in this area. They did so through the appeal of more luxuriously-appointed new ships, greater speed brought about by improved engine technology and the invigorating air enjoyed on a sea cruise.

Two important points come out of these minutes. Firstly that on this long-haul route the railways and steamboat companies quite normally consulted and informed each other of changes in freight rates and tried to keep some sort of balance between the two, though the coaster rate was always below that of the railway. Secondly, that even in the sort of commodities which should have been the most ready to switch to the train, the railway companies had no easy or lasting victory. Through at least until the 1890s the steamer continued to carry a significant share of such traffic. This certainly confirms Channon's view, confined to the cattle and meat trade, that the competition between rail and steamboat 'was very real and very effective'.[28] When the sheep and

---

[24] Ibid., minute 1646.2.

[25] Ibid., minute 1673.

[26] PRO, RAIL 727/2, minute 2420.

[27] PRO, RAIL 1080/514, minute 6291.

[28] G. Channon, 'The Aberdeenshire Beef Trade with London: A Study in Steamship and Railway Competition 1850–69', in *Transport History*, 2 (1969) p. 18.

pig traffic is included the steamboat carried the lion's share in some years.

Collaboration between the coaster and the railway companies on the very long haul Aberdeen to London route seems to have been informal, sporadic and uncertain. However, there is one example of long lasting formal collaboration between the railways and a coastal company. As Philip Bagwell pointed out in his work on the RCH, from about 1855 the Dundee, Perth and London Shipping Company (DPLS) was brought into the English and Scotch Traffic Agreement. This included all railway companies in the cross-border trade, pooled receipts and then divided them between the various railways. [29] The DPLS ran steamers and sailing smacks between London and the two Scottish towns. The railways and steamboat company had a formal agreement in which they collaborated on fixing rates for bale traffic and also agreed to pool the receipts from this traffic and divide it between the two modes in pre-arranged proportions. Philip Bagwell was mainly concerned to show the role of the RCH in collecting statistics, calculating apportionments and acting as an objective arbitrator to promote through traffic. He did not deal with the significance of this agreement for the coaster or the light it threw on inter-modal collaboration and competition.

There were, in fact, three separate but contiguous agreements between the DPLS and the railways, which gave a continuous period of twenty-four years of collaboration from 1856 to 1879. There were some common features in all three agreements. Each ran for a set period: fourteen years for the first, five years for both the second and third. Freight rates were determined mutually for each mode and could not then be altered without joint consultation. However, the rates fixed were not the same for both forms of transport, the steamboat charge being always considerably less than the railway's rate. This policy of rate fixing did not prove so rigid as to prevent a rapid response when competition by sea occurred. On several occasions a rival shipping firm entered the trade, offering lower freight rates than the DPLS, but each time the competition was shortlived for the sea freights were cut and the opposition soon withdrew. For instance in May 1876 the *Brigadier* was put on the route charging only 14s. per ton, 1s. less than the DPLS. [30] The latter immediately cut their rate to 12s. 6d.

[29] Bagwell, *The Railway Clearing House*, pp. 254–55.
[30] PRO, RAIL 1080/510, minute 1616.

and then, as the owners of the *Brigadier* went to 10s, matched that rate. By mid August the intruding steamship had been withdrawn and the sea freight returned to its normal 15s per ton.[31] All three agreements contained 'joint purse' pooling arrangements. At the end of each half year the RCH presented statistics of the tonnage carried by each mode and worked out how much was due to whom.

Table 1

Freight Carried from Dundee to London, 1856–79

Six Months Ending	Tonnage Carried By Sea	Percentage off Total Traffic
31.8.1856	7,041	78
31.3.1857	6,250	84
30.6.1870	7,572	
31.12.1870	8,367	92
31.12.1872	11,716	92
30.6.1873	10,478	92
31.12.1873	12,543	93
30.6.1874	12,215	93
31.12.1874	10,723	93
30.6.1875	5,075	87
31.12.1875	5,825	88
30.6.1876	5,175	89
31.12.1876	4,945	88
30.6.1877	4,346	87
31.12.1877	4,354	90
30.6.1878	4,870	87
31.12.1878	5,758	92
30.6.1879	6,299	90
31.12.1879	5,715	90

Source: PRO, RAIL 1080/509–512.

The changes that were implemented in successive agreements were partly a matter of detail. For instance the freight rate by ship in the first term was 15s. whereas in the second and third it was 25s. Similarly the rail rate rose from 37s. 6d. to 41s. 8d. at the same time.[32] While the first agreement was current the rate for calculating the transfer payment from

[31] Ibid., minute 1713.
[32] Ibid., minutes 2154 and PRO, RAIL 1080/511, minute 3155.

the transport mode which carried more than its agreed share to that which was under-subscribed was set at 1s. 6d. per barrel bulk, roughly 16s. 6d. per ton, minus 20 per cent for working expenses.[33] In the second and third agreements the transfer price was set at 15s. per ton less 20 per cent to cover the working expenses.[34] Of more significance, perhaps, was the changing share of the total traffic allocated to each form of transport. In the first agreement the split was 25 per cent to the railway, 75 per cent to the shipping company.[35] In the second agreement, from 1870, the railways' share was reduced to 10 per cent with the coaster raising its proportion to 90 per cent.[36] The third agreement, in force from 1875 to 1879, saw the railway's share increased to 12.5 per cent.[37]

The earliest agreement, as well as fixing freight rates jointly, also set passenger fares in collaboration. This practice ceased with the first agreement and was never renewed.[38] Similarly, during the first period, the railway companies guaranteed a minimum sum for cattle traffic receipts to the shipping company. That too was not incorporated into the second agreement.[39] Admittedly the sum guaranteed was quite small, £500 each half year, equal to £1,000 per annum. However, on the two occasions when the committee received information on the cattle trade, in 1856 and 1857, the railways paid £315 and £491 respectively to the coastal company. It seems likely that similar payments were made in other six-month periods, though the minutes are silent on the topic. The logic of the railway companies in guaranteeing a minimum income for cattle traffic to the shipping firm seems obscure, until two clauses in the third agreement are added into the conundrum. These read, 'The shipping company to discourage as far as possible any Meat or Fish traffic being sent by their steamers' and, 'The Shipping Coy to discourage cattle traffic being sent by their route'.[40] The £1,000 per annum was compensation paid by the railways to the steamers for allowing the meat, fish and cattle traffic to go predominantly by the railway. The justification for this may have been speed, since if the railway ran special fast ice-cooled trains, rather than using the regular freight trains, they could cover the distance much

---

[33] Ibid., minute 243.
[34] PRO, RAIL 1080/511, minute 2378.
[35] PRO, RAIL 1080/510, minute 1713.
[36] Ibid., minute 2298.
[37] PRO, RAIL 1080/511, minute 3945.
[38] PRO, RAIL 1080/510, minute 2226.
[39] Ibid., minute 2154.
[40] PRO, RAIL 1080/511, minutes 3155 and 3189.

faster than the coastal ship. This also allowed the railway to cream off the higher-rated traffic, leaving the bulkier, lower-rated goods such as bales of jute, pieces of cloth and hanks of yarn to the steamers.

To those who espouse the conventional wisdom that the railways superseded the coaster because of their lower costs and charges, the proportions officially allocated to the coaster may come as a surprise, for it was expected to carry the vast majority of the cargo. Even more surprising from this viewpoint, as shown in table 1, is that, for those years where the tonnages are recorded, the coaster consistently carried more than its official share and ended each half year owing money to the railways. Thus the vast majority of customers preferred to send their goods by the cheaper sea route rather than by the dearer railway, even if the train was faster.

The agreement between the DPLS was the most formal sort of collaboration between the railway companies and a coastal liner business. There was also mutuality of price fixing between the railway conference and two other companies, both sailing between the Firth of Forth and London. These were the General Steam Navigation Co. (GSN) and the London and Edinburgh Shipping Co. (LES). As early as 1866 the rail companies were writing to the owners of the London and Edinburgh steamers (as well as those plying from Dundee and Aberdeen) to inform them that the railway rate on cattle was to be advanced as from 1 December, in the hope that the steamer companies would follow suit.[41] Similarly in April 1872 the railway companies set up a sub-committee to call upon the two steamer firms plying between Edinburgh and London to try and arrange for the freight rates by both modes to be advanced.[42] After detailed negotiations it was agreed by the railway companies, the GSN and the LES, to raise rates in conjunction as from 1 November 1872.[43] Appended to the agreement is a long list of rates for a range of commodities which indicates that the steamboat price was always lower than that by railway. Although the differential varies from commodity to commodity, the premium charged by the railway lay in the range of 20 to 35 per cent. The variety of products for which steamer rates were quoted, including manufactured goods such as biscuits, books, pianos and drapery, perishables such as oranges, lemons and meat and frangibles such as glass chimneys and globes, indicates that the coastal liners were not

---

[41] PRO, RAIL 1080/509, minute 1498.
[42] PRO, RAIL 1080/511, minute 2577.
[43] Ibid., minute 2634.

confined to bulky, low-value commodities but were carrying a wide range of high value goods as well. In 1873 the two steamboat companies and the railway companies party to the conference again made minor adjustments to the agreed rates.[44] Throughout 1875 and 1876 tripartite talks took place between the two coastal liner firms and the railways making detail alterations mutually to freight rates. Sometimes this was done at meetings, at other times by an exchange of letters.[45]

The agreement between the two transport modes was sufficiently flexible to allow the steamer companies to respond to threatened competition. For instance, in April 1875 the London Leith and Glasgow Steam Shipping Company threatened a twice weekly steam service between Leith and London in direct opposition to the GSN and LES. As a result the coastal companies wrote to the railway conference requesting a suspension of their agreement. In this the railways concurred.[46] This opposition by Messrs Burrell and Son proved long lived and it was not until January 1877 that the coastal firms could report that the competition had ceased and they were willing to revert to the rates agreed in October 1875.[47] Only a few months later, in May 1878, opposition was threatened again and in response the rail and shipping companies cut the rates both by rail and sea by about 10 per cent to maintain their share of the traffic.[48] Again in April 1879 a new shipping company was offering to carry paper from Edinburgh to London at a lower rate than that in force, so the railway companies agreed to the steamer firms reducing their rate by 1s per ton.[49] This agreement between the two shipping firms and the railway conference was still in existence in September 1886 when it was cited by the railways as an exemplar of its kind.[50] By then it also included the Carron Company which ran a liner trade between the Firth of Forth and London.[51] There is also evidence of this agreement continuing, essentially unchanged, until the spring of 1889 at least,[52] by when it had been superseded by the agreement discussed below.

---

[44] Ibid., minutes 2708 and 2709.
[45] PRO, RAIL 1080/512, minutes 3135, 3168 and 3198.
[46] Ibid., minutes 3194 and 3211.
[47] Ibid., minute 3573.
[48] Ibid., minute 3895.
[49] PRO, RAIL 1080/513, minute 4117.
[50] Ibid., minute 4276.
[51] I. Bowman, 'The Carron Line', in *Transport History*, (1979).
[52] PRO, RAIL 1080/514, minute 6693.

The east coast agreement between railway and steamboat was to act as a model for the west coast and was to usher in an even larger grouping; in September 1886, the railway companies in the Anglo-Scotch Conference were negotiating with firms operating on the Glasgow to London route to bring them into an agreement.[53] The Clyde Shipping Company joined in talks with the railway companies, the GSN, LES, and Carron Company. The aim of these discussions was to agree a set of freight rates for both the east and west coast routes between London and Scotland by both rail and sea. After some months of meetings and negotiations an agreement was drawn up with mutually agreed freight rates to be effective from 1 March 1887.[54] The agreement was subject to three months notice of intention to withdraw. The terms were similar to those which had applied to the east coast trade. A schedule of freight rates was drawn up collaboratively by the various parties and no unilateral alterations could be made in them. The rates by the various routes and types of transport were not identical. The railway rate was the most expensive with the east coast sea route being on average between 25 and 50 per cent less than the railway rate. Generally the steamboat enjoyed a larger differential on the more expensive rates. The freight charges by the west coast steamboats were in all cases slightly less than by the east coast sea route. The discount enjoyed by the west coast over the east was quite small, varying from 4 to 11 per cent with the larger discount on the higher rated commodities. The reason given for this additional discount was that the west coast was the 'long sea route' which would mean greater time taken in transit; hence the lower freight rate was to compensate for the slower speed of delivery.[55]

This agreement was still in force in June 1888 when Paisley and Greenock were brought into the group of stations and ports which were included in the definition of Glasgow.[56] The concord was also sufficiently alive and healthy for it to be worthwhile, in October 1893, to reprint the lists of rates applying to the various routes, as there had been numerous changes in individual charges.[57]

Collaboration between the two modes was still going strong in January 1895 when the railway companies agreed to the shipping firms temporarily reducing their rates on some products because of 'competition by outside

53 Ibid., minute 5969.
54 Ibid., minutes of meeting of 21 December 1886.
55 Ibid., minute 6179.
56 Ibid., minute 6494.
57 Ibid., minute 7713.

steamers', that is, not members of the rates conference.[58] This opposition was long lasting, for these exceptional rates stayed in force until December 1898. In the autumn of 1899 and spring of 1900 the conference agreed to rises in freight rates of between 2 and 7 per cent on both modes[59]. Various references in the minutes indicate that this concord between railways and coastal liners continued at least until the spring of 1911,[60] and that in 1908 there was an attempt to implement identical terminal rebates:[61] that is where the customer was given a discount from published rates because they did their own collection or delivery or unloaded directly, not using the transport mode's carts or labour. This was to remove hidden price competition and so eliminate another element of discretion in rate making. By 1911 the concord between the coastal liner companies had become further formalised, for there was a body in Glasgow known as the London Shipping Conference which acted for those companies trading between the Clyde and Thames in negotiations with the railway conference.[62] Although it is not absolutely clear, it seems likely that this cooperation between railways and coasters on both the east and west coast routes between Scotland and London continued until at least the First World War.

Railway-coaster cooperation was a normal part of business life on the long-distance east coast route between Scotland and London from the mid-nineteenth century. From at least the 1880s this was extended to embrace liner companies plying the west coast route to the Thames. The pattern was similar in all cases, collaboration to fix freight rates and then alteration only by mutual agreement. Competition was restrained essentially to non-price competition via speed and frequency. This did not deny choice to the intending shipper, for the freight rates were not identical. The merchant could decide between the cheaper sea route, which was a little riskier and might be marginally slower and less frequent, or the dearer railway rate which might be faster, more frequent and more reliable. The difference in price probably reflected the difference in costs of the two modes.

There is plenty of evidence of railway-steamboat collaboration on the west coast. Specifically the trade between the Clyde and the Mersey was the

---

[58] PRO, RAIL 1080/516, minutes 8010 and 8055.
[59] Ibid., minutes 9569 and 9656.
[60] PRO, RAIL 1080/518, minute 12891.
[61] Ibid., minute 12103.
[62] Ibid., minutes 12891, 12948 and 13130.

subject of formal cooperation between the two transport modes for at least twenty years from 1858 to 1878. In the former year the railway companies met with Messrs G. and J. Burns and Messrs Langlands to negotiate over the trade.[63] Few details seem to have survived of their agreement, but it is highly likely that it included the mutual fixing of freight rates with a differential, giving the railways a premium price for what was perceived as a superior service: in 1862 the two steamboat companies wrote to the West Coast Conference about the 'differential rates for traffic between Glasgow and Liverpool and Manchester by railway and steampacket',[64] suggesting that the 1858 agreement was still in force and was concerned, inter alia, with such matters. What is certain is that the railway monitored the traffic between Liverpool and Glasgow from 1860 to 1863 very closely, comparing the number of passengers by rail and steamboat.[65] The latter carried twice as many as the former. These comparative figures are likely to have come from the coastal companies themselves further supporting the idea of collaboration.

In February 1867 a formal agreement was drawn up between the four railway companies (LNWR, Caledonian, North British, and Glasgow and South Western) and Messrs Burns and Langlands and Son.[66] By then the steamer companies were operating a daily service each way and in addition there was a weekly service by the steamer *Jacinth* operated by McArthur Brothers and a regular service by sailing schooners operated by Lewis Potter and Co. The 1867 agreement is quite explicit. The parties drew up a list of differential freight rates for a whole range of goods. The basis of these rates was the five classes of the RCH classification. However, the differential between the railway and steamer rate was much greater than that on the Edinburgh to London route, for on the west coast the steamer rates lay normally in the range 40 to 56 per cent of the railway price, giving the railway a premium of 45 to 60 per cent for its service. It was also agreed that these rates should apply to Manchester-Glasgow traffic, giving both sides through rates to the inland town, the steamer traffic using the canal to maintain an all water route. The only goods for which a special rate was quoted was box and bale goods – essentially

[63] PRO, RAIL 1080/511, minute 2616; on Messrs G. & J. Burns, see A. Slaven and S. Checkland (eds), *Dictionary of Scottish Business Biography, 1860–1960*, 2. (Aberdeen, 1990) pp. 266–7.

[64] PRO, RAIL 727/1, minute 185.

[65] Ibid., minutes 152, 172 and 256.

[66] PRO, RAIL 1080/511, minute 2616.

textiles – where the steamer rate was set at two-thirds of the railway rate. The agreement was not for any particular fixed period but simply terminable on one month's notice by any of the parties to it. Here again the pattern was confirmed: railway and coastal liner collaborating to regulate traffic by fixing mutually agreed freight rates with a premium differential in favour of the railways.

These agreements were not set in tablets of stone and when one side felt aggrieved it was likely to request a reconsideration. This occurred in April 1870 when the railways considered 'the present arrangement with the Glasgow and Liverpool Steam Boats [has] been found unsatisfactory, especially with respect to the down traffic from Liverpool to Glasgow'.[67] They consequently approached the coastal liner companies to discuss the matter. The basis of the railway's complaint was that the shipping companies had extended their operations 'by quoting through rates to the interior of England'.[68] The steamers were now using various canal carriers such as on the Duke of Bridgewater's canal to enable them to quote all-water through rates to inland towns in Staffordshire and the Midlands at much lower prices than the through railway rate.[69] This had diverted a significant amount of the traffic, hence the railway businesses' unease. Eventually, in January 1871, the steamboat proprietors agreed to a meeting [70] and were willing to negotiate on the through rates.[71] These negotiations dragged on through 1871 and well into 1872. Eventually in September 1872 a new agreement was drawn up whereby both railway and steamboat rates were raised 'in consequence of the serious increase in working expenses' as from 2 September 1872.[72] At this time the class rates were not altered but rather the special rates, running to fourteen printed pages, were altered individually and the bale and box rate was increased by 2s. 6d. per ton by both means of transport. As in the case of the DPLS, the variety of goods for which steamer rates were quoted supports the idea that the coastal liner was carrying not only bulky, low-value goods, but a wide range of commodities including perishables, such as apples and damsons; manufactured goods, such as bottled lemonade and ketchup; fragile products, such as window glass and empty jars; and high value goods, such as sewing machines, macaroni and lithographic stones.

[67] PRO, RAIL 727/1, minute 804.
[68] Ibid., minute 928.
[69] PRO, RAIL 1080/510, minute 2228.
[70] Ibid., minute 2296.
[71] Ibid., minute 2372.
[72] PRO, RAIL 1080/511, minute 2616.

In late 1872 negotiations resumed over the knotty problem of the shipping firms quoting through rates to the Midlands. [73] For example Burns were carrying sugar from Greenock to Birmingham and Wolverhampton. [74] The railway companies wished the ships to confine their through rates to Liverpool and Manchester at the one end and Glasgow and Greenock in Scotland in order that all traffic bound for inland destinations should travel by railway. [75] The shipping companies desired some latitude as to which final destinations were covered by a through rate, suggesting that any place within a radius of twenty-five miles of Liverpool and Glasgow should be 'grouped' as within the scope of these rates. They declined to cease offering through rates to inland towns, preferring to set up a separate conference, to include the Bridgewater Navigation Co. as well as the railway and steamboat firms, and suggesting a general rise in rates, which they considered 'unremunerative'. [76] Negotiations were terribly slow, many meetings being postponed or inconclusive. [77] The railway and steamer companies continued to collaborate in setting freight rates for the Liverpool-Glasgow run but could not agree which towns should be included in each grouping or on the scale of steamer through rates to the inland towns of the Midlands. [78] The cause of this was that the railway which worked the area around the Scottish terminus, the Glasgow and South Western railway, refused to bring nearby stations into the grouping, presumably because it would lose the extra freight revenue for the local carrying.

The railway companies still felt that the agreement was not working in their favour. In autumn 1876 they were so concerned by the cheap passenger fares offered by the steamboat companies during the summer that they contemplated running special excursion trains or offering cheap fares themselves. In the end they decided against any reduction because of the effect this would have on other through passenger fares which included the Liverpool-Glasgow leg. [79] In June 1878 the railway companies made a last effort to resolve the problem. They proposed a general rise in rates, a strict definition of Liverpool and Glasgow so that nearby towns were

---

73 Ibid., minute 2705.
74 Ibid., minute 2941.
75 Ibid., minute 2705.
76 Ibid., minute 2744.
77 For example see ibid., minutes 2792, 2818 and 2845.
78 PRO, RAIL 1080/512, minute 3247.
79 PRO, RAIL 727/1, minutes 1445, 1470, 1479 and 1492.

not included, and that coastal liners should not charge less for through traffic on the Liverpool to Glasgow part than the agreed rates. The latter would have ruled out the steamers offering any special rates for long distance traffic. Since they already had arrangements with the Bridgewater Navigation Company for through rates to inland cities such as Manchester, Warrington, Birmingham and Wolverhampton, the coastal firms refused this suggestion. Upon inspecting the new rates proposed by the railway companies the shipping lines also discovered that the differential between the railway and steamer rates had been much narrowed.[80] The railways felt that they had been receiving too small a share of the traffic and that a larger proportionate rise in the steamer freight rates would reduce their attractiveness to shippers, so diverting traffic onto the railways. It might be seen as an admission by the railways that the service they now offered was proportionately not so superior to the steamboat as it had been when the agreement was drawn up in 1867. Certainly the average speed of coastal liners was increasing as improvements in engine technology came through. From the 1870s the railways' determination to carry even small consignments may have slowed down the speed of freight trains, as more time was spent shunting and marshalling wagon loads rather than train loads.

The result was stalemate between the two sides: the steamers being unwilling to cease their through rates to the interior or to accept the drastic narrowing of the differential; the railways insisting on both and that the agreed rates should apply to only Glasgow, Liverpool and Birkenhead. As a result, on 25 October 1878, the railway companies gave notice of termination of the agreement as of 25 November. Attempts were made to find an 'amicable arrangement' and there was an extensive exchange of letters and many meetings at which disputes arose over the share of total traffic each mode had enjoyed, whether or not shippers insured, and precisely which goods attracted Town and Dock dues.[81] No resolution was found and from 1 April 1880 the railways introduced new, lower rates in consequence of the breakdown of these talks.[82] These seemed to be of little short-term advantage to the railways: in June 1881 the conference was complaining of 'the falling off' in the weight of goods carried by rail between stations in the Manchester and Glasgow groups because of the

---

[80] PRO, RAIL 1080/512, minutes 3956 and 3989.
[81] PRO, RAIL 1080/513, minutes 4041, 4060, 4097 and 4116.
[82] Ibid. minute 4334.

'low rates charged by the shipping company throughout, using the canal from Manchester to Liverpool and then the steamer to Glasgow'.[83]

The conclusions to be drawn from this incident are that the railway companies preferred to fix prices with the steamboat companies rather than engage in price competition. When this failed, because the railways considered they were not getting their fair share and that 'the Water Route practically enjoys a monopoly of the traffic to the exclusion of the Railway Route',[84] their initial reaction was to attempt a reduction in the differential between the railway and the water rates and so attract customers to the railways. After the steamboat owners refused this, the railways reluctantly accepted that they must act separately and reduced their rates. This was to little avail, as about a year later they still felt that they were losing traffic to the steamers.

On routes such as Glasgow to Liverpool, or the east coast, the distance by sea was little different from that by rail, since both modes had a fairly direct route. This is patently not true for traffic moving from one coast to another. Here the inland route had a direct line whereas the coaster had to go around the coast, travelling a much greater mileage than the railway route. Thus for the journey from Liverpool to Aberdeen or Dundee the coaster had a distinct disadvantage, the distance by land being respectively 330 and 270 miles, whereas by sea it was 648 and 714 miles: the coaster had twice as far to go. While it might be thought that the railway had nothing to fear from the coaster on this sort of route, this was not the case.

As early as October 1858 the English and Scotch Traffic Committee was considering concluding long term agreements with merchants because of a threatened service by steamer between Dundee and Liverpool.[85] By January 1859 this threat had partly materialised.[86] From at least 1863 the railways found their through traffic affected by the North British Railway Company (NBR) collaborating with a steamboat service between Liverpool and Silloth to offer cheap rates, not just between Cumberland and Dumfrieshire but also for traffic from Dundee to Liverpool. The railway steamboat rate was less than the through rail rate and the conference felt

<hr />

83 Ibid., minute 4593.

84 Ibid., letter of 5 May 1879 from E.G. Rider, Secretary of English and Scotch Traffic Rates Conference to Messrs Burns and Messrs Langlands & Sons.

85 PRO, RAIL 1080/509, minute 549.

86 Ibid., minute 584.

compelled to match this price.[87] To try and eliminate this competition, the West Coast Conference requested the NBR in 1866 to discontinue the steamer service and send all its traffic by rail. The rail rates would then be raised to remunerative levels and the NBR would be given facilities via the LNWR's tracks through Lancaster and Preston.[88] No changes had occurred by February 1867 [89] but in June 1868 the rates between Silloth and Liverpool were raised mutually by the railway companies and the steamboat, giving a differential in favour of the coastal ship. Again here is an example of the two transport modes collaborating to fix freight rates to provide reasonable returns and eliminate competition. The railway conference anticipated that the steamboat would soon be withdrawn,[90] but this hope was not realised, for in October 1869 the steamboat was still plying and the West Coast Conference noted 'the very great falling off in jute between Liverpool and Dundee and in other traffic between Liverpool and Manchester and Dundee'.[91] The railways faced not merely steamboat competition on the west coast but also on the east, so that goods could travel from Liverpool to Dundee in three stages: by steamboat from Liverpool to Silloth; then by rail to Newcastle; and from there to Dundee by steamer, hence maximising the cheaper water rate.[92] Additionally there was now a new threat: steamers plying direct from east to west coast via the north of Scotland.

In 1870 the railways noted that traffic between Liverpool and the east coast Scottish ports was 'still unsatisfactory'.[93] This was because the NBR was now running a daily steamer service between Liverpool and Glasgow whereas in 1867, when the agreement on differential rates had been concluded, the coastal service had been thrice weekly;[94] and because of the direct steamer which had been recently put on the route.[95] By the autumn of 1871 the direct steamer was doing so well that in a four-month period it carried nearly 7,000 tons of goods between Liverpool and Dundee and Aberdeen, equivalent to more than 20,000 tons per annum.[96] Throughout

---

[87] PRO, RAIL 727/1, minute 319.
[88] Ibid., minute 372.
[89] Ibid., minutes of meeting of 16 February 1867.
[90] Ibid., minute 444.
[91] Ibid., minute 691.
[92] Ibid., minute 692.
[93] Ibid., minute 904.
[94] PRO, RAIL 1080/510, minute 2066.
[95] PRO, RAIL 727/1, minute 999.
[96] Ibid., minute 1050.

1872 the Liverpool to Aberdeen and Dundee traffic by rail continued 'to show a decrease' because of 'the competition by direct steamer'[97] so that in the autumn the railway companies commenced negotiations with Messrs Langlands and Sons, who ran the direct steamer, to try to get the freight rates by both modes of transport raised.[98]

On this route the railway companies faced a double difficulty for they had competition from one of their number – the NBR operating in conjunction with the steamboat between Liverpool and Silloth – as well as the direct steamer operated by Langlands. Hence the all-rail share of the traffic was negligible. By the autumn of 1874 the railway conference was reporting 'a large falling off in the goods traffic carried by the rail through route' and blaming it on 'the increased number of steamers between Liverpool and Aberdeen and Dundee'.[99] In December of that year Langlands stole a march on the railways by having a steamer built especially for this trade that could travel by the Caledonian Canal, cutting the mileage by sea drastically. As a result in the autumn of 1874 the coaster was carrying over 1,700 tons per month between Liverpool, Aberdeen and Dundee whereas the direct rail route was carrying about 200 tons per month.[100] The coaster was not confined to low-value, high-bulk commodities, carrying syrup, oils and rice as well as soda and jute from Liverpool and mostly 'bale goods' – manufactured textiles – back.

In order to compete, the railway conference recommended a reduction in their freight rates, as from January 1875, to a flat rate of £1 per ton, station to station, for a whole range of commodities, as 'it would result in Messrs Langlands seeking an interview with the companies to arrange differential rates on a fair basis as between sea and railways'.[101] This proved of no avail and in January 1875 the flat rate was reduced to 15s., per ton.[102] Even this drastic reduction did not benefit the railways, for they calculated that in the first quarter of 1875, the direct steamer increased the tonnage it carried from Dundee to Liverpool by about 400 tons per month, whereas the direct railway route carried 700 tons *less* per month.[103] Since outright price competition was not working in the railways' favour and

---

[97] Ibid., minute 1125.
[98] PRO, RAIL 1080/511, minute 2659.
[99] PRO, RAIL 1080/551, minute 2659.
[100] Ibid., minute 1339; PRO, RAIL 1080/511, minute 3095.
[101] Ibid.
[102] PRO, RAIL 1080/512, minute 3136.
[103] PRO, RAIL 727/1, minute 1374.

since Langlands were now running their direct steamer on to Leith as well as Aberdeen and Dundee, the railways felt their only option was to come to an arrangement with Langlands. Consequently, in July 1875, a formal agreement was drawn up between Langlands and the English and Scotch Conference whereby the former agreed virtually to abandon the trade with Leith, except where the quantities offered were in excess of 50 tons, for the coaster agreed to charge the same rate as the direct rail route. For lots of 50 tons or more of one article the steamboat charged a price lower than the direct rail route by 6s. 8d. per ton. For the Liverpool to Dundee and the Liverpool to Aberdeen routes the parties agreed a series of rates based on the RCH classification, in which the steamers enjoyed a differential of between 10 and 32 per cent below the railway rate for the class rates. The differential in favour of the coastal ship was rather greater for some 'exceptional rates'. The differential was greatest on the lower rates and narrowed as the freight rate rose for higher valued commodities. [104] The railways then cancelled their special 15s. rate and the parallel £1 to Inverness. [105]

Even this agreement seems to have benefited the railway companies very little. For in 1881 the conference was complaining that the direct steamers were carrying about 2,000 tons of bale goods per month from Scotland to Liverpool whereas the direct railway line was carrying only about 650 tons, a quarter of the total traffic. In part they blamed this on the increased frequency of the steamboat service, now running twice a week. [106] Having reached an agreement with Langlands on freight rates, they could not reduce these and considered improving the service. At the same time the English and Scotch Conference still had the problem of the rail-steamer route offered by the NBR via the steamboats from Liverpool to Silloth. Although a formal agreement had been reached in 1868 between the NBR and the conference, in 1877 the latter complained that the NBR was not sticking to the rates agreed then and hence was carrying too large a proportion of the traffic. Its daily steamboat service was seen as too frequent. [107] Not merely this, but the NBR was quoting lower through rates to a large number of destinations in Scotland, such as Edinburgh and Leith, as well as those cities further north. [108] In addition there was obviously non-price competition between the through railway and steamer-rail routes

[104] PRO, RAIL 1080/512, minute 3242.
[105] Ibid., minute 3297.
[106] PRO, RAIL 727/1, minute 1938.
[107] PRO, RAIL 1080/512, minute 3707.
[108] Ibid., minute 3820.

in terms of the terminal services they offered. In 1878 the Liverpool agents for the Silloth steamers, Messrs Johnson Grainger and Co., were charging only 1s. 3d. per ton for cartage in Liverpool, whereas the railway conference charged 1s. 8d. Also the steamboat allowed its men to stillage ale in the consignee's cellars, whereas the railway normally charged for this another 5d. per ton.[109] The conference, thus, urged the NBR to bring its rates into line with those of the conference. However, even if these methods of non-price competition were eliminated, the railway conference remained unhappy about the quantity of freight going via the Silloth Steam Packet Co., rather than using the all-rail route.[110] In 1884 it tried to get the NBR to cancel the price differential in favour of the steamboat which had been agreed in 1868.[111]

There is one further set of Railway Clearing House records which shed light on the nature of railway and coaster cooperation. In 1902 a conference existed dealing with goods traffic between London and the West Riding of Yorkshire; the parties to this conference included ten railway companies, seven coastal shipping firms and two canal businesses.[112] It is clear that this organisation had been in existence for a number of years, at least since 1897, and that it continued until at least mid 1904.[113] However, because only one volume of minutes survives, the date of establishment is unknown and its history before 1902 remains a mystery. A number of significant points, germane to the theme of this essay, emerge from the one surviving volume of the West Riding, London Shipping Traffic Conference (WRLSTC).

Firstly, it is obvious that collaboration between the two transport modes involved a larger number of separate firms than any of the previously cited agreements. Although there was some variation at the margins there was a hard core of ten railway companies (the Great Central, Great Eastern, Great Western, Hull & Barnsley, Great Northern, Midland, Lancashire & Yorkshire, Cheshire, London & North Western, and North Eastern); seven firms involved in the coastal liner trade (the General Steam Navigation Company, Jescott Steamers, George R. Haller, France Fenwick & Co., Sollas & Sons, the London Yorkshire & Lancashire

---

109 Ibid., minute 3878.
110 PRO, RAIL 727/2 minutes 1949 and 1966.
111 Ibid., minute 2088.
112 PRO, RAIL 1080/465.
113 Ibid., meeting of 17 June 1903.

Carrying Co., and Fisher, Renwick & Co.), and two inland waterway businesses (the Rochdale Canal Co. and the Aire & Calder Navigation) who were in the conference.[114] There were also additional companies for some of the time, for example the Crofton Shipping Co. joined in June 1902 while the Merchants Carrying Co., another coastal shipper, was in negotiation to join in November 1903.[115]

The agreement was a formal, written document with a code of conference regulations stating its objectives, membership and procedural rules. Its main aim was to facilitate long-distance traffic between London and the West Riding of Yorkshire whether via the Humber or Manchester by sea and rail, rail direct, sea and canal, or any combination of the three transport modes. The freight rates were set by the West Riding Conference and were mutually agreed and binding on conference members once approved. As in other agreements that we have examined, the rates by each method of transport were not identical, but rather the all water route was cheaper than the direct rail rate. The discount in favour of the shipping companies varied within the range 14 to 21 per cent with the average being about 17 per cent.[116] Again this was, no doubt, meant to reflect both the lower cost structure of the coaster in long-distance freight haulage compared to the train and the superior service which the railways claimed to offer in terms of speed and frequency.

Mutually enforced freight rates were not enough. A whole host of ancillary services and drawbacks had to be mutually priced and agreed by all parties to ensure that these did not become back-door methods of giving discounts on agreed freight rates as, we saw above, the railway companies had claimed the Silloth steamer was doing in its charges for cartage in Liverpool and its free stillage of ale. The WRLSTC's solution to this was to draw up a long appendix to the code listing the agreed rates of as many of these types of ancillary charges as possible.[117] For instance, the scale of drawbacks to be paid when the public did their own carting or barging in London but where the agreed rates included collection or delivery were laid down; the normal practice on the cost of customs entries and clearances, cost of insurance on cargoes, the cost of marking and carding imported colonial wool in London and where separate deliveries were needed because consignments were sent in separate batches were all codified.

---

[114] Ibid., various minutes.
[115] Ibid., minutes 630 and 746.
[116] Ibid., minutes 591 and 686.
[117] Ibid., appendix to minute 582.

By drawing up such a detailed set of regulations the conference hoped to eliminate all forms of price competition, not merely the main freight rate.

Further to reduce competition between the various transport modes, the WRLSTC agreed to divide up the traffic in one major commodity. This was for raw wool brought into London from the colonies or foreign parts and then moved to the West Riding as a raw material for the woollen and worsted industries. There were two categories involved – 'overside' and 'sales' wool. The coaster's allocated share of each in December 1901 was 75 per cent and 38 per cent respectively, giving it a slightly larger slice of the traffic than the railways. [118] If either mode carried more than its share in any given quarter then it had to pay a levy per ton on the 'excess carryings' to the other route. In the summer of 1903 there was some discussion of this split between modes but after some bargaining, there was no real change in these, the coaster retaining 75 and 37.5 per cent respectively. [119]

It is also clear that the coaster was not pushed out of carriage of the high value commodities. The conference appointed a number of inspectors to check that the goods at the quays were as described in the manifests and that higher rated goods were not being passed off as commodities which incurred a lower freight rate. Thanks to these returns we get quarterly snapshots of some of the goods which were being carried by the coasters between London and Humber ports such as Hull, Grimsby and Goole, and also Manchester. These commodities included manufactured goods such as Bovril, Vaseline, Spratts dog food and sewing machines, and frangible products such as lamps and glass tumblers. [120] Thus the coastal liners were carrying a wide variety of products including the more valuable and higher rated goods on this route, just as we have discovered on other routes.

Although neither aggregate figures nor quantities of specific cargoes carried by the two transport methods are given, there is one exception which indicates that the coaster was not necessarily relegated to carrying a tiny proportion of total traffic while the railway moved the lion's share. This is suggested by the split agreed by the conference, referred to above, where the coaster was assigned slightly more than 50 per cent of wool traffic. This allocation was borne out in practice. For in 1901–3 the coaster increased consistently the proportion of 'overside' wool which it carried from 74 per cent to 92 per cent and kept its proportion of 'sales'

[118] Ibid., minutes of meeting of 17 December 1901.
[119] Ibid., minutes of meeting of sub-committee on 12 June 1903 appointed by minute 704.
[120] Ibid., minutes 592 and 664.

wool between 45 and 49 per cent. Overall the coaster carried 47 per cent of all wool traffic in 1901 and 55 per cent in 1902 and 1903.[121] This is not consistent with the hypothesis of a transport method beaten into submission by the technologically superior railway. Rather it suggests a rough parity between the two types of transport with a margin of superiority for the coaster.

This conclusion is borne out by the only other direct observation in this file of relative traffic carried by direct rail compared to the coasters. For the first half of 1903 the WRLSTC monitored the quantities of rags, hides and kips carried between London and the West Riding. They discovered that the coasters carried 53 per cent of all rags and 58 per cent of all kips and hides.[122] Admittedly these were not high value goods and indeed kips and hides could be a smelly, unpleasant cargo and hence the railway may not have been sorry to see them go by sea, but certainly this reinforces the view that the coaster was able to hold its own against the railways and indeed carry slightly over half the total traffic. The WRLSTC bears out the findings of the other examples examined earlier. Namely that collaboration between railway companies and coastal liners to eliminate price competition was normal and formal. This could also be extended to include inland navigation firms as well. The essence of the agreement was mutually approved freight rates with a small premium in favour of the railways. The coaster did carry high value commodities such as manufactured goods and was able to attract a significant share of total traffic on-long distance routes, perhaps slightly more than half.

A number of important points emerge from this story that are of relevance to railway coaster competition. Firstly, there is no question but that the steamboats were able to compete successfully with the railways long after the latter had through rail routes. Secondly, the railways did not cream off all the high-value freight relegating the coastal liner to low-value bulk goods. The coaster continued to carry high-value commodities such as manufactured goods and exotic imports. Thirdly, the railway conferences considered it quite reasonable to try to eliminate competition by fixing freight prices with rival steamboat companies so that the rates were mutually remunerative. This is quite contrary to the view propounded recently by one transport historian. He believed

[121] Ibid., minutes 662 and 771.
[122] Ibid., minute 764.

'Coasting was excepted [from conference agreements] because railway competition made rate-fixing impossible'.[123] These findings suggest that the railways were no hindrance to rate-fixing but rather that they encouraged collaboration between coastal liner companies and themselves to fix mutually agreed rates. These agreements took the form of either formal written documents, some of them highly codified, or less formal ad hoc cooperation through an exchange of letters or meetings as and when necessary. This cooperation was not restricted to rates conferences but in some cases involved pooling of traffic receipts and division among the parties on a prearranged basis. Fourthly, the steamboat was perceived as having lower costs than the railways, which was reflected in its lower freight rate compared to the railway, when the agreed schedules were drawn up. The railway was accepted as having higher costs and thus needing a higher freight rate to remunerate it. In theory such a premium price should have been reflected in a higher quality service but, on their own evidence, the railways seemed to be suggesting that many shippers did not see it this way for long-distance traffic and preferred to send their goods via the coaster. Finally, when agreement had been reached on freight rates so that price competition had been eliminated, the two transport modes continued to try to outdo each other via service competition. This could take the form of frequency of sailings, differences in terminal charges or the level of service offered within such charges, and of specialised vessels allowing shorter and therefore faster journeys, such as via the Caledonian Canal.

There are many lacunae in this essay and some of the issues which remain unresolved are of major importance. Perhaps the most significant is to assess the outcome of the cooperation and competition between the two modes of transport. Did collaboration pay off for each form of transport, or did one benefit at the expense of the other? Did the steamboat make higher profits when collaborating with the railway companies or when competing? It would be a little easier to attempt an answer to some of these questions if we had runs of figures on how much of what goods were carried between which destinations. However there is a dearth of precisely this material. The railway records do not contain such data for their own network let alone the potential competitors. The few coastal companies for which records survive do not normally include even the aggregate tonnage carried in any given year, let alone any breakdown of

---

[123] S.P. Ville, *Transport and the Development of the European Economy 1750–1918* (London, 1990) p. 95.

commodities and routes. These are difficult to get around and must mean that our picture of nineteenth-century transport remains broad brush and rather impressionistic.

It should also be stressed that although much of this essay has been devoted to discussing the extent of collaboration between the coaster and the railway, this only applies to coastal liner services. There is no evidence of any such activity between the tramping coaster and the railway company and indeed none is to be expected, since the tramp was offering a totally different service to the liner or railway. In terms of the quantity of cargoes carried the tramp section of the coastal trade was almost certainly the largest. The single largest commodity conveyed was coal and this was entirely inappropriate to liners. Hence the liner trade was the smaller in quantitative terms but carried the higher value commodities and could command a premium price over the tramp ship because of the higher quality of the service it provided. Thus it was the smaller but up-market segment of the coastal sector which collaborated with the railways.

The RCH records also support some of the generalisations made elsewhere about the economic characteristics of the coastal trade. They reinforce the view that the coaster was particularly able to compete in long distance goods transport and that the average haul of the coastal ship was likely to be well in excess of 100 miles. This suggests that the idea of a freight market segmented in part by distance with the coaster filling the long haul niche while the railway's average haul was much shorter, is not unreasonable. It also confirms that there was normally a significant differential between the price charged by the coasting liner and the railway train for carrying an identical commodity between the same two points, and that this discount offered by the coaster was normally in the range from 25 to 50 per cent. Finally it also reinforces the idea that coastal liner companies were likely to cooperate with each other in setting freight rates, arranging timetables mutually and even agreeing to some prearranged division of the traffic and revenue. For all of these elements were present in at least one of the examples of railway-coaster collaboration, and cooperation with other lines was obviously a normal part of coastal liner operations.

Such inter-modal collaboration is in line with previous thinking on railway policy in the last quarter of the nineteenth century. A number of writers, including Philip Bagwell, have shown that the railways virtually eliminated competition in freight rates in this period[124] and that service competition,

---

[124] Bagwell, *The Railway Clearing House*, p. 263.

in terms of facilities, frequencies, speed, and willingness to move small consignments, was the extent of inter-company rivalry.[125] If the railways were to eliminate price competition completely then they needed to include any competing mode which offered a similar service. The coastal liners did just this, hence the railway companies' eagerness to bring them into agreements to fix freight rates and cooperate.

[125] P. Cain, 'Private Enterprise or Public Utility? Output, Pricing and Investment on English and Welsh Railways, 1870–1914', *The Journal of Transport History*, 3rd ser., 1 (1980) pp. 18–19.

6

Birth of a Holiday: The First of May*

E.J. Hobsbawm

Michael Ignatieff, writing about Easter in the *Observer* observed that 'secular societies have never succeeded in providing alternatives to religious rituals'.[1] And he pointed out that the French Revolution 'may have turned subjects into citizens, may have put liberté, egalité and fraternité on the lintel of every school and put the monasteries to the sack, but apart from the Fourteenth of July it never made a dent on the old Christian calendar'. My present subject is perhaps the only unquestionable dent made by a secular movement on the Christian or any other official calendar; a holiday established not in one or two countries, but in 1990 officially in 107 states. What is more it is an occasion established not by the power of governments or conquerors, but by an entirely unofficial movement of poor men and women. I am speaking of May Day, or more precisely of the First of May, the international festival of the working-class movement, whose

* This paper was first given as the S.T. Bindoff Memorial Lecture at Queen Mary and Westfield College, University of London on 3 May 1990, and is here published, in a slightly modified form, by kind permission of the College. For a full bibliography, A. Panaccione, 'I 100 anni del 1º maggio nella storiografia' in A. Panaccione (ed.) *I luoghi e i soggetti del 1º maggio* (Venice, 1990).
[1] Michael Ignatieff, 'Easter has become Chocolate Sunday', *Observer*, 15 April 1990.

centenary ought to have been celebrated in 1990, for it was inaugurated in 1890.

'Ought to be' is the correct phrase, for, apart from the historians, few have shown much interest in this occasion, not even in those socialist parties which are the lineal descendants of those which, at the inaugural congresses of what became the Second International, in 1889 called for a simultaneous international workers' demonstration in favour of a law to limit the working day to eight hours to be held on 1 May 1890. This is true even of those parties actually represented at the 1889 congresses, which are still in existence. These parties of the Second International or their descendants today provide the governments or the main oppositions or alternative governments almost everywhere in Europe west of what until recently was the self-described region of 'really existing socialism'. One might have expected them to show greater pride, or even merely greater interest in their past.

The strongest political reaction in Britain to the centenary of May Day came from Sir John Hackett, a former general and former head of a college of the University of London, who called for the abolition of May Day, which he appeared to regard as some sort of Soviet invention. It ought not, he felt, to survive the fall of international communism. However, the origin of the European Community's Spring May Day holiday is the opposite of Bolshevik or even socialdemocratic. It goes back to the anti-socialist politicians who, recognising how deeply the roots of May Day reached into the soil of the western working classes, wanted to counter the appeal of labour and socialist movements by coopting their festival and turning it into something else. To cite a French parliamentary proposal of April 1920, supported by forty-one deputies united by nothing except *not* being socialists: This holiday, they argued,

> should not contain any element of jealousy and hatred [the code word for class struggle EJH]. All classes, if classes can still be said to exist, and all productive energies of the nation should fraternise, inspired by the same idea and the same ideal.[2]

---

[2] Maurice Dommanget, *Histoire du Premier Mai* (Paris, 1953), pp. 350–51. Dommanget's book, one of the few to deal with the subject before the late 1970s, remains important, but lacks the strong iconographical orientation of the recent literature.

Those who, before the European Community, went furthest in coopting May Day were on the extreme right, not the left. Hitler's government was the first after the USSR to make the First of May into an official National Day of Labour.[3] Marshal Pétain's Vichy government made the First of May into a Festival of Labour and Concord and is said to have been inspired to do so by the Falangist May Day of Franco's Spain, where the Marshal had been an admiring ambassador.[4] Indeed, the European Economic Community which made May Day into a public holiday was not, in spite of Mrs Thatcher's views on the subject, a body composed of socialist but of predominantly anti-socialist governments. Western official May Days were recognitions of the need to come to terms with the tradition of the unofficial May Days and to detach it from labour movements, class consciousness and class struggle. But how did it come about that this tradition was so strong that even its enemies thought they had to take it over, even when, like Hitler, Franco and Pétain, they destroyed the socialist labour movement?

The extraordinary thing about the evolution of this institution is that it was unintended and unplanned. To this extent it was not so much an 'invented tradition' as a suddenly erupting one. The immediate origin of May Day is not in dispute. It was a resolution passed by one of the two rival founding congresses of the International – the Marxist one – in Paris in July 1889, centenary year of the French Revolution. This called for an international demonstration by workers on the same day, when they would put the demand for a Legal Eight Hour Day to their respective public and other authorities. And since the American Federation of Labor had already decided to hold such a demonstration on 1 May 1890, this day was to be chosen for the international demonstration. Ironically in the USA itself May Day was never to establish itself as it did elsewhere, if only because an increasingly official public holiday of labour, Labor Day, the first Monday in September, was already in existence.

Scholars have naturally investigated the origins of this resolution, and how it related to the earlier history of the struggle for the Legal Eight Hour Day in the USA and elsewhere, but these matters do not concern us here. What is relevant to the present argument is how what the

[3] Cf. Helmut Hartwig, 'Plaketten zum 1. Mai 1934–39', *Aesthetik und Kommunikation* vii, 26 (1976), pp. 56–59. A Riosa (ed.), *Le metamorfosi del l⁰ maggio* (Venice, 1990) contains essays on the Italian, Nazi and Salazarist attempts to co-opt May Day.

[4] Dommanget, pp. 301ff.

resolution envisaged differed from what actually came about. Let us note three facts about the original proposal. First, the call was simply for a single, one-off, international manifestation. There is no suggestion that it should be repeated, let alone become a regular annual event. Second, there was no suggestion that it should be a particularly festive or ritual occasion, although the labour movements of all countries were authorised to 'realise this demonstration in such ways as are made necessary by the situation in their country'. This, of course, was an emergency exit left for the sake of the German Social Democratic Party which was still at this time illegal under Bismarck's anti-socialist law. Third, there is no sign that this resolution was seen as particularly important at the time. On the contrary, the contemporary press reports mention it barely if at all and, with one exception, curiously enough a bourgeois paper, without the proposed date.[5] Even the official Congress Report, published by the German Social Democratic Party, merely mentions the proposers of the resolution and prints its text without any comment or apparent sense that this was a matter of significance. In short, as Edouard Vaillant, one of the more eminent and politically sensitive delegates to the Congress recalled a few years later: 'Who could have predicted . . . the rapid rise of May Day?'[6]

Its rapid rise and institutionalisation was certainly due to the extraordinary success of the first May Day demonstrations in 1890, at least in Europe west of the Russian empire and the Balkans.[7] The Socialists has chosen the right moment to found, or if we prefer, reconstitute an International. The first May Day coincided with a triumphant advance of labour strength and confidence in numerous countries. To cite merely two familiar examples: the outburst of the New Unionism in Britain which followed the Dock Strike of 1889, and the Socialist victory in Germany, where the Reichstag refused to continue Bismarck's anti-socialist law in January 1890, with the result that a month later the Social Democratic Party doubled its vote at the general election and emerged with just under 20 per cent of the total vote. To make a success of mass demonstrations at such a moment was not difficult, for both activists and militants put their hearts

[5] Ibid., pp. 100–1.

[6] Ibid., p. 102.

[7] The fullest international treatment is Andrea Panaccione (ed.), *The Memory of May Day. An iconographic history of the origin and implanting of a workers' holiday* (Venice, 1989) (hereafter cited as *The Memory*). For the first May Day see the same author's *Un giorno perche. Cent'anni di storia internazionale del 1° maggio* (Rome, 1990), cap. iv.

into them, while masses of ordinary workers joined them to celebrate a sense of victory, power, recognition and hope.

And yet, the *extent* to which the workers took part in these meetings amazed those who had called upon them to do so, notably the 300,000 who filled Hyde Park in London which thus, for the first and last time, provided the largest demonstration of the day. For while all socialist parties and organisations had naturally organised meetings, only some had recognised the full potential of the occasion and put their all into it from the start. The Austrian Social Democratic Party was exceptional in its immediate sense of the mass mood, with the result that, as Frederick Engels observed a few weeks later, 'on the continent it was Austria, and in Austria Vienna, which celebrated this festival in the most splendid and appropriate manner'.[8]

Indeed, in several countries, so far from throwing themselves wholeheartedly into the preparation of May Day, local parties and movements were, as usual in the politics of the Left, handicapped by ideological arguments and divisions about the legitimate form or forms of such demonstrations – we shall return to them below – or by sheer caution. In the face of a highly nervous, even on occasion hysterical, reaction to the prospect of the day by governments, middle-class opinion and employers who threatened police repression and victimisation, responsible socialist leaders often preferred to avoid excessively provocative forms of confrontation. This was notably the case in Germany, where the ban on the party had only just been revoked after eleven years of illegality. 'We have every reason to keep the masses under control at the First of May demonstration', wrote the party leader August Bebel to Engels. 'We must avoid conflicts.' And Engels agreed.[9]

The crucial matter at issue was whether the workers should be asked to demonstrate in working time, that is to go on strike, for in 1890 the First of May fell on a Thursday. Basically, cautious parties and strong established trade unions – unless they deliberately wanted to, or found themselves engaged in industrial action, as was the plan of the American Federation of Labor – did not see why they should stick their own and their members' necks out for the sake of a symbolic gesture. They therefore tended to opt for a demonstration on the first *Sunday* in May and not on the first

---

[8] Marx-Engels, *Werke*, 22 (Berlin, 1963), p. 60.
[9] Dieter Fricke, *Kleine Geschichte des Ersten Mai* (Frankfurt, 1980), pp. 30–1.

day of the month. This was and remained the British option, which was why the first great May Day took place on 4 May. However, it was also the preference of the German party, although there, unlike Britain, in practice it was the First of May that prevailed. In fact, the question was to be formally discussed at the Brussels International Socialist Congress of 1891, with the British and Germans opposing the French and Austrians on this point, and being outvoted.[10] Once again this issue, like so many other aspects of May Day, was the accidental by-product of the international choice of the date. The original resolution made no reference at all to stopping work. The problem arose simply because the first May Day fell on a weekday, as everybody planning the demonstration immediately and necessarily discovered.

Caution dictated otherwise. But what actually *made* May Day was precisely the choice of symbol over practical reason. It was the act of symbolically stopping work which turned May Day into more than just another demonstration, or even another commemorative occasion. It was in the countries or cities where parties, even against hesitant unions, insisted on the symbolic strike that May Day really became a central part of working-class life and of labour identity, as it never really did in Britain, in spite of its brilliant start. For refraining from work on a working day was both an assertion of working-class power – in fact, the quintessential assertion of this power – and the essence of freedom, namely *not* being forced to labour in the sweat of one's brow, but choosing what to do in the company of family and friends. It was thus both a gesture of class assertion and class struggle and a holiday: a sort of trailer for the good life to come after the emancipation of labour. And, of course, in the circumstances of 1890 it was also a celebration of victory, a winner's lap of honour round the stadium. Seen in this light May Day carried with it a rich cargo of emotion and hope.

This is what Victor Adler realised when, against advice from the German Social Democratic Party, he insisted that the Austrian party must provoke precisely the confrontation which Bebel wanted to avoid. Like Bebel he recognised the mood of euphoria, of mass conversion, almost of messianic expectation which swept through so many working classes at this time. ('The elections have turned the heads of the less politically educated (*geschult*) masses. They believe they have only to want something and

10 Dommanget, p. 156.

everything can be achieved', as Bebel put it.)[11] Unlike Bebel, Adler still needed to mobilise these sentiments to build a mass party out of a combination of activists and rising mass sympathy. Moreover, unlike the Germans, Austrian workers did not yet have the vote. The movement's strength could not therefore be demonstrated electorally as yet. Again, the Scandinavians understood the mobilising potential of direct action when, after the first May Day, they voted in favour of a repetition of the demonstration in 1891, 'especially if combined with a cessation of work, and not merely simple expressions of opinion'.[12] The International itself took the same view when in 1891 it voted (against the British and German delegates as we have seen) to hold the demonstration on the First of May and 'to cease work wherever it is not impossible to do so'.[13]

This did not mean that the international movement called for a general strike as such, for with all the boundless expectations of the moment, organised workers were in practice aware both of their strength and their weakness. Whether people should strike on May Day, or could be expected to give up a day's pay for the demonstration, were questions widely discussed in the pubs and bars of proletarian Hamburg, according to the plain-clothes policemen sent by the Senate to listen to workers' conversations in that massively 'red' city.[14] It was understood that many workers would be unable to come out, even if they wanted to. Thus the railwaymen sent a cable to the first Copenhagen May Day which was read out and cheered: 'Since we cannot be present at the meeting because of the pressure exerted by those in power, we will not omit fully supporting the demand for the eight-hour working day'.[15] However, where employers knew that workers were strong and solidly committed, they would often tacitly accept that the day could be taken off. This was often the case in Austria. Thus, in spite of the clear instruction from the Ministry of the Interior that processions were banned and taking time off was not to be permitted; and in spite of the formal decision by employers *not* to consider the First of May a holiday – and sometimes even to substitute the day *before* the first of May as a works holiday – the State Armaments Factory in Steyr, Upper Austria, shut down on the First of May 1890 and every year

[11] Fricke, p. 30.

[12] Dommanget, p. 136.

[13] Ibid., p. 156.

[14] R. Evans (ed.), *Kneipengespräche im Kaiserreich. Stimmungsberichte der Hamburger Politischen Polizei, 1892–1914* (Reinbek, 1989), pp. 20, 253–57.

[15] *The Memory*, p. 247.

thereafter. [16] In any case, enough workers came out in enough countries to make the stopwork movement plausible. After all, in Copenhagen about 40 per cent of the city's workers were actually present at the demonstration in 1890. [17]

Given this remarkable and often unexpected success of the first May Day it was natural that a repeat performance should be demanded. As we have already seen, the united Scandinavian movements asked for it in the summer of 1890, as did the Spaniards. By the end of the year the bulk of the European parties had followed suit. That the occasion should become a regular annual event may or may not have been suggested first by the militants of Toulouse who passed a resolution to this effect in 1890, [18] but to no one's surprise the Brussels Congress of the International in 1891 committed the movement to a regular annual May Day. However, it also did two other things, while insisting, as we have seen, that May Day must be celebrated by a single demonstration on the first day of the month, whatever that day might be, in order to emphasise 'its true character as an economic demand for the eight-hour day and an assertion of class struggle'. [19] It added at least two other demands to the eight-hour day: labour legislation and the fight against war. Although it was henceforth an official part of May Day, in itself the peace slogan was not really integrated into the popular May Day tradition, except as something that reinforced the international character of the occasion. In addition to expanding the programmatic content of the demonstration the resolution included another innovation. It spoke of 'celebrating' May Day. The movement had come officially to recognise it not only as a political activity but as a festival.

Once again this was not part of the original plan. On the contrary, the militant wing of the movement and, it need hardly be added, the anarchists, opposed the idea of festivities passionately on ideological grounds. May Day was a day of struggle. The anarchists would have preferred it to broaden out from a single day's leisure extorted from the capitalists into the great general strike which would overthrow the entire system. As so often, the most militant revolutionaries took a sombre view of the class struggle, as the iconography of black and grey masses lightened by no more

[16] Kurt Greussing (ed.), *Die Roten am Land. Arbeitsleben und Arbeiterbewegung im westlichen Österreich (Steyr, 1989), pp. 58–59.*

[17] Calculated from *The Memory*, p. 247.

[18] Dommanget, p. 155.

[19] Ibid., p. 156.

than the occasional red flag so often confirms.[20] The anarchists preferred to see May Day as a commemoration of martyrs – the Chicago martyrs of 1886 – and as 'a day of grief rather than a day of celebration'.[21] Where they were influential, as in Spain, South America and Italy, the martyrological aspect of May Day actually became part of the occasion. Cakes and ale were not part of the revolutionary game-plan. As a recent study of the anarchist May Day in Barcelona brings out, refusing to treat it or even to call it a *Festa del Treball*, a labour festival, was one of its chief characteristics before the Republic.[22] To hell with symbolic actions: either the world revolution or nothing. Some anarchists even refused to encourage the May Day strike, on the grounds that anything that did not actually initiate the revolution could be no more than yet another reformist diversion. The revolutionary syndicalist French Confédération Générale du Travail (CGT) did not resign itself to May Day festivity until after the First World War.[23]

The leaders of the Second International may well have encouraged the transformation of May Day into a festival, since they certainly wanted to avoid anarchist confrontational tactics and naturally also favoured the broadest possible basis for the demonstrations. But the idea of a class

[20] Cf. the comparison of Social-Democratic and Communist May Day iconography in Weimar Germany in W.L. Guttsman, *Workers' Culture in Weimar Germany: Between Tradition and Commitment* (New York-Oxford-Munich, 1990), pp. 198–99. The finest example of this colour-scheme I know is Th.A. Steinlen's undated 'La Manifestation', No. 314 in *Le Bel Heritage: Th.A. Steinlen Retrospective 1885–1922* (Montreuil, 1987). For comparison: a real workers' May Day demonstration at a time of revolutionary struggle, Kustodiev's 'Demonstration at the Putilovskij factory for May Day 1906' in *The Memory*, pp. 530–31. While obviously influenced by the black-red convention, the painter clearly reflects the wider range of colours on such occasions in real life. For this artist's other contributions to radical iconography, see David King and Cathy Porter, *Images of Revolution: Graphic Art from 1905 Russia* (New York, 1983).

[21] Lucia Rivas Lara, 'El Primer de Maig a Catalunya, 1900–1931' in *L'Avenc* (May, 1988), p. 9. The substance of this is taken from the same author's *Historia del 1o de mayo en España: desde 1900 hasta la 2a Republica* (Madrid, 1987), which is the fullest treatment of the theme for that country.

[22] Ibid., *passim*. See also Lucia Rivas Lara, 'Ritualizacion socialista del 1O de mayo. Fiesta, huelga, manifestacion?' in *Historia Contemporànea de la Universidad del Pais Vasco*, 3 (1990). I owe this reference to Paul Preston.

[23] For a (failed) anarchist attempt to turn the demonstration into the Revolution, see David Ballester and Manuel Vicente, 'El Primer de Maig a Barcelona. Vuit Hores de Treball, d'Instrucció i de Descans', *L'Avenc* (May, 1990), pp. 12–17: a study of the 1890 May Day in that city. For the French CGT, see Maxime Leroy, *La Coutume Ouvrière*, 1, (Paris, 1913), p. 246 who notes that, once the CGT took over the occasion from the socialists after 1904, 'plus de fête du travail'. Dommanget, p. 334.

holiday, both struggle and a good time, was definitely not in their minds originally. Where did it come from?

Initially the choice of date must, almost certainly, have played a crucial role. Spring holidays are profoundly rooted in the ritual cycle of the year in the temperate northern hemisphere, and indeed the month of May itself symbolises the renewal of nature. In Sweden, for instance, the First of May was already by long tradition almost a public holiday.[24] This incidentally was one of the problems about celebrating wintry May Days in otherwise militant Australia. From the abundant iconographical and literary material at our disposal, which has been made available in recent years,[25] it is quite evident that nature, plants and above all flowers were automatically and universally held to symbolise the occasion. The simplest of rural gatherings, like the 1890 meeting in a Styrian village, shows not banners but garlanded boards with slogans, as well as musicians.[26] A charming photograph of a later provincial May Day, also in Austria, shows the social-democratic worker-cyclists, male and female, parading with wheels and handlebars wreathed in flowers, and a small flower-decked May child in a sort of baby seat slung between two bicycles.[27]

[24] For a most interesting account of (a) the transfer (under Peter the Great) of the western spring festival to Russia, via the German suburb of Moscow, and (b) the merger of this *maevka* with the tiny socialdemocratic workers' demonstrations of the 1890s, for which they provided a cover, see Vjaceslav Kolomiez, 'Dalla storia del 1o maggio a Mosca tra la fine del ottocento e gli inizi del novecento: i luoghi delle manifestazioni' in Panaccione (ed.) *I luoghi*, pp. 105–22. See pp. 110–11 for the use of the simile of spring in a political context.

[25] Among this literature, the following deserve to be noted: André Rossel, *Premier mai. 90 ans de lutte populaire dans le monde* (Paris, 1977), Udo Achten, *Illustrierte Geschichte des Ersten Mai* (Oberhausen, 1979), U. Achten, *Zum Lichte Empor: Maifestzeitungen der Sozialdemokratie 1891–1914* (Berlin-Bonn, 1980), Sven Bodin and Carl-Adam Nycop, *Första Maj 1890–1980* (Stockholm, 1980), *Upp till kamp . . . Socialdemokratins första maj-märken 1894–1986* (Stockholm, 1986) (hereafter *Upp till kamp*), U. Achten, M. Reichelt, R. Schultz (eds), *Mein Vaterland ist international. Internationale illustrierte Geschichte des ersten Mai von 1886 bis heute* (Oberhausen, 1986), Fondazione Giangiacomo Feltrinelli, *Ogni anno un maggio nuovo: il centenario del Primo Maggio* (Milano, 1988), Comune di Milano, Fondazione Giangiacomo Brodolini, *Per i cent'anni della festa del lavoro* (Milano, 1988) (hereafter *Per i cent'anni*), Maurizio Antonioli, Giovanna Ginex, *1o Maggio. Repertorio dei numeri unici dal 1890 al 1924* (Milano, 1988) and, above all, *The Memory*. See also for Switzerland, Bildarchiv & Dokumentation zur Geschichte der Arbeiterbewegung, Zürich, *1.Mai/1er mai: Mappe zur Geschichte des 1.Mai in der Schweiz*, (Zürich, 1989).

[26] *The Memory*, pp. 356–57.

[27] Greussing, p. 168.

Flowers appear unselfconsciously round the stern portraits of the seven Austrian delegates to the 1889 International Congress, distributed for the first Vienna May Day. Flowers even infiltrated the militant myths. In France the *fusillade de Fourmies* of 1891 with its ten dead, is symbolised in the new tradition by Maria Blondeau, eighteen years old, who danced at the head of 200 young people of both sexes, swinging a branch of flowering hawthorn which her fiancé had given her, until the troops shot her dead. Two May traditions patently merge in this image. What flowers? Initially, as the hawthorn branch suggests, colours suggestive of spring rather than politics, even though the movement soon to settle on blossoms of its own colour: roses, poppies and, above all, red carnations. National styles vary. But flowers and those other symbols of varied but burgeoning growth, youth, renewal and hope, namely young women, were central. It is no accident that the most universal icons for the occasion, reproduced time and again in a variety of languages, come from Walter Crane – especially the famous young woman in the Phrygian bonnet surrounded by garlands. The British socialist movement was small and unimportant and its May Days, after the first few years, were marginal. However, through William Morris, Crane and the arts-and-crafts movement, inspirers of the most influential 'new art' or *art nouveau* of the period, it found the exact expression for the spirit of the times. The British iconographic influence is not the least evidence for the internationalism of May Day.

The idea of a public festival or holiday or labour arose, once again, spontaneously and almost immediately – no doubt helped along by the fact that in German the word *feiern* can mean both 'not working' and 'formally celebrating'. (The use of 'playing' as a synonym for 'striking', common in England in the first part of the century, no longer seems common by its end.) In any case it seemed logical on a day when people stayed away from work to supplement the morning's political meetings and marches with sociability and entertainment later; all the more so as the role of inns and restaurants as meeting-places for the movement was so important. Publicans and *cabaretiers* formed a significant section of socialist activists in more than one country. [28]

One major consequence of this must be immediately mentioned. Unlike politics which was in those days 'men's business', holidays included women and children. Both the visual and the literary sources demonstrate the

[28] Claude Willard, *Les Guesdistes* (Paris, 1964), p. 237 n; W.L. Guttsman, *The German Social Democratic Party, 1875–1933*, (London, 1981), p. 160.

presence and participation of women in May Day from the start.[29] What made it a genuine class display, and incidentally, as in Spain, what increasingly attracted workers who were not politically with the socialists,[30] was precisely that it was not confined to men but belonged to families. And in turn, through May Day, women who were not themselves directly in the labour market as wage-workers, that is to say the bulk of married working class women in a number of countries, were publicly identified with movement and class. If a working life of wage-labour belonged chiefly to men, refusing to work for a day united age and sex in the working class.

Practically all regular holidays before this time had been religious holidays, at all events in Europe, except in Britain where, typically, the European Community's May Day has been assimilated to a bank holiday. May Day shared with Christian holidays the aspiration to universality, or, in labour terms, *internationalism*. This universality deeply impressed participants and added to the day's appeal. The numerous May Day broadsheets, often locally produced, which are so valuable a source for the iconography and cultural history of the occasion – 308 different numbers of such ephemera have been preserved for pre-fascist Italy alone – constantly dwell on this. The first May Day journal from Bologna in 1891 contains no less than four items specifically on the universality of the day.[31] The analogy with Easter or Whitsun seemed as obvious as that with the spring celebrations of folk custom.

Italian socialists, keenly aware of the spontaneous appeal of the new *festa del lavoro* to a largely Catholic and illiterate population, used the term 'the workers' Easter' from at the latest 1892, and such analogies became internationally current in the second half of the 1890s.[32] One can

---

[29] Cf Renata Ameruso, Gabriela Spigarelli, 'Il 1° maggio delle donne' in Panaccione (ed.), *I luoghi*, pp. 9–104.

[30] L. Rivas Lara, pp. 7–8.

[31] Antonioli, Ginex, pp. 4–5. Ballester, Vicente, p. 13 for the (typically) strong sense of the *internationality* of the 1890 demonstration in Barcelona. F. Giovanoli, *Die Maifeierbewegung. Ihre wirthschaftlichen und soziologischen Ursprünge und Wirkungen* (Karlsruhe, 1925), pp. 90–91, stresses the unexpected strength of this international feeling as revealed by the first demonstrations.

[32] The anarchist poet Pietro Gori created his famous Mayday hymn ('Sweet Easter of the Workers'), to be sung to the music of the chorus in Verdi's *Nabucco*, in 1896, as part of a one-act play on May Day. F. Andreucci, T. Detti (eds), *Il movimento operaio italiano. Dizionario biografico*, 2, (Roma, 1976), p. 526. See E.J. Hobsbawm, *Worlds of Labour* (London, 1984), p. 77.

readily see why. The similarity of the new socialist movement to a religious movement, even, in the first heady years of May Day, to a religious revival movement with messianic expectations, was patent. So, in some ways, was the similarity of the body of early leaders, activists and propagandists to a priesthood, or at least to a body of lay preachers. We have an extraordinary leaflet from Charleroi, Belgium in 1898, which reproduces what can only be described as a May Day sermon: no other word will do. It was drawn up by, or in the name of, ten deputies and senators of the Parti Ouvrier Belge, undoubtedly atheists to a man, under the joint epigraphs 'Workers of all lands unite (Karl Marx)' and 'Love One Another (Jesus)'. A few samples will suggest its mood:

> This is the hour of spring and festivity when the perpetual Evolution of nature shines forth in its glory. Like nature, fill yourselves with hope and prepare for The New Life.

After some passages of moral instruction ('Show self-respect: Beware of the liquids that make you drunk and the passions that degrade' etc.) and socialist encouragement, it concluded with a passage of millennial hope:

> Soon frontiers will fade away! Soon there will be an end to wars and armies! Every time that you practise the socialist virtues of Solidarity and Love, you will bring this future closer. And then, in peace and joy, a world will come into being in which Socialism will triumph, once the social duty of all is properly understood as bringing about the all-round development of each.[33]

Yet the point about the new labour movement was not that it was a faith, and one which often echoed the tone and style of religious discourse, but that it was so little influenced by the religious model, even in countries where the masses were deeply religious and steeped in church ways.[34] Moreover, there was little convergence between the old and the new faith except sometimes (but not always) where Protestantism took the form of unofficial and implicitly oppositionist sects rather than churches, as in

---

[33] Jules Destrée & Emile Vandervelde, *Le Socialisme en Belgique* (Paris, 1903), pp. 417–18. Giovanoli, pp. 114–15, notes the religious element in the language.

[34] See Hobsbawm, *Worlds of Labour*, cap. 3 ('Religion and the rise of socialism').

England. Socialist labour was a militantly secular, anti-religious movement which converted pious or formerly pious populations *en masse*.

We can also understand why this was so. Socialism and the labour movement appealed to men and women for whom, as a novel class conscious of itself as such, there was no proper place in the community of which established churches, and notably the Catholic church, were the traditional expression. There were indeed settlements of 'outsiders', by occupation as in mining or proto-industrial or factory villages, by origin like the Albanians of what became the quintessentially 'red' village of Piana dei Greci in Sicily (now Piana dei Albanesi), or united by some other criterion that separated them collectively from the wider society. There 'the movement' might function as *the* community, and in doing so take over many of the old village practices hitherto monopolised by religion. However, this was unusual. In fact a major reason for the massive success of May Day was that it was seen as the *only* holiday associated exclusively with the working class as such, not shared with anyone else and, moreover, one extorted by the workers' own action. More than this: it was a day on which those who were usually invisible went on public display and, at least for one day, captured the official space of rulers and society.[35] In this respect the *galas* of British miners, of which the Durham Miners' Gala is the longest survivor, anticipated May Day, but on the basis of one industry and not by the working class as a whole.[36] In this sense the only relation between May Day and traditional religion was the claim to equal rights. 'The priests have their festivals', announced the 1891 May Day broadsheet of Voghera in the Po valley, 'The Moderates have their festivals. So have the Democrats. The First of May is the Festival of the workers of the entire world'.[37]

But there was another thing that distanced the movement from religion. Its key word was 'new' as in *Die Neue Zeit* (New Times), title of Kautsky's Marxist theoretical review, and as in the Austrian labour song still associated with May Day, whose refrain runs: 'Mit uns zieht die neue Zeit' ('The new times are advancing with us'). As both Scandinavian and Austrian

---

[35] The sense of May Day as the *only* holiday exclusively associated with the workers, and its consequent effect in forming class consciousness, was noted from the start: 'This day is theirs. It is theirs alone', J. Diner-Denes 'Der erste Mai' (*Der Kampf*, Vienna, 1 May 1908). The author also notes the conquest of public space by the workers on this day.

[36] Hobsbawm, *Worlds of Labour*, p. 73 and more generally cap. 5 ('The transformation of labour rituals').

[37] Antonioli, Ginex, p. 23

experience show, socialism often came into the countryside and provincial towns literally with the railways, with those who built and manned them, and with the new ideas and new times they brought.[38] Unlike other public holidays, including most of the ritual occasions of the labour movement up till then, May Day did not commemorate anything; at all events outside the range of anarchist influence which, as we have seen, liked to link it with the Chicago anarchists of 1886. It was about nothing but the future, which, unlike a past that had nothing to give to the proletariat except bad memories ('Du passé faisons table rase' sang the Internationale, not by accident), offered emancipation. Unlike traditional religion, 'the movement' offered not rewards after death but the new Jerusalem on this earth.

The iconography of May Day, which developed its own imagery and symbolism very quickly, is entirely future-oriented.[39] What the future would bring was not at all clear, only that it would be good and that it would inevitably come. Fortunately for the success of May Day, at least one way forward to the future turned the occasion into something more than a demonstration and a festival. In 1890 electoral democracy was still extremely uncommon in Europe, and the demand for universal suffrage was readily added to that for the eight-hour day and the other May Day slogans. Curiously enough, the demand for the vote, although it became an integral part of May Day in Austria, Belgium, Scandinavia, Italy and elsewhere until it was achieved, never formed an ex-officio international part of its political content like the eight-hour day and, later, peace. Nevertheless, where applicable, it became an integral part of the occasion and greatly added to its significance.

In fact, the practice of organising or threatening general strikes for universal suffrage, which developed with some success in Belgium, Sweden and Austria, and helped to hold party and unions together, grew out of the symbolic work stoppages of May Day. The first such strike was started by the Belgian miners on 1 May 1891.[40] On the other hand trade unions were far more concerned with the Swedish May Day slogan 'shorter hours and higher wages' than with any other aspect of

[38] Greussing. pp. 18–21.

[39] The most interesting analysis of May Day symbolism is Giovanna Ginex, 'L'immagine del Primo Maggio in Italia (1890–1945)' in *Per i cent'anni*, pp. 37–41, and the same, 'Images on May Day Single Issue Newspapers (1891–1924): Their function and meanings' in A. Panaccione (ed.), *May Day Celebration* (Venice, 1988), pp. 13–25.

[40] The role of May Day in advancing and catalysing the idea of the General Strike – not only for universal suffrage – was already brought out in Giovanoli.

the great day. [41] There were times, as in Italy, where they concentrated on this and left even democracy to others. The great advances of the movement, including its effective championship of democracy, were not based on narrow economic self-interest.

Democracy was, of course, central to the socialist labour movements. It was not only essential for its progress but inseparable from it. The first May Day in Germany was commemorated by a plaque which showed Karl Marx on one side and the Statue of Liberty on the other. [42] An Austrian May Day print of 1891 shows Marx, holding *Das Kapital*, pointing across the sea to one of those romantic islands familiar to contemporaries from paintings of a mediterranean character, behind which there rises the May Day sun, which was to be the most lasting and potent symbol of the future. Its rays carried the slogans of the French Revolution: Liberty, Equality, Fraternity, which are found on so many of the early May Day badges and mementoes. [43] Marx is surrounded by workers, presumably ready to man the fleet of ships due to sail to the island, whatever it might be, their sails inscribed: 'Universal and Direct Suffrage, Eight Hour Day and Protection for the Workers'. This was the original tradition of May Day.

That tradition arose with extraordinary rapidity – within two or three years – by means of a curious symbiosis between the slogans of the socialist leaders and their often spontaneous interpretation by militants and rank-and-file workers. [44] It took shape in those first few marvellous years of the sudden flowering of mass labour movements and parties, when every day brought visible growth, when the very existence of such movements, the very assertion of *class* seemed a guarantee of future triumph. More than this: when it seemed a sign of imminent triumph as the gates of the new world swung open before the working class.

Yet the millenium did not come and May Day, with so much else in the labour movement, had to be regularised and institutionalised, even though something of the old flowering of hope and triumph returned to it in later years after great struggles and victories. We can see it in the mad futurist May Days of the early Russian Revolution, and almost everywhere in Europe in 1919–20, when the original May Day demand of

[41] *Up till kamp*, p. 12.

[42] *The Memory*, p. 223.

[43] Ibid., p. 363.

[44] E.J. Hobsbawm, '100 Years of May Day' in *Liber*, 8 June 1990 (distributed with *Times Literary Supplement*), pp. 10-11.

the Eight Hours was actually achieved in many countries. We can see it in the May Days of the early Popular Front in France in 1935 and 1936, and in the countries of the Continent liberated from occupation, after the defeat of fascism. In most countries of mass socialist labour movements May Day was routinised sometime before 1914.

Curiously, it was during this period of routinisation that it acquired its ritualistic side. As an Italian historian has put it, when it ceased to be seen as the immediate antechamber of the great transformation, it became 'a collective rite which requires its own liturgies and divinities',[45] the divinities being usually identifiable as those young women in flowing hair and loose costumes showing the way towards the rising sun to increasingly imprecise crowds or processions of men and women. Was she Liberty, or Spring, or Youth, or Hope, or rosy-fingered Dawn or a bit of all of these? Who can tell? Iconographically she has no universal characteristic except youth, for even the Phrygian bonnet, which is extremely common, or the traditional attributes of Liberty, are not always found. We can trace this ritualisation of the day through the flowers which, as we have seen, are present from the beginning, but become, as it were, officialised towards the end of the century. Thus the red carnation acquired its official status in the Habsburg lands and in Italy from about 1900, when its symbolism was specially explicated in the lively and talented broadsheet from Florence named after it. (*Il Garofano Rosso* appeared on May Days until the First World War.) The red rose became official in Sweden in 1911–12.[46] And, to the grief of incorruptible revolutionaries, the entirely unpolitical lily-of-the-valley began to infiltrate the French workers' May Day in the early 1900s, until it became one of the regular symbols of the day.[47]

Nevertheless, the great era of May Days was not over while they remained both legal – i.e. capable of bringing large masses onto the street

---

[45] Ginex in *Per i cent'anni*, p. 40.

[46] The rise of the red carnation in Italy is most easily followed in *Ogni Anno* (which includes the collection of Single Issues in the Feltrinelli Library, containing, it appears, some not listed in Antonioli, Ginex) and has numerous illustrations. The first reference to the flower as 'official' seems to be a poem in an issue from 1898 (p. 94), though other flowers do not disappear until 1900. For *Il Garofano Rosso*'s explication ibid., p. 105 and Antonioli, Ginex, p. 130. For the Swedish rose, *Upp till kamp*, pp. 21–3.

[47] At least, so Dommanget, pp. 361–63. But Dommanget himself traces the political use of the lily-of-the valley back to an Austrian print of the early 1890s (pp. 175–76), i.e. a time when the political association was with spring flowers, not necessarily symbolically red ones. For a German May Day image of a small girl selling these flowers, which was taken up internationally, *Ogni Anno*, p. 100 (*Der Wahre Jacob*, 26 April 1898).

– and unofficial. Once they became a holiday given or, still worse, enforced from above, their character was necessarily different. And, since public mass mobilisation was of their essence, they could not resist illegality, even though the socialists (later communists) of Piana degli Albanesi took pride, even in the black days of fascism, in sending some comrades every First of May without fail to the mountain pass where, from what is still known as Dr Barbato's rock, the local apostle of socialism had addressed them in 1893. It was in this same location that the bandit Giuliano massacred the revived May Day community demonstration and family picnic after the end of fascism in 1947.[48] Since 1914, and especially since 1945, May Day has increasingly become either illegal or, more likely, official. Only in those comparatively rare parts of the Third World where massive and unofficial socialist labour movements developed in conditions that allowed May Day to flourish, is there a real continuity with the older tradition.

May Day has not, of course, lost its old characteristics everywhere. Nevertheless, even where it is not associated with the fall of old regimes which were once new, as in the USSR and Eastern Europe, it is not too much to claim that for most people even in labour movements the word May Day evokes the past more than the present. The society which gave rise to May Day has changed. How important, today, are those small proletarian village communities which old Italians remember? 'We marched round the village. Then there was a public meal. All the party members were there and anyone else who wanted to come'?[49] What has happened in the industrialised world to those who in the 1890s could still recognise themselves in the Internationale's 'Arise ye starvelings from your slumbers'? As an old Italian lady put it in 1980, remembering the May Day of 1920 when she carried the flag as a twelve-year old textile worker, just started at the mill: 'Nowadays those who go to work are all ladies and gentlemen, they get everything they ask for'.[50] What has happened to the spirit of those May Day sermons of confidence in the future, of faith in the march of reason and progress? 'Educate yourselves! Schools and courses, books and newspapers are instruments of liberty! Drink at the fountain of Science and Art: you will then become strong enough to bring about

---

[48] The incident is vividly recaptured in Franco Rosi's superb film *Salvatore Giuliano*.

[49] *Un altra Italia nelle bandiere dei lavoratori: Simboli e cultura dall'unità d'Italia all'avvento del fascismo* (Turin, 1980), p. 276. This catalogue of an exhibition of workers' flags confiscated by the fascists is a superb contribution to the art history of popular ideology.

[50] Ibid., p. 277.

justice.'[51] What has happened to the collective dream of building Jerusalem in our green and pleasant land?

And yet, if May Day has become no more than just another holiday, a day – I am quoting a French advertisement – when one need not take a certain tranquilliser, because one does not have to work, it remains a holiday of a special kind. It may no longer be, in the proud phrase 'a holiday outside all calendars',[52] for in Europe it has entered all calendars. It is, in fact, more universally taken off work than any other days except the 25th of December and the first of January,[53] having far outdistanced its other religious rivals. But it came from below. It was shaped by anonymous working people themselves who, through it, recognised themselves, across lines of occupation, language, even nationality as a single *class* by deciding, once a year, deliberately *not* to work: to flout the moral, political and economic compulsion to labour. As Victor Adler put it in 1893: 'This is the sense of the May holiday, of the rest from work, which our adversaries fear. This is what they feel to be revolutionary'.[54]

The historian is interested in this centenary for a number of reasons. In one way it is significant because it helps to explain why Marx became so influential in labour movements composed of men and women who had not heard of him before, but recognised his call to become conscious of themselves as a class and to organise as such. In another, it is important because it demonstrates the historic power of grass-roots thought and feeling, and illuminates the way men and women who, as individuals, are inarticulate, powerless and count for nothing, can nevertheless leave their mark on history. But above all this is for many of us, historians or not, a deeply moving centenary, because it represents what the German philosopher Ernst Bloch called (and treated at length in two bulky volumes) *The Principle of Hope*: the hope of a better future in a better world. If nobody else remembered it in 1990, it was incumbent on historians to do so.

---

[51] Destrée & Vandervelde, p. 418.

[52] *L'Aurora del 1º Maggio* (1905), p. 290. Paradoxically this was anticipated by the Weberian bourgeois of Barcelona in 1890 who predicted, bitterly, that if the workers insisted on striking on May Day this would mean 'the addition of another holiday to the many which tradition and the Church have saddled the calendar with'. Ballester, Vicente, p. 14.

[53] T. Ferenczi, 'Feastdays' in *Liber*, 8 June 1990, p. 11.

[54] Victor Adler's *Aufsätze, Reden und Briefe*, I (Vienna, 1922), p. 73.

7

Railway Safety and Labour Unrest: The Aisgill Disaster of 1913

David Howell

The Settle to Carlisle railway with its impressive viaducts and many tunnels is a fine monument to the creativity of Victorian railway engineers. It reaches its highest point at Aisgill, almost on the border between Westmorland and North Yorkshire and 1,169 feet above sea level. From the south, trains have climbed the Long Drag through Upper Ribblesdale before entering the Blea Moor tunnel and emerging high above Dentdale. From the north, the line begins at near sea level in Carlisle and follows for the most part the Eden Valley. Aisgill has always been a quiet place, a road paralleling the railway, a few cottages; to the west and to the east, the fells reach over 2,000 feet. It is even quieter now that Aisgill signalbox has gone with a decline in traffic, transferred to a preservation site in Derbyshire.

Just north of the summit, the road crosses the railway. At this point, just after three o'clock on the morning of September 2, 1913, there occurred an accident that cost sixteen lives. The Aisgill disaster became a *cause celèbre* in the labour and socialist press; its consequences included the threat of a national railway strike and hurried consultations between senior government ministers. The tragic affair illuminates wider themes: the pressures on Edwardian railway management and divisions within the newly-formed National Union of Railwaymen. In turn consideration of these questions perhaps offers some insight into the complexities of the pre-war labour unrest.

Appreciation of the wider debates requires an examination of the events leading up to the disaster.[1] Soon after midnight on 1/2 September 1913 two footplate crews signed on at the Midland Railway's locomotive sheds in Carlisle, prior to working express trains to the south. Driver William Nicholson and Fireman James Metcalf were booked to take engine No. 993 on the 1.35 a.m. departure from Carlisle: Driver Samuel Caudle and Fireman George Follows would follow fifteen minutes later. Each crew would work their train as far south as Leeds.

All the men were highly experienced. Nicholson was forty-nine years old and had been a driver for twelve; he had driven expresses for the previous two years. Caudle was ten years older; his driving experience went back for twenty-nine years and his service with the Midland Railway for about forty.[2] He had received seven awards for vigilance. That night he saw the coal tipped into his locomotive's tender. The quality of the fuel provided for the Midland's Carlisle depot had recently become a matter of concern and Caudle's response was critical:

> It struck me that the coal was worse than usual as regards its size; it was very small . . . Engine No. 446 is a good steamer and it struck me when I saw the coal that if she would steam with this description of coal she would do well with anything.[3]

The coal supplied to Nicholson and Metcalf was of the same character.[4]

The 1.35 a.m. train was assembled at Carlisle Station from portions originating at Glasgow and Stranraer. No. 993 was one of the most powerful passenger engines owned by the Midland, but over the steep gradients of the Settle and Carlisle, its maximum load unassisted was laid down as 230 tons. When Nicholson found that his train had 13 tons excess weight, he asked for a pilot engine, but was told that none was available. In fact the judgement made by the platform Inspector was that

---

[1] For accounts of the accident see amongst others L.T.C. Rolt *Red For Danger* (London 1955); O.S. Nock *Historic Railway Disasters* (London 1966); Peter E. Baughan *North of Leeds* (Hatch End 1966); E.G. Barnes *The Midland Main Line, 1875–22* (London 1969). The principal contemporary source is the report prepared by Major Pringle on behalf of the Railway Department of the Board of Trade. This contains the Inspector's findings and the evidence given by witnesses without the inclusion of Pringle's questions. It was published as *Command Paper*, 7153 (1913).

[2] Ibid., p. 26 and p. 33.

[3] Ibid., p. 34.

[4] Ibid., p. 27 and p. 29.

more time would be lost waiting for a pilot than in climbing to Aisgill with a train overloaded by 13 tons.[5]

No. 993 with Nicholson and Metcalf on the footplate left three minutes late. Initially they coped well; over the first thirty miles to Appleby only one more minute was lost, but then the poor quality of the coal began to have its effect. Metcalf was emphatic:

> He had more trouble with the coal that night than ever before. The coal was a great deal more dusty and he had to pour water on it. This clogged the coal into cakes which lay dead on the fire generating no heat.[6]

Time began to be lost as steam pressure fell; most critically the falling pressure eroded the vacuum in the train pipe and the brakes began to leak on. The train came to a standstill at about 2.57 am. about half a mile short of Aisgill summit.

The 1.35 a.m. should have been secure; it was protected in the rear by the signals at Mallerstang about three miles to the north. The Mallerstang signalman, George Sutherland, had returned these to danger after Nicholson's train had passed. He was not permitted to allow any following train to go forward until he had been notified that its predecessor had passed the next signalbox at Aisgill. The next southbound train was that driven by Caudle. This had left Carlisle five minutes late at 1.54 a.m. No. 446 was a smaller engine than No. 993 but in this case there was no question of a pilot. Although 446 was limited to 180 tons over this steeply-graded line, the train composed of sections from Aberdeen, Inverness and Edinburgh was 23 tons under the maximum.[7]

Initially Caudle and Follows travelled more slowly than their predecessor and at one stage the gap between the trains was nineteen minutes.[8] However this began to narrow as the second train's lighter load proved less onerous on the steepening gradients. One of the driver's responsibilities under the Company's regulations was to ensure that his locomotive's bearings were adequately lubricated. Failure to do so could result in their

---

[5] *Carlisle Journal*, 24 October 1913 – report of Caudle's trial for the availability question, evidence of Inspector Jefferson; also the comment of Cecil Paget Ibid, 5 September 1913 and in *Command Paper*, 7153, p. 37.

[6] *Carlisle Journal*, 21 October 1913.

[7] For the trains' formations see *Command*, 7153, pp. 3–4.

[8] Ibid., p. 8 for details of the two trains' performances.

running hot and the incurring of a fine. This had happened to Caudle in the previous year. Some of the oil wells on No. 446 had been sealed up fifteen months previously and the Midland's official view was that an amended system of lubrication involving the gradual and automatic syphoning of oil into the bearings had solved the problem. This claim was not endorsed by Midland drivers. Caudle suggested a scepticism about the merits of so-called automatic lubrication:

> I make it a practice to go round the engine to oil the auxiliary boxes. They start with a certain amount of oil, and this may be enough to take us through to Skipton or Leeds, but sometimes it is not. If it is very low in the cup, there is not so much syphoned as if the cup is full and I prefer to go round for my own sake and the Company's.[9]

He took the classic footplateman's pride in his engine:

> I think as much of my engine as I do of myself.
> Nothing shall go wrong if I can help it.[10]

That night Caudle, choosing a stretch of line where the speed was likely to be relatively low, left the footplate to the north of Mallerstang and made his way round the outside of the locomotive. It was a windy night and the fifty-nine-year-old driver found that the journey took him longer than usual. When he returned to the footplate he faced a new problem.

Follows was familiar with the type of engine but not with No. 446. During Caudle's absence from the footplate, the fireman noticed that the supply of water to the boiler was insufficient. Since leaving Carlisle, water had been supplied through the use of the left-hand injector, but the poor coal and the consequentially inferior steaming had reduced its efficiency. Follows tried to activate the auxiliary right hand injector:

> I could not get it to work. Sometimes the steam does not catch behind the water properly, for the first time or two and you have to go through the operation again. We had just come out of the tunnel and I was engaged in working at the right-hand injector when the driver

---

[9] Ibid., p. 34. See also his comments at p. 35. Caudle's trial produced strong claims by Nicholson and himself as to the need for lubrication. *Carlisle Journal* 21 and 24 October 1913. For a Midland head office circular see *Command*, 7153 p. 55.

[10] *Manchester Guardian*, 19 September 1913 report of Kirkby Stephen inquest.

came in off the outside of the engine to the footplate. He took the injector in hand and I started firing . . . .[11]

Caudle's concern with the supply of water to the boiler was based in part on the disciplinary consequences of an injector failure:

If he had burned his fire box, he might as in the old days have been discharged or severely punished, though he had not heard of this being done lately.[12]

The crisis preoccupied Caudle and Follows on their approach to Mallerstang and to the last set of signals before the stalled train. Sutherland in the Mallerstang box had three signals to protect the line to Aisgill in sequence from north to south: a distant signal which a driver could pass at caution; a home signal which could be lowered to green in the event of the line ahead being blocked only when a driver had brought a train to a halt or had almost done so; and finally a starting signal which must not be lowered until the line was clear to Aisgill. When it became apparent to Sutherland that the first train was taking an unusually long time to reach Aisgill, he phoned his colleague there, but was told that the position of the 1.35 was not known. Clearly something was amiss and on the approach of Caudle's train Sutherland initially kept his signals at danger. However his first sight of the train suggested that it was slowing down and therefore he lowered his middle signal to green. He apparently intended to minimise any delay by allowing Caudle to draw up to the starting signal. This was a normal practice but it rapidly became clear to Sutherland that the train was not obeying the signals. He threw the lowered signal back to danger and waved a red hand lamp, but No. 446 and its six coaches continued up the bank.[13]

During his journey around the outside of the engine Caudle had believed that he had spotted the Mallerstang distant and that it was showing green. Throughout all the subsequent investigations he continued to insist on this point.[14] He also admitted that the injector crisis had meant that he had failed to take his customary second look at the Mallerstang distant and he had

---

[11] *Command*, 7153, p. 36.

[12] *Carlisle Journal*, 24 October 1913; see also *Manchester Guardian*, 9th September 1913.

[13] For Sutherland's evidence see *Command*, 7153, pp. 21–22.

[14] See *Carlisle Journal*, 24 October 1913.

seen neither of the other signals – one of which had shown a green light for a brief period. Instead he realised on resolving the injector problem that he had just passed the final Mallerstang signal. Three miles away stood the stalled train.

The Midland Railway's regulations did not rely only on the security of the signals for the protection of a train that had come unexpectedly to a standstill between signal boxes. Rule 217(a) prescribed that such a train be *immediately* protected in the rear by detonators as a second safeguard against a following train running through signals.[15] On this occasion the precaution was not immediately taken and it is easy to see how inflexible adherence to such a rule could produce what seemed to be unwarranted delays. Some ambiguity surrounds the failure to comply with the rule. The 1.35 train had two guards. Following the unexpected stop the front guard, Donnelly, asked Nicholson what had happened. The driver said that they were short of steam, but they'd only be a minute and he should get back to his van. Donnelly conveyed only part of this information to the rear guard, Whitley. He suggested the stop would be brief but not that they were short of steam:

> I did not tell Guard Whitley what the driver told me, that the engine . . . was stopped for want of steam, because he must have known it himself already. The train had been travelling so slowly for such a distance.[16]

Whitley later claimed ignorance on this point and insisted that had he been aware of the cause of the delay, he would have protected the train immediately.[17] Certainly there remains in all the testimony a degree of doubt about how rapidly these exchanges were carried out. Subsequently it was estimated that the train stood for six or seven minutes before the collision; only when the train crew heard and then saw Caudle's engine climbing the bank did Whitley run back with lamp and detonators. He went less than 200 yards; no detonators were put down. At the last minute Follows saw the tail lamps of the preceding train; his initial judgement that they were Aisgill signal lights was quickly abandoned as he saw

[15] For appropriate sections of Rule 217 see *Command* 7153, p. 54.

[16] For Donnelly's evidence *ibid*, p. 31 and p. 43–44 the specific quotation is on p. 43. Nicholson's recollection is at p. 27.

[17] For Whitley see pp. 32–33, also *Carlisle Journal*, 23 September and 21 October 1913; *Manchester Guardian* 18 September 1913.

Whitley's lamp. Caudle made an emergency brake application; but there was insufficient distance and his engine ploughed into the rear of the first train. The last vehicle was a van and was completely demolished, the next one was a third-class carriage and all the fatalities occurred amongst its occupants. Fourteen died on the spot and two more later in hospitals at Leeds and Carlisle. Each train was gas lit; the last three vehicles of the stalled train were completely burned out, although witnesses disagreed how far the fire was a consequence of ignited gas and how far of spillages of hot coals.

Public concern about the disaster was perhaps intensified by the fact that its location was only two miles away from the scene of another fatal collision early on Christmas Eve 1910.[19] When an official Midland Railway statement suggested, contrary to the claims of some witnesses, that all the deceased had been dead or unconscious before the fire reached them, an accusatory postcard arrived at the company's Derby headquarters:

WHAT A LYING STATEMENT TO MAKE. WHAT HAVE YOU DONE SINCE THE LAST DISASTER. NEARLY NIL. FROM A PASSENGER.[20]

Both disasters could be linked to wider features of company policy; in the aftermath of the 1910 accident, the connections were barely hinted at. Less than three years later they became the subject of angry debate.

An understanding of these exchanges necessitates some analysis of the Midland Railway's response to the problems facing Edwardian railways. Some generalisations about this predicament are possible. Companies faced a rise in the proportion of costs to receipts; they were unable to make a direct response because legislation placed severe obstacles in the way of raising charges. Particularly after the Conciliation Agreement of 1907, the Companies faced a further constraint in the growing self-confidence and combativity of many railway trade unionists. Some companies responded by initiating schemes of 'scientific' management, whilst some leading figures in the railway world were increasingly sceptical about the alleged benefits of competition. Instead they claimed that a

[19] For the circumstances of the earlier collision see the secondary works cited in above; also the official report again by Major Pringle with evidence published as *Command Paper*, 5587 (1911).

[20] PRO, RAIL 491/791, a collection of press cuttings, telegrams etc relating to Hawes Junction and Aisgill disasters.

more efficient system would result from amalgamations or traffic-sharing agreements.[21]

Within this general experience, the distinctive features of the Midland's position must be located. In one tradition of railway literature, that of history written by enthusiasts and for enthusiasts, the Midland has typically enjoyed a good press. Photographic collections highlight immaculate crimson locomotives, comfortable carriages and architecturally striking buildings. Commentaries are often uncritical. But the limitations of this literature are often acute, neglecting the harsh experiences of company employees and ignoring the economic pressures on railway companies even before the start of serious road competition. From its formation in 1844, the Midland had enjoyed the strength and faced the weakness of its geographical location. Centred in the Midlands with its headquarters at Derby, it was close to several areas of industrial development yet its position meant that it could never count on any monopoly traffic of significance. Much of its early expansion involved a series of attempts to escape from a limited provincial status. On May Day 1876 passenger trains began to use the Settle and Carlisle and the Midland began a competitive service between London and Scotland. The line was expensive to construct and to maintain; at one stage the Midland had wished to abandon its construction but had been blocked by a parliament concerned about anything that hinted at a railway monopoly.[23]

The Midland faced the problem that many of its main routes were longer than its rivals'. Its mileages to Scottish destinations were greater than from Euston and King's Cross; the same was true of its London to Leeds traffic. At least to Manchester its distance from London was little more than that of its principal competitor, but the severe gradients in the Derbyshire Peak made its access to Lancashire more difficult. Even in its heartland the Midland system had structural limitations. These meant that it was very difficult for a Midland express to serve both Leicester and Nottingham on its way to the North. Moreover Sheffield was not on the original mainline at all, but on a steeply-graded loop. Trains to Leeds and Scotland could call at the city only with some extension of journey time. These deficiencies mattered more from 1899 when Britain's last main line was opened by

[21] On general developments see Geoffrey Alderman, *The Railway Interest* (Dawlish 1973) and for a detailed analysis of a large but atypical company, R.J. Irving *The North Eastern Railway* (Leicester 1976).

[23] For a detailed study of the layout and development of the line see David Jenkinson, *Rails in the Fells* (Beer 1980).

the Great Central Railway from Sheffield via Nottingham and Leicester to London Marylebone. It was an invasion of the heart of the Midland empire by a rival determined to compete hard.

An attempt to respond by introducing a remodelled passenger timetable in 1901 was only a qualified success.[24] Punctuality remained far from perfect and the whole of the Midland's operations were threatened with acute congestion because of heavy and ill-organised freight operations. Much Midland traffic was provided by the Yorkshire and East Midlands coalfields, and this was often subject to acute delay. Coal coı ld take several days to reach London; staff overtime assumed monumental proportions. These inefficiencies remained in spite of sizeable capital works around the turn of the century. Some kind of initiative was needed to loosen the log jam.

This came with a senior appointment from outside the railway service. W. Guy Granet was born in 1867 and educated at Rugby and Balliol.[25] His college career was highly conventional: he was captain of the college boat club and his tutor later suggested that his social life could explain his failure to achieve a First.[26] After some years as a barrister, he became in 1900 the first salaried secretary of the Railway Companies Association. From this position he was head-hunted by someone within the Midland hierarchy. One who wished to recruit him warned against the contrast with his previous experiences:

. . . socially. I could only regard it as purgatory . . . In a service which has necessarily made promotion a feature, fancy yourself brought in as an outsider to the whole staff, with a totally different social status and far wider ideas.[27]

In 1905 Granet became the Midland's Assistant General Manager; the following year he was appointed General Manager. He set out to reorganise

---

[24] For Midland passenger services see the series of articles in the *Railway Magazine* during 1947–48 by R.E. Charlewood, especially the piece in *Railway Magazine* for July-August 1947.

[25] For an outline of his career see the entry in David Jeremy and Chrstine Shaw (ed.), *Dictionary of Business Biography*, 2 (London 1984), pp. 20–23, entry by Henry Parris, note also comments following his death in *Railway Gazette*, 15 and 22 October 1943.

[26] Copy of letter written by A.L. Smith of Balliol College 21 November 1897 in *Granet Papers*, MSS 191/3/1. (Modern Records Centre, University of Warwick).

[27] H.C. Beale to Granet, 2 May 1904; loc. cit.

the Midland's management structure; his main policy objectives were to expand turnover and to cut costs to a minimum.

Granet saw himself as a moderniser, perhaps something of a benevolent despot. His impact on Midland practices was radical. Within a year he had been instrumental in creating the new post of General Superintendent responsible to the General Manager for the running of all trains. This appointment went to Cecil Paget, seven years Granet's junior. Whereas Granet was a suave and assured meritocrat, Paget was something of a card. An Old Harrovian and the son of Sir Ernest Paget, the Midland Chairman, he had served his time as an apprentice at Derby Works and had eventually became Works Manager. As a locomotive engineer, he had a creativity that some commentators have seen as verging on genius. In 1907 his drive and enthusiasm, together with his understanding of recent American practices, were transferred to the Traffic Department.[28]

For lengthy periods he lived in a coach by the line side at Rotherham in the Midland's congested central section. The results of this experiment were seen in January 1909 in a scheme of centralised traffic control for freight traffic. This was applied experimentally to the congested lines of South Yorkshire and North Derbyshire. The apex of the control network was at Derby. Instructions on loadings and paths were passed down to local offices and then forwarded to train crews. Eventually the system was expanded to cover freight operations through the Midland system with the employment of twenty-four local control offices.[29]

The result of the reform was a huge drop in overtime and a reduction in freight train mileage that assisted the economy drive. The more rational structuring of freight services helped to improve passenger train punctuality and this was also facilitated by the introduction of more scientific timetabling techniques. His drive for rationalisation involved a system of loadings for each class of engine over each stretch of line. Excess weight required the provision of a pilot to keep to scheduled times. This systematisation lay behind Nicholson's unsuccessful request for a pilot prior to the Aisgill tragedy.[30]

This and other controversies lay in the future when Sir Ernest Paget

[28] For Paget see obituary in *Railway Gazette*, 18 December 1936; also the pen portrait of Paget by Kenneth Leech in James Clayton, *The Paget Locomotive* reprinted from the Railway Gazette, 2 November 1945.

[29] For a detailed exposition see *The Train Control System of the Midland Railway* reprinted from *Railway Gazette*, 1921.

[30] For loadings over the Settle and Carlisle see *Command*, 7153, p. 55.

commented on the initial impact of the reforms to a meeting of Midland shareholders in February 1910:

> The Midland Railway is better operated now than I believe it has ever been since its construction. It has been brought about by refusing to agree that old methods had been used for years by men of undoubted experience, that therefore they must not be questioned, and when those old methods would not stand the test of investigation, they have been ruthlessly thrown aside and better ones put in their place. [31]

The drive for efficiency had already produced a rift in the Derby hierarchy. A further reorganisation of the management structure had led in 1909 to the resignation of the Midland's Locomotive Engineer, Richard Deeley. He objected to the proposal, subsequently carried out, to remove the running side of the Locomotive Department from his jurisdiction and place it under Paget's control. Beyond this demarcation dispute there lay a lengthy battle over the Midland's policy on locomotive construction. Deeley had favoured a strategy of larger, more powerful engines, an option vetoed by the Board to avoid an expensive programme of bridge reconstruction. As a result, the Midland's locomotives remained small compared with those of its principal competitors. This policy was strengthened with the appointment of Deeley's successor, the amenable Henry Fowler. The operational consequences of this policy were a service of light, frequent trains and the widespread use of pilots. [32]

The drive for economy also left its first sombre impact on the Settle and Carlisle. The Christmas Eve 1910 disaster had as its immediate cause, an error by a busy signalman nine hours into a ten-hour shift. Most expresses in the busy Christmas season required pilots up to Aisgill. In order to save mileage the pilots were detached at the summit and ran three miles south to Hawes Junction where they could use a turntable and then return to their home stations. Early that morning the Hawes Junction signalman had to deal with no fewer than nine such engines whilst attending to many other tasks. He forgot about two of the locomotives standing on the mainline and ready to return to Carlisle. They were run into by a London to Glasgow

[31] *Railway News*, 19 February 1910.

[32] The enthusiasts' literature contains many references to a Deeley-Paget feud for example C. Hamilton-Ellis *The Midland Railway* (London 1953); for a more sober assessment see the comments of Deeley's nephew in *Trains Illustrated*, May 1956 (article by C.J. Allen).

express. The policy of cost cutting did not leave its mark on this tragedy solely through the small-engine policy. Fifteen months earlier, the Midland Traffic Committee had approved a proposal to replace the two existing signal boxes at Hawes Junction by one new installation. The remodelling had been carried out in the summer of 1910 at a cost of £770 but with an annual saving of £164 in signalmen's wages. At the subsequent inquiry, little was made of the wider issues: a man with a previously unblemished record accepted responsibility for twelve deaths.[33]

Aisgill in 1913 was to a very different aftermath. This cannot be separated from the increasingly adversarial character of the Midland's industrial relations.[34] The threat of a national railway strike in 1907 had brought Granet a significant role during the negotiations as secretary to the employers' committee. The settlement involved a complex system of Conciliation Boards for each company with arbitration as the last resort. Over the next few years the Midland acquired a bad reputation in trade union circles as a company which was unwilling to settle by conciliation and which then sought to evade sections of arbitration awards by regrading apparent beneficiaries. Paget certainly seems to have had a hostile approach to trade unions. When the Royal Commission set up after the 1911 strike to assess the working of the conciliation system heard Midland witnesses, this was a recurrent theme. One referred to 'innumerable complaints' from his colleagues:

> when they have to go before the General Superintendent, he himself wants to know whether they are members of the Amalgamated Society of Railway Servants. The result is that these men do not care to assist us on the conciliation boards . . .[35]

The allegation of intimidation was repeated by Jimmy Thomas, a rising union official and the Labour Member for Derby.[36] It was given more graphic form by a former Midland driver and union activist.

[33] The rationalisation is referred to by the Inspecting Office, *Command* 5587, p. 6 and by witnesses at pp. 25 and 30. The reference to the expected economy is in *Midland Railway Company Traffic Committee Minutes*, 30 September 1909, Rail 491/165 (PRO).

[34] For examples on the general theme see P. Bagwell, *The Railwaymen* (London 1963), pp. 277–83, 339–40.

[35] Report of the Royal Commission on the Working of the Railway Conciliation Scheme of 1907 – Evidence, *Command Paper*, 6014 at paragraph 1153 (witness John White of Toton).

[36] Ibid at Paragraph 1188.

He recalled how Paget had harangued him on the footplate of his locomotive in Derby Station:

> you and men like you, are a disgrace to the company's service and the sooner you are out of it, the better.

This railwayman soon quit:

> . . . if I made the slightest mistake, I should be discharged and out of employment . . . I have a wife and four children dependent on me, so I got another job as soon as I possibly could.

Granet's attitude towards trade unionism was more ambiguous. Compared with the sentiments of many senior railway officers, his comments to the 1911 Royal Commission seemed to be those of a 'progressive'. He claimed not to be opposed to railway unions in principle; yet he argued that they could not credibly claim recognition because of the their alleged minority status and also because recognition would subvert the supposed bargain of 1907. Granet claimed that the companies had accepted arbitration and the consequential erosion of their managerial prerogatives precisely because it was an alternative to recognition.[38] In the crisis of August 1911 it had been Granet, along with Sir Gilbert Claughton of the London and North Western, who had met union officials without, in the view of the companies, conceding recognition. Moreover Granet's actions during and after the strike had made him an object of suspicion to some of the more reactionary chairmen and managers. But Granet's vision of a high wage and efficient railway service did not mean that he was always conciliatory in his industrial relations policy. As the probability of a strike grew in 1911 he had proclaimed that the Midland would fill the place of every striker.[39] He also found time to write to Winston Churchill at the Home Office about a German waiter at a Glasgow railway hotel who was allegedly an agent disbursing funds to trade union leaders.[40]

---

[38] Ibid., especially Paragraph 12914.

[39] See *Derby and Chesterfield Reporter*, 18 August 1911.

[40] See Granet to Winston Churchill, 15 August 1911 in Randolph Churchill, *Winston Churchill Companion Volumes*, 2, pp. 1271–72 (London 1969). From another angle note the later positive view of Granet taken by Jimmy Thomas in his preface to G.W. Alcock, *Fifty Years of Railway Trade Unionism* (1922) at p. viii.

Whatever the nuances of style and opinion amongst Midland management over the trade union question, there was abundant evidence that many employees were becoming estranged from the company: the drive for economy involved regradings with loss of wages; the bureaucracy of the control system could be authoritarian; and many railwaymen felt that the company abused the conciliation system. The cautious Derbyshire Miners MP W. E. Harvey referred to 'seething discontent with the management'.[41] The Railway Servants MP Walter Hudson acknowledged the desirability of more effective control of traffic but claimed that on the Midland it was administered 'with a ruthless hand and reckless as to how much men suffer in consequence'.[42]

The brief 1911 strike severely disrupted Midland services in the industrial centres of the North and the Midlands. Many Midland men left work before the official strike call. In the North West they often struck as the dispute in its first unofficial phase spread outwards from Merseyside; on the Sheffield loop traffic came to a halt as the whole afternoon shift of signalmen failed to appear on account of local grievances. Some Midland installations were attacked: an assault on Chesterfield Station led to the reading of the Riot Act. Even in the Midland capital there were disturbances as the company attempted to remove perishables from its Derby warehouses.[43]

Significantly, relationships remained strained after the strike had ended. The Midland return to work was protracted since in some places men found that their jobs had been filled by strike-breakers or that they had lost their seniority and faced reductions.[44] Although the immediate issues seemed to be settled, claims that strikers were suffering victimisation soon emerged. The Railway Servants took up some of the cases and early in 1913 a Board of Trade official carried out a detailed investigation. In all cases but one the allegations were dismissed, but the report noted that Midland personnel records identified in red ink each employee who had struck in 1911. Despite the generally favourable verdict the inquiry had not been an easy one for Midland management witnesses. They had been thoroughly and

---

[41] Volume 15, *H.C. Deb.* 5th Series at Col. 878; the same debate contained an attack by Thomas on Midland responses to arbitration awards. (21 March 1910).

[42] Volume 27, *H.C. Deb,* 5th Series, Col. 1059 (4 July 1911).

[43] On the strike see for example the columns of the *Derby and Chesterfield Reporter* during August 1911.

[44] *Manchester Guardian,* 22 and 23 August 1911.

effectively cross-examined by Jimmy Thomas; it was not an experience they wished to be repeated.[45]

Within weeks the Midland control system almost produced a strike. A Goods Guard called Richardson refused the instruction of a Chesterfield foreman acting on control orders that he add more waggons to his train. The guard argued that any additional load would be in breach of the regulations for the line in question. Richardson was subsequently dismissed, his case receiving sympathetic coverage in both national and labour presses. After representations by union officials and expressions of rank and file anger, he was reinstated.[46]

This embittered industrial atmosphere provides the necessary backdrop to the Aisgill disaster. Significantly, at the time of the accident, the Midland's Carlisle cleaners were on strike over managerial behaviour and remained out for much of September.[47] In the aftermath of the accident, the recently formed National Union of Railwaymen rapidly became involved. Several of the principal figures were NUR members; in particular all four footplatemen were members of the union's Carlisle No. 1 Branch. They asked that Jimmy Thomas travel to Kirkby Stephen to represent them at the Board of Trade enquiry.[48] This investigation was a statutory requirement carried out by an officer drawn from the Royal Engineers and acting on behalf of the Railway Department of the Board of Trade. A union official had standing with such an enquiry only if one or more railwaymen asked for union representation.

Antagonism between the NUR and Midland management soon reappeared. The Company provided a special train to carry the Board of Trade investigator, Major Pringle, several of the railwaymen and Company officials from Leeds to Kirkby Stephen. Thomas approached Cecil Paget requesting that he be allowed to travel by the special

the next I saw of him, he was in consultation with the drivers, firemen and guards of both trains . . . he informed me that he had talked

[45] The minutes are available – 248 pages in all – in the NUR Records for 1913 (Modern Records Centre, University of Warwick).

[46] *Railway Review* 28 February, 7 and 14 March 1913; *Manchester Guardian* 4 and 26 March.

[47] See *Carlisle Journal* through September 1913 for progress of strike.

[48] See General Secretary's Report to *NUR Executive Committee*, 15 September 1913. The report notes that one guard and one signalman were also NUR members.

to the men and they had decided they were not going to have me to represent them.

The memory of the victimisation enquiry perhaps rankled

We are not going to have a repetition of your cross-questioning if we can help it. The men and we (the Company) are going to stick together.

Thomas travelled by the special after representations had been made by Major Pringle. When the train stopped at Aisgill and later at Mallerstang, inspections were made but Thomas was forbidden to leave his carriage. The final scene took place on the station platform at Kirkby Stephen. Pringle asked the railwaymen if they wished Thomas to represent them. They stuck to their newly negative position: 'The poor devils were frightened to death.'

Thomas quickly revealed the gifts that made him such an astute negotiator. He refused to attend the Enquiry as a silent spectator and instead presented his views not to the Board of Trade investigator inside the station building but to the press on the platform. Reporters besieged him as he announced that the 'real cause of the accident was shortage of steam.' Allegations were made about inferior coal. If Paget had attempted to exclude the union as a damage limitation exercise, the strategy proved a disastrous failure. The General Superintendent responded to journalists' questions by simply refusing to speculate on the causes of the accident.[49] It was an insufficient response; concern was articulated across much of the press. The first session of the Board of Trade enquiry had been held in private at Kirkby Stephen; in response to the widespread concern later sessions were held publicly in Leeds and London.

The enquiry heard evidence from railwaymen, Midland officials and a few passengers; then Pringle set about writing his report. The intervening weeks were filled with dramatic events arising out of the inquests. There were three since passengers had died in three different places. Following the events at Kirkby Stephen Station, the footplate men seem to have shifted their position on union representation. A week after the disaster they all attended a NUR branch meeting in Carlisle and explained the

[49] *Manchester Guardian*, 5 September 1913; also report to NUR E.C., 15 September 1913.

retraction of their requests for union assistance.[50] Perhaps the atmosphere of the branch meeting left its mark. When the first inquest met again in Kirkby Stephen, Thomas appeared as representative of the Carlisle railwaymen.[51]

Thomas used the opportunity to broaden the issue beyond the conduct of individual railwaymen. He focused not just on the question of coal but also on the lubrication issue and the failure to provide a pilot. The jury's response was protracted. They were sent out three times before returning a verdict of death by misadventure with observations on Caudle and Follows added as a rider. The next inquest in Leeds produced a slightly more pointed verdict: the cause of death was the failure to observe the Mallerstang signals, but given the circumstances this could not be regarded as culpable negligence.[52]

The railwaymen had to face one last legal hurdle. One passenger, Sir Arthur Douglas, previously Defence Under-Secretary in New Zealand, had died in hospital at Carlisle. At this hearing the railwaymen were represented by the Midland's solicitor. The Deputy Coroner made his position clear. The broader questions were 'minor matters'

If a driver knowing how serious the consequences must be, were allowed to drive past signals at danger merely because various parts of his engine required attention, there would be an end to all sense of security in railway travelling.

For Deputy-Coroner Strong, the verdict was a foregone conclusion

I think you cannot avoid finding – in fact the driver has admitted – that he did not carry out his duties and from that it is a pure question of deduction that the accident arose from that neglect.

The jury, given such directions, reached a speedy verdict. Caudle should be indicted on a manslaughter charge. His case was committed to the next Cumberland Assizes with bail set at £50.[53]

---

[50] *Railway Review*, 12 September 1913.

[51] For material on Kirkby Stephen inquest see *Carlisle Journal*, 23 September 1913; *Manchester Guardian* 18th–20 September 1913.

[52] *Carlisle Journal*, 23 September 1913.

[53] Ibid., 26 September 1913.

Caudle's trial opened in Carlisle on 20 October 1913. The prosecution was led by Gordon Hewart recently elected as a Liberal MP, the NUR had retained a Conservative member, Alfred Tobin, to defend Caudle. The union had briefed him on the wider questions of company policy, but the judge, Mr Justice Avory, opposed any broadening of the argument. Thus when the question of piloting was raised he intervened

> . . . this was all beside the question. Everybody knew that if the first train had not stopped, there would have been no accident, but the question they were trying was whether the driver of the second train was guilty of negligence in not observing the signals.

In such circumstances, the defence counsel's concluding speech with its insistence that Caudle's employers should have freed him from the stresses imposed by poor coal and the need for lubrication, was not likely to influence the judge. Avory had a reputation as a cold and stern figure and his summing-up was unsympathetic to Caudle. The jury's verdict was one of guilty but given the wider context, with a plea for clemency. Avory's remarks on sentencing were not calculated to assuage the anger of railwaymen. Caudle wept as he was reminded that the burden of his mistake would remain with him for the rest of his life. Avory insisted on the need for a custodial sentence on the ground of deterrence. This was a bizarre contention since presumably errors by footplate staff put their own safety at risk more than anyone's. Caudle was sentenced to two months imprisonment in the Second Division.[54]

Only once in the previous forty years had a railway driver been found guilty on a manslaughter charge. In that case arising out of an accident at near Arbroath in December 1906, there had been evidence that alcohol might have been a minor factor; even then, union pressure had helped in the reduction of the original five-months sentence to three. Some critics of the Caudle verdict drew a stark contrast. H.J. Pearce of the Manchester Fabians argued:

> Driver Caudle's fault was a fault of judgement. The fault of the management was a deliberate and considered fault solely in the interests of the money profits of the railway proprietors.[55]

---

[54] Ibid., 21 and 24 October 1913. The judge's comment is from the report of the 24.

[55] Letter in *Manchester Guardian*, 23 October 1913.

A cartoon in the NUR journal *Railway Review* portrayed a harsh dichotomy – Caudle in his cell, Midland directors dining in style. Beneath was Paget's maxim that they'd all stand together.[56]

Yet any attempt by the NUR to act effectively on Caudle's behalf would raise a strategic controversy within the union. The Aisgill disaster had been contemporaneous with the violent beginning of the Dublin lockout. Shortly afterwards some British railway men stopped work; some struck in sympathy with the Dublin workers, others were concerned with local grievances. Either way this spate of unofficial action was unwelcome to the NUR's full-time officials, and gradually the strikes were terminated.[57] Leaders such as Thomas argued that the doctrine of the sympathetic strike, if applied to the railway industry, was of almost unlimited relevance and was therefore a destabilising and destructive influence.[58] In response, the Left within the NUR influenced by 'direct action' and syndicalist sentiments attacked the timidity of their officials.

Caudle's conviction reopened the argument; he seems to have been a highly-respected figure in Carlisle railway circles and local emotions ran high. R.D. Denman the Liberal MP for Carlisle, wrote that the town's railwaymen were 'naturally furious . . . I listened to a good deal of ugly talk after the sentence had been passed'. He also emphasised the wider industrial context:

> Railwaymen . . . are not in too good a temper at present and the feeling that one of the most respected of their body has been imprisoned . . . does not allay bitterness of feeling.[59]

This assessment was borne out in the resolutions that began to be passed by NUR Branches and District Councils. Several called specifically for a strike to release Caudle. The *Daily Herald* at that time the scourge of cautious officialdom published the strike calls.[60] The anger was evident at

---

[56] *Railway Review*, 31 October 1913. Material was also included in *Daily Herald, Daily Citizen* and *Labour Leader*.

[57] This controversy can be traced in the *Daily Herald* and also in the minutes of the NUR.

[58] For a near-contemporary analysis see G.D.H. Cole and R. Page Arnot *Trade Unionism on the Railways Its History and Problems* (London 1917).

[59] R.D. Denman to Reginald McKenna, 21 October 1913. H.O. 144/1292 file 132928 (PRO).

[60] See *Daily Herald* columns for last week of October 1913.

the Carlisle mass meeting when a member of the audience asked: if this petition on behalf of Caudle is not successful are the railwaymen prepared to strike for him? The response was robust: 'Loud shouts of "yes everyone of them" and cheers.'[61]

The reference to a petition signposted the alternative strategy favoured by the NUR's national leadership. Thomas revealed a distaste for 'direct action' that foreshadowed his position in 1921 and in 1926. A strike was seen as not 'a real remedy' since Caudle had not been sentenced by the railway company. He drew a contemporary parallel that highlighted the liberal constitutionalism that influenced so much of the British Labour tradition: Whatever Sir Edward Carson might preach in Ulster . . . it would be a bad thing for the country for a Home Secretary to be intimidated in a matter of that kind.[62] Instead Thomas suggested that it would be preferable to lobby the Home Secretary with a view to demonstrating an injustice and thereby persuading him to recommend a pardon.

This strategy involved the presentation of a petition originated by the Carlisle railwaymen. Its language was far removed from the class-conscious militancy of some trade-union resolutions. Attention was paid to Caudle's previously good record and to the exceptional difficulties under which he had had to work; no reference was made however to any alleged corporate failings. Instead emphasis was placed on the jury's recommendation for clemency and on Justice Avory's comment that Caudle's awareness of his error would stay with him.[63] The petition quickly attracted over 23,000 signatories. Most were from Carlisle and demonstrated the degree to which, in his own community, Caudle's plight had evoked sympathy across social and political boundaries.

The petition and its signatures landed on the desk of the Home Secretary, Reginald McKenna. So did letters from Denman and Thomas. McKenna's time at the Home Office was not notable for its liberality. He presided over the forcible feeding of imprisoned suffragettes and had ministerial responsibility for the associated 'Cat and Mouse' legislation. Essentially an economist and an administrator he hardly evinced the passions of a civil libertarian. The initial advice from his officials was unsympathetic to Caudle's case. The official Home Office view was that the sentence was entirely proper; it met the jury's recommendation for

[61] *Carlisle Journal*, 28 October 1913.
[62] Ibid.
[63] Ibid.

clemency and secured a balance between protecting the public and giving due weight to Caudle's previous record.[64]

McKenna contacted Mr Justice Avory for his views and received a predictably bleak response. The judge claimed that any justification had to be on the basis of Caudle's previous record. Any remission of sentence would be

> an encouragement of the doctrine which apparently is beginning to prevail that the members of the class to which an offender belongs are entitled to arrogate to themselves the functions of the judicial tribunal.[65]

Nevertheless the political pressures intensified, NUR officials visited McKenna and he seems to have felt a need for wider ministerial consultations. Asquith was out of town and telegraphed suggesting discussions with Haldane, the Lord Chancellor, and Rufus Isaacs, the Attorney-General.[66] In fact eight, days after Caudle's sentencing McKenna met with a wider group of ministers. The meeting included many of the leading figures in the Cabinet – Haldane, Grey, Lloyd George, Runciman and Simon were all present. They unanimously agreed to a radical step. Caudle should be granted an immediate pardon rather than any remission of sentence.[67]

The decision ran contrary to Asquith's own preference. He had been opposed to any executive intervention and had felt that judicial proprieties would be served better by an application to the Court of Criminal Appeal.[68] Something of McKenna's own position comes through in a draft memorandum intended apparently for Asquith. He distanced himself from the position of the Permanent Under-Secretary in the Home Office, Sir Edward Troup, in that he felt that the prosecution had been ill-advised. McKenna noted not just the great rarity of such cases in the railway service but also that manslaughter charges would not be brought in similar situations – for example in the merchant navy. Within the privacy of a memorandum, McKenna felt free to criticise the judiciary. There was no evidence of criminal intent therefore Avory would have been better

---

[64] Departmental minutes in HO 144/1291 file 243938.

[65] Avory to McKenna, 25 October 1913, loc. cit.

[66] See telegrams from Asquith, 30 October 1913, loc. cit.

[67] Pencilled note, *loc cit.* The reference to 'Lord C' was probably to Lord Crewe.

[68] See translation of cipher telegram from Asquith no date loc. cit.

advised to impose a formal penalty simply binding the defendant to come up for judgement and sentencing if required. Against these legal criticisms McKenna was sensitive to the charge of political interference with judicial discretion; he felt between a rock and a hard place:

> Whichever cause is taken there will be much dissatisfaction. On the whole, I think the public would prefer an immediate remission. On the other hand, this course would be condemned by the Judges and much weighty official opinion. [69]

Backed by his Ministerial colleagues, McKenna completed the formalities for a free pardon. Early on 1 November 1913 Caudle was released from Carlisle Prison and was escorted through the streets by a large and welcoming crowd. [70] Thomas claimed that the release marked a victory for his policy of advocacy rather than militancy:

> It was not true that the Home Secretary had set Caudle free because of the threat of a railway strike. Neither would it be honourable to anyone holding the position of Home Secretary in this country. To have a strike in these circumstances would be to prostitute the power of the strike and to bring into absolute contempt the whole system of government. [71]

As the commendation of one trade union strategy and the dismissal of another, this was intelligible given the arguments within the NUR in the Autumn of 1913. The release of Caudle came as the debate over support for Dublin workers was about to become even more impassioned with James Larkin's attacks on trade union officials. But was Thomas's judgement based on an accurate interpretation of ministerial motivations? Following the decisive conclave of Cabinet ministers McKenna had noted that the decision to grant a pardon could stand on its own merits but that wider considerations had had a strong influence – 'the state of p.o.' (i.e. public opinion) 'and industrial situation'. [72] The Liberal backbencher, Denman had advised McKenna of the feelings of Carlisle railwaymen and had referred

---

[69] See four page typescript loc. cit.

[70] *Carlisle Journal*, 4 November 1913.

[71] *Railway Review*, 7 November 1913 (speech at Liverpool).

[72] See the pencilled note on the ministerial meeting of 30 October 1913, in H.O. 144/1291 file 243938.

to the general mood of the industry. Indeed he had suggested that a failure to respond to the reasoned lobbying of NUR leaders could render strike action more likely.

Caudle's release did not terminate the arguments over Aisgill. Late in November the Board of Trade published Major Pringle's report on the disaster. His conclusions acknowledged that the problems with piloting, coal and lubrication had contributed to the accident but he insisted that their importance was secondary. For him the responsibility lay with individuals. He criticised Sutherland for dropping a signal prematurely, although acknowledging that this was irrelevant to the outcome; he held those in charge of the first train, and especially Whitley, responsible for the lack of protection in the rear, but above all Pringle's view was that of Deputy-Coroner Strong and of Mr Justice Avory

'After giving the fullest consideration to all the circumstances and making every allowance possible for difficulties on the journey . . . the main responsibility for this deplorable accident rests upon Driver Caudle'.[73]

The response from within the Labour movement was hostile. Thomas argued that Pringle's analysis of the broader issues contained inaccuracies;[74] more radically a *New Statesman* editorial headed 'Whitewash' extended the indictment. It was not simply that Pringle's Report misrepresented the situation in specific respects; it was also that the document systematically served the interests of the railway company. The leader concluded with heavy sarcasm:

Is it worthwhile . . . spending public money on these enquiries? Is any purpose served thereby that would not be served by allowing the Railway Company itself to hold the enquiry and publish its own report at its own expense?'[75]

The attack provoked protective responses within the Board of Trade, 'a bitter and I think, most unfair attack' was one verdict.[76]

[73] *Command*, 7153 p. 12; for criticism of Sutherland p. 10; and Whitley and his colleagues pp. 11, 12.

[74] *Morning Post*, 27 November 1913.

[75] *New Statesman*, 29 November 1913.

[76] Departmental minute, 2 December 1913, MT 6/2361/10 (PRO)

Even such a respectable and cautious Labour figure as Arthur Henderson was moved to criticism. The inquiry had been 'little more than a farce'. The outcome was inequitable: 'The Company is saved from serious criticism while the servants are severely indicted.' The Report was 'worthless' except as a demonstration of 'an obsolete system'. It highlighted 'beyond contest the predominating influence of the railway companies. They are all-powerful before the supine and inept administration of the Board of Trade.'[77] For Henderson, this was a robust reaction. In part it perhaps reflected the place occupied by railway companies not just in Labour but also in much Liberal demonology. They were seen as powerful and often autocratic corporations, which were unenlightened on labour questions and ready to place shareholders' interests above everything else. Within the House of Commons the 'railway interest' was dominated by reactionary Tories. Henderson, after all had once been a thorough Radical Liberal and this left its legacy long after he had given his organisational loyalty to Labour. His criticism of Pringle's report also exemplified a theme that was central to Edwardian Labour politics the protection and enhancement of the conditions of organised workers, coupled with the claim that such improvement would raise the standard of public service. Once again the wider context is significant. A week before Caudle's trial 439 men died in the Senghenydd pit disaster. The safety question was at the centre of both Labour and wider public debate. When Parliament met early in 1914 the Parliamentary Labour Party focused on the issue in its amendment to the King's Speech. Senghenydd and to a lesser degree Aisgill provided the sombre motifs in the debate.[78]

The controversy over Aisgill ended in this unsatisfactory fashion with recriminations and unresolved differences. In part the arguments indicated that the disputants asked different questions of the complex causal chains that produced a tragedy. Pringle, Avory and Strong insisted that without Caudle's contribution the general circumstances would not have produced an accident; their critics argued that the behaviour of Caudle and other railwaymen could be explained only in the context of the broader questions and that a thorough understanding would dissolve any belief in individual blame. It is worth noting the readiness with which officers of the state embraced the notion of individual responsibility but besides

[77] *Derby Daily Telegraph*, 8 December 1913.

[78] *58 HC Deb*, 5th Series for example Thomas at Col 477 on lubrication question and defence of Caudle by the Conservative Member, Lord Henry Cavendish-Bentinck at Col 485 (13 February 1914).

this preference there remained controversy over evidence in three crucial areas.

The material on the provision and non-provision of pilots contained one significant inconsistency. Pringle in his report accepted the testimony given by Cecil Paget. The General Superintendent had outlined the strict regulations that governed train loadings under the Midland system:

'Every train has a scheduled timing and according to the timing certain loads are regulated for the engine . . . If it is thought necessary, and we are very particular about punctuality, to rigidly maintain our scheduled timing a pilot engine becomes necessary in order to do that, but only in order to do that.'[79]

This piloting was to achieve punctuality, not to ensure safety. Paget also insisted that footplate crews would not be blamed for any loss of time attributable to overloading and the lack of a pilot. This claim was supported at the Board of Trade enquiry by Caudle.[80]

Nevertheless the evidence of the Carlisle Locomotive Superintendent, Edward Carey, suggested that such an immunity was not automatic. Unpunctuality would lead to an investigation and any failure to furnish a persuasive explanation could lead to punishment.[81] More significantly the Kirkby Stephen inquest with Thomas cross-examining witnesses produced a claim at odds with the official version. Nicholson responded to a question from Thomas by agreeing that there had been a notice displayed at the Carlisle locomotive sheds indicating that crews were expected to keep time in the absence of a pilot, even if their train was a few tons overloaded. Carey, cross-examined by Thomas, claimed a loss of memory on this point; there was certainly no firm denial.

The discrepancy was never resolved; the allegation about the notice was emphasised by Thomas in his attack on Pringle's report. He added the claim that the notice had been removed after the accident. The union restricted its attack in this area to the suggestion of a cover-up; the wider implications of the Midland's heavy dependence on piloting were not explored. But in the evidence given to Pringle, there was one comment by William Nicholson that was highly suggestive. He acknowledged that

[79] *Command* 7153, p. 37.

[80] Ibid., p. 33.

[81] Ibid., p. 37 In his evidence before the Board of Trade inquiry Carey did not refer specifically to loss of time due to lack of a pilot but to a 'reasonable explanation'.

given normal conditions including fine weather, a Class Four locomotive such as No. 993 could take a few extra tons up to Aisgill without much difficulty. But weather conditions on the Settle and Carlisle were often far from ideal: 'If the night is rough, difficulty is experienced even with a load of 230 tons'.[83]

In an experienced driver's judgement the Midland's most powerful passenger type, specially designed for the Settle and Carlisle, could lose time with a permitted load given weather conditions that were far from unusual. Here was an indication of company policy that extended far beyond allegations of a local cover-up. The small locomotive and light train policy might seem viable over much of the Midland system; on the long tough gradients up to Aisgill and in harsh Pennine weather, the policy could mean problems for footplate staff and perhaps some erosion of safety standards.

One crucial contribution to the failure of Caudle to observe the Mallerstang signals was his protracted journey around the outside of his locomotive to ensure adequate lubrication. Pringle asserted that the practice was no longer necessary

'A receptacle is now filled with oil before a journey is commenced, and the lubricant is syphoned, drop by drop, from wicks onto the bearings. Provided that the receptacle is large enough to supply all the oil likely to be syphoned, there is no actual necessity for the driver to renew the supply during the journey.'[84]

However Pringle noted that drivers habitually oiled the bearings during a journey; but he insisted that this was not essential. Attention has been paid earlier to the considerations that led Caudle to leave his footplate, and evidence given to the Board of Trade investigation underlined the extent to which such action was common practice. Graphic testimony on the issue was provided at Caudle's trial. Nicholson emphasised that the class of engine driven by Caudle needed special attention: 'Only a limited amount of oil was supplied, and whether the weather was hot or cold, the oiling was a source of constant anxiety to drivers'.[85] Once again there is the hint of economy. Caudle at his trial remained sceptical about the effectiveness

[83] *Command*, 7153, p. 28.
[84] Ibid., p. 9.
[85] *Carlisle Journal*, 21 October 1913.

of supposedly automatic lubrication: 'In summertime the oil was so thin that you could hardly keep it in the boxes. In the wintertime the oil was thick so that it would not syphon through properly'.[86] The anxieties of the men at the front end suggested that more was at stake than attachment to an anachronistic tradition.

The controversy continued following the publication of Pringle's report. Thomas attacked the claim that lubrication during a journey was no longer necessary, and much of the *New Statesman's* onslaught concentrated on the question. It alleged that the lubrication system on 446 had been amended in the interests of economy. This journalistic attack was taken with some seriousness within the Board of Trade. Pringle's report had been based solely on the evidence submitted to him and several significant claims about the continuing need for lubrication had been made at the Kirkby Stephen inquest and at the trial where Thomas and Tobin respectively could develop the theme through cross-examination. A Board of Trade official, Sir William Marwood, wrote therefore to the Midland's solicitor for clarification. The reply claimed that the alteration in the lubrication method was based not on a search for savings but on its greater effectiveness. Under the old system 'there was a tendency for the big reservoir to get filled with water and dirt which led to the engine running hot when either the water or the dirt or both worked through'.[87] Careful testing had demonstrated that the modified arrangements provided sufficient lubrication and lessened the load on drivers. The gap between managerial decisions and judgements and the realities of footplate work on the climb to Aisgill offered one more illumination of the discontents within the railway service.

Above all, there was the question of the coal – the factor stressed by Thomas at his impromptu press conference at Kirkby Stephen. Metcalf and Follows had spoken of their firing problems; the former had recalled a verbal complain to a Carlisle locomotive inspector a fortnight before: 'I told him that the coal was very bad indeed and not good enough for passenger service'.[88] Nicholson and Caudle also claimed to have made complaints. The former suggested that on the day prior to the accident another express had stopped twice due to shortage of steam.[89] The arguments over the coal raised most directly the question of managerial economies.

[86] Ibid., 24 October, 1913.

[87] H.C. Beale to William Marwood, 8 December 1913; along with Marwood's, request for clarification 4 December 1913 in MT 6/2361/10.

[88] *Command*, 7153, p. 29.

[89] Ibid., p. 27 and p. 33.

One of Pringle's judgements was uncontroversial, the coal provided was of inadequate size, a point freely admitted by the Midland's officers. Beyond this point of agreement, Pringle considered claims that the coal contracts had been made with an eye to saving money and with quality as a secondary consideration. On this highly-charged matter, Pringle accepted Sir Guy Granet's refutation.[90] The General Manager made a lengthy contribution to the enquiry in pursuit of two objectives. One was to demonstrate how comprehensively the Midland had acted upon the safety recommendations made following the earlier accident in 1910; the other was to refute allegations about cheap and inferior coal.[91] Stylistically, Granet was an impressive witness:

'He had a weight and deliberation of utterance, a massive normality of demeanour which although they owed something to the art which conceals art, inspired confidence and bred conviction'.[92]

He set out his stall to defend Company policy:

'The suggestions . . . which I resent very much is [sic] that the coal was of a very inferior quality, that the contract was made negligently or carelessly or without proper tests as to whether the coal was a proper sort for use on the railway and that it was bought for reasons of economy. This is absolutely without foundation . . .'[93]

The coal loaded onto the two locomotives' tenders had come from two sources, the Blackett and South Tyne Collieries Ltd. and from the Naworth Colliery in Cumberland. The Midland had dealt with the Blackett firm for five years. An initial analysis of its coal by the Midland's chemist had noted its high calorific value, but had warned of its tendency to form a clinker. Granet's presentation concentrated on the Naworth coal, supplied by a Newcastle firm, J. Fenwick only since 1st July 1913. The Derby analyst's verdict on an earlier sample had been impressive. The coal had a very high calorific value equalling that of the best Welsh coals. Its sulphur content – unlike that of the Blackett coal – was low. Tests on the road between Carlisle and Leeds produced a largely favourable Inspector's

90 Ibid., pp. 8–9.
91 Ibid., pp. 44–48; see also the text in *Railway News*, 20 September 1913.
92 *Times*, 14 October 1943.
93 *Command*, 7153, p. 47.

report. This emphasised its cleanliness; it did not require blending with Yorkshire coal. It was 'a splendid fuel for use on the Carlisle road.' There was one reservation: 'It is rather small'. [94]

This qualification proved of course to be crucial, but in most respects the preliminary tests seemed to suggest that the coal's quality could justify a contract. Granet insisted that the price fixed was in no sense cheap. At 13s. a ton, it was 6d. above the South Yorkshire price and 1s 6d more than the price of the best East Midlands coal. The contract was given in evidence as for 300 tons a week with the requirement that the coal be passed over $\frac{3}{4}$ inch screens to prevent the inclusion of slack.

On this point Granet's account is inaccurate. The initial contract with J. Fenwick was approved by the Midland's Stores Committee on 5 June 1913. This was for 100 tons a week – not 300 – at 13s. a ton; the stipulation was for $1\frac{1}{4}$ screens not – a more effective safeguard against the risk of small coal. Three weeks later the Stores Committee accepted the offer from J. Fenwick of a further 200 tons a week again at 13s. a ton – but this time the screening was to be over $\frac{3}{4}''$ bars. Eventually on 10 July the committee said that the colliery could not supply 100 tons a week on the basis of the $1\frac{1}{4}''$ screening requirement. Instead the Midland accepted a modified contract. All 300 tons would be subject to the $\frac{3}{4}''$ screening but the price would be dropped to 12s. 9d. a ton. The Midland's eventual screening requirement was a second best for a coal acknowledged to be 'rather small'. The price was 3d. a ton less than the General Manager had stated. [95]

Fenwick's inability to meet the initial contract was perhaps a consequence of the obsolescent state of Naworth Colliery. It was a small pit and its screening facilities were old-fashioned. Granet acknowledged this, suggesting that the screens became clogged and as a result slack ended up in the waggons and eventually at the Carlisle coaling stage. [96] The locomotive men soon began to be critical of the coal's size. By August 1 Derby had received an official complaint from the Carlisle Locomotive Superintendent and an Inspector sent to investigate confirmed the complaint. In response colliery representatives promised

[94] For Inspector's comments see Ibid., for chemist's comments Ibid., p. 55.

[95] See Midland Railway Store Committee Minutes for 5 June, 26 June and 10 July 1913. Rail 491/221 (PRO). This renegotiation is noted by Baughan op. cit. p. 402 but without comparing it with Granet's evidence to the inquiry.

[96] *Command* 7153 p. 48; also the evidence of Arthur Bancroft, clerk in charge of the Coal Office at Derby, Ibid., p. 38. He noted that the Blackett screen was larger – $1\frac{1}{2}$ to 2 inches.

to adjust their screening mechanism, a later sampling of deliveries on 21 August suggested at least to Derby that the problem had been solved.[97] In contrast the Carlisle Superintendent suggested that any improvement was not maintained,[98] a judgement supported by Metcalf's complaint. Perhaps the most appropriate comment came from Cecil Paget three days after the disaster: 'We have stopped the supply of coal to Carlisle from these two collieries, so that this particular coal will not be used in future for locomotive purposes'.[99]

The making of this coal contract was not a simple case of parsimony. There seemed to be plausible grounds for using Naworth coal – the assessment of quality was favourable, and the Midland had good reason to purchase local coal for its Carlisle locomotives. The alternative was to purchase in the south and to bear the cost of transporting the coal to Carlisle. Here was another omission from Granet's justification of the contract, an absence that distorted his presentation of comparative costings. The difficulties came when the Midland ignored warning signals about the competence of the supplier. The modification of the first contract – not revealed to the Board of Trade investigator – suggests some readiness to lower standards, if there was a compensating fall in costs. The subsequent problems with size were viewed not as an endemic problem with an old-fashioned producer but as teething difficulties which could be removed. It is a matter for judgement how far the Midland response reflected the Granet regime's passion for economy and how far it reflected the inflexibility of the company bureaucracy.

Aisgill aroused public controversy for a brief period, it is recalled only by railway historians. Yet the tragedy offers insights from a novel angle into the character of Edwardian industrial relations and political argument. The successful agitation surrounding the conviction and release of Caudle demonstrates the dilemmas facing pragmatic trade union officials such as Jimmy Thomas. Whatever their desire for constructive relationships with Government and employers, such leaders had to reckon with the temper of many of their own members. This could be aroused easily by demonstrations of managerial insensitivity and authoritarianism or by a judicial decision that seemed draconian. Indeed the credibility of such officials could be enhanced by a belief that in the absence of concessions,

---

[97] Ibid., p. 38 (Bancroft); p. 47–8 (Granet).
[98] Ibid., p. 37.
[99] Ibid.

there could be a shift to a more radical, less accommodating style of trade unionism. Against this pressure from the left the conception of a Progressive Alliance incorporating a broad section of trade union opinion together with many Liberals remained a meaningful notion. Denman represented an important element within Liberal politics; he cultivated close links with the railway unions and saw the Liberal Government as an appropriate vehicle for advancing the aspirations of decent respectable workers. [100] Samuel Caudle, the senior railwayman with a lengthy record of service to his company, was a most suitable focus for such sentiments, whether articulated by a Liberal or by a Labour leader such as Arthur Henderson.

Any characterisation must involve an emphasis on the distinctiveness of the industrial politics of these pre-war years. They should not be approached through the transformed political alignments of the 1920s. Yet those who were to dominate British politics in the immediate post-war decade were already heavily involved and some continuities can be grasped at the level of individuals' priorities and styles. Jimmy Thomas emerges as a talented trade union leader. He showed flexibility in defending his members and a flair for effective publicity; he rode the tide of militancy within the NUR to win concessions. The image of Thomas wrong-footing Cecil Paget on Kirkby Stephen Station platform helps to illuminate the basis of his continuing dominance within the NUR. Yet Thomas's career ended tragically and some of the limitations were already apparent even before the flattery of the fashionable had its corrosive effect. The controversies within his union allowed Thomas to demonstrate his distaste for strikes and his uncritical constitutionalism. Above all, he was concerned to obtain a fair deal for Caudle and the other Midland men. He acted on the presumption that significant progress could be made within the existing structure of railway ownership. There was nothing beyond an adept pragmatism.

Yet the most fundamental theme is not concerned with political configurations nor with patterns of trade union leadership; rather it is one of the awesome responsibility placed on an often ill-paid railway staff. They had to cope with the consequences of remote managerial decisions taken in the optimistic belief that efficiency, economy and safety were always compatible. When a hard choice had to be made, it was the worker

---

[100] Subsequently Denman joined the Labour Party and was Labour Member for Central Leeds 1929–31. He then went with MacDonald – and Thomas – and remained a Leeds M.P. until 1945.

on the spot who had to make it. So Caudle at Mallerstang had to choose between observing signals and coping with a steam shortage and the risk of a hot boiler produced by poor coal. Yet in the subsequent enquiry inquests and trial, the experiences and anxieties of Caudle and his colleagues were marginalised. There was no conspiracy between Board of Trade and the Midland management, but senior civil servants and senior railway figures spoke the same language and shared standards of reasonableness.

The recovery of the experiences of Caudle, Nicholson and the other Midland men has relevance for the continuing debate about the tensions within Edwardian society; arguably it also strikes a contemporary chord with those tragedies of 1987 and 1988 – the grim images of the wreck of the Herald of Free Enterprise, the King's Cross fire, the Clapham Junction disaster. Once again the question is posed as to whether managerial pressures for profitability reduce safety standards; once again the harsh choices rest with workers on the spot.

This links back to the core of the Aisgill disaster. Beyond the consultations of urbane politicians and measured public servants, the austere verdicts of courts, there stand the rank and file railwaymen. They encountered daily the pressures of their jobs and at a moment of crisis responded creatively and effectively to assist a colleague. Here perhaps is an optimistic signpost.

8

Trade Unionists, Employers and the Cause of Industrial Unity and Peace, 1916–1921

Chris Wrigley

The often dramatic industrial clashes of 1917–21 have loomed large over the trade union history of the period. This is not surprising given the impact of the strikes, or even threats of strikes, on the political as well as the industrial history of those years. The trade unions emerged from the First World War strong both in membership and in finance. The threat of coordinated action by the Triple Alliance unions (miners, railwaymen and transport workers) to achieve sizeable improvements in pay and working hours and to prevent the reversion of their industries to private ownership – outlined and analysed skilfully by Philip Bagwell[1] – was a source of very considerable concern to the government and the propertied classes between the Armistice in 1918 and the coal lock-out of 1921.

Yet the First World War also left a very different legacy. Among a significant number of trade unionists the experience of wartime cooperation with employers, combined with a distaste for the new militancy, reinforced a pre-war taste for joint committees and for the settling of industrial differences within industries without recourse to Whitehall. This tendency also revealed itself in the participation of many trade unionists, nationally and locally, in forming alliances with employers' organisations in order to

---

[1] P.S. Bagwell, 'The Triple Industrial Alliance, 1913–1922' in A. Briggs and J. Saville (eds.), *Essays in Labour History, 1886–1923* (London, 1971), pp. 96–128.

propagate the cause of industrial peace and cooperation. During the period of maximum industrial and social unrest bodies such as the National Alliance of Employers and Employed (NAEE) and the Industrial League campaigned vigorously in many of Britain's industrial centres. While the trade unionists of national standing who busied themselves in these organisations were often of second or third rate importance, leading Labour Party figures – notably J.R. Clynes and Arthur Henderson – did bless these organisations and their efforts.[2]

What was unusual about 1916–21 was the proliferation of such alliances and the amount of support they gained. Before the First World War there had been not only many joint councils in individual industries but also a few attempts to form employer-employee alliances at national level. In 1895–96 there had been a short-lived Industrial Union of Employers and Employed which had seen itself as a means to 'emphasise the underlying common interests of both classes . . . and cultivate the feeling of goodwill on both sides'. This had been followed in 1900 by the National Industrial Association, which described itself as 'a National Association of Employers' Associations and Trade Unions'.[3] Such moves reached their pre-war apogee in 1911 with Sir Charles Macara's proposal that the government should support the setting up of a National Industrial Council. During the acute industrial unrest of the pre-war years such a marshalling together of centre opinion in British industry – the bringing together of all those who shared the ideal of 'the substitution in the industrial sphere of cooperation for antagonism in relations between employers and employed' – proved attractive also to the Liberal ministers who desired to reassure the public that something was being done.[4]

There was a marked continuity in representation on the trade union side, both of unions and of individuals, between the pre-war alliances and pre-war industry based conciliation schemes and those of the post-1916 period. Thus, for example, W.J. Davis of the Brassworkers was a key figure in the 1895–96 body and an early prominent figure in the NAEE. Davis was not

[2] C.J. Wrigley, *Lloyd George and the Challenge of Labour* (Hemel Hempstead, Wheatsheaf, 1990), pp. 185–87 and *Arthur Henderson* (Cardiff, 1990), pp. 140–41.

[3] H.A. Clegg, A. Fox and A.F. Thompson, *A History of British Trade Unions since 1889*, 1 (Oxford, 1964), pp. 175–76.

[4] The best account of the Industrial Council is R. Charles, *The Development of Industrial Relations in Britain, 1911–1939* (London, 1973), pp. 37–74. On Macara see A.J. McIvor, 'Sir Charles Wright Macara (1845–1929)' in D. Jeremy (ed.), *Dictionary of Business Biography*, 4 (London, 1985), pp. 7–14.

only the founder and first secretary of the Brassworkers' Union (1872–83, 1889–1920) but he was also instrumental in securing the formation of the employers' organisation for the industry in 1897, seven years after he had achieved recognition and sole bargaining rights for his union. The official history of the Master Brass Founders' Association observed of Davis at roughly the time of the turn of the century that though he was 'then regarded as a wild radical' he was 'in fact a moderate Liberal and a personal friend of King Edward VII'.[5] There was a similar continuity among the industrial sectors that participated in such bodies.

For instance, the iron and steel trade unions were frequently involved. The iron trade unions had been prominent in the conciliation movement of the late nineteenth century, feeling that such an industrial relations strategy made sense for unions which had been battered in open conflict with employers in the 1860s and early 1870s and had remained weak in the subsequent decade. In 1894 Edward Trow, the secretary of the Associated Iron and Steel Workers of Great Britain, was a member of the committee which set up the Industrial Union of 1895–6, as was David Dale, the ironmaster. Dale was president of the Board of Arbitration and Conciliation for the Manufactured Iron Trade of the North of England, and Trow was one of its joint secretaries. Eric Taylor has commented of Trow's union that it was 'little more than an instrument of the Board'.[6] Trow was well-known to the young Iron Founders' official, Arthur Henderson, not just in his trade union capacity, but as vice-president of Darlington Liberal Association when Henderson was elected, in effect, as a Lib-Lab to both Darlington Council and Durham County Council in 1898.

Well after his death, his union joined with the British Steel Smelters' Association in 1916 and the National Steel Workers' Association to form a new union, the British Iron, Steel and Kindred Trades Association, to recruit new members in the trades and to form the Iron and Steel Trades Confederation to represent the constituent unions. Setting up two bodies made it easier to, in effect, amalgamate under the existing trade union legislation. The British Steel Smelters had been built up by John Hodge (general secretary 1886–1918, President of the Iron and Steel

[5] E.N. Hiley, *Brass Saga* (London, 1957), pp. 25–27. M. Espinasse and J. Saville, 'William John Davis (1848–1934)' in J. Bellamy and J. Saville (eds.), *Dictionary of Labour Biography*, 6 (London, 1982), pp. 92–98.

[6] E. Taylor, 'Edward Trow (1833–99)' in Bellamy and Saville (eds), 3 (1976), pp. 187–92. J.H. Porter, 'The Iron Trade' in C.J. Wrigley (ed.), *A History of British Industrial Relations, 1875–1914* (Hassocks, 1982), pp. 253–65.

Trades Confederation 1917–31 and Labour MP 1906–23). He, just like Arthur Henderson, had been a Liberal councillor in the 1890s, was a Wesleyan, a temperance advocate and also a supporter of collaborative policies with employers (including negotiating a sliding scale agreement in 1905). Indeed, Hodge and Henderson were often politically close before 1919, from the time Henderson was Hodge's agent in a 1903 by-election until at least when Henderson rescued Hodge from deselection as candidate for Gorton in mid 1918. Hodge served on the executive of the NAEE and, even more controversially, he was president of Lord Milner's 'patriotic labour' organisation, the British Workers' National League, from 1916 until he resigned in mid1918 rather than be forced out of the Labour Party.[7]

One of Hodge's closest associates was Arthur Pugh, assistant secretary of the Smelters from 1906, secretary of The Iron and Steel Trades Confederation from its formation until 1936 and chairman of the TUC during the 1926 General Strike. Hodge testified of Pugh that he:

> . . . became a strong adherent of Arbitration and Conciliation Boards; strong on the necessity of collective bargaining and equally strong on the adamant necessity of constitutional methods. No one could have practised these principles as administrative officer more strongly than he did.[8]

Pugh took the highest NAEE posts afforded to the trade union side – being both a joint vice-chairman and a joint treasurer. He was accompanied to the general council meetings of the NAEE not only by Hodge but also by Robert Dennison and James Gavin of the Iron and Steel Trades Federation.

The example of the iron and steel trade links with such movements could be elaborated further. One of the few trades councils to support the Industrial Union was Sheffield, with its Nonconformist and Liberal president – Charles Hobson – serving on its executive.[9]

One further example of such continuity on the trade union side deserves particular mention: that is the role of the General Federation of Trade

---

[7] Wrigley, *Henderson*, pp. 19, 28–33, 41, 85 and 121. D. Howell and J. Saville, 'John Hodge (1855–1937)' in Bellamy and Saville (eds.), 3, pp. 109–15. J. Hodge, *Workman's Cottage to Windsor Castle* (London, 1931), pp. 59–61 and 145–49. Sir Arthur Pugh, *Men of Steel by One of Them* (London, 1951), pp. 255–81.

[8] Hodge, p. 360.

[9] Hobson advocated industrial conciliation in 1919. H. Mathers, 'Charles Hobson (1845–1923)' in Bellamy and Saville (eds.), 7 (1984), pp. 121–23.

Unions (GFTU). This had been set up in 1899 to deal purely with industrial, not political, matters; with the desire to provide mutual assistance during industrial disputes being a prime motive. Two of the key figures in its formation, Robert Knight (general secretary of the Boilermakers, 1871–99) and Alexander Wilkie (general secretary of the Associated Shipwrights Society, 1882–1928) were prominent supporters of the National Industrial Association founded in 1900. While the GFTU as a body was critical of the structure of the Association, it nevertheless, in its 1901 annual report, declared the need for some such organisation 'if Britain is to be freed from the irritating and unbusinesslike stoppages which periodically hamper her productivity'.[10] In 1917 the GFTU was one of the key supporters of the NAEE; so much so that the *Cotton Factory Times* deemed the trade union side of it to be like 'a gathering of the executive council of the General Federation of Trade Unions'.[11] These included W.A. Appleton, the GFTU's dominating secretary (1899–1938), on its executive, and James O'Grady MP (secretary of the National Federation of General Workers, 1917–24), its wartime chairman. By this time the GFTU was weakened, representing the smaller craft unions while the major powerful unions went their own way. W.A. Appleton was out of tune with the collectivist sentiments which predominated in the labour movement during the First World War. He was an opponent of state intervention in industrial relations and critical of mixing trade unionism and politics (by which he meant socialism, for he himself was a great maker of political comments). In 1919, having taken over the GFTU's insolvent journal *The Federationist* and renamed it *The Democrat*, he used it to condemn vigorously Smillie and Direct Action while praising Liberal policies.[12]

The special conditions of the wartime economy and the immediate post-war period gave a considerable boost to this always significant tendency within British trade unionism. For a period the NAEE, in particular of the bodies which preached industrial peace, made a considerable impact in industrial politics, not just at the national level but also across the country. It became a relatively well funded propaganda organisation, with aspirations even to a mass membership.

[10] Clegg, Fox and Thompson, p. 176.

[11] H.A. Clegg, *A History of British Trade Unions since 1889*, 2 (Oxford, 1985), p. 231.

[12] A. Prochaska, *History of the General Federation of Trade Unions, 1899–1980* (London, 1982), pp. 157–64.

The NAEE's creation followed on shortly from the formation of the Federation of British Industries (FBI) in the autumn of 1916. In both the same industrialists and employers' organisations were active; the latter including the Engineering and National Employers' Federation, the National Federation of Iron and Steel Manufacturers, the Shipbuilding Employers' Federation and the Master Cotton Spinners. These employers' organisations were matched in the NAEE by the presence of leading figures from the appropriate trade unions. In a special trade fair edition of the FBI's *Bulletin*, published in March 1919, it was claimed that the FBI 'was largely instrumental in founding the National Alliance of Employers . . . The Federation works in close cooperation with this body, the influence of which is a daily growing factor in industrial politics'.[13]

While identifying the FBI as the main instigator of the NAEE is straightforward, the reasons for setting up such a body, and for its relative success for a while, were more varied. The most important of these were: concern about post-war reconstruction, and in particular the return of those who had left industry because of the war; a desire to build on wartime attitudes which favoured cooperation rather than confrontation in industry; worries about the competitiveness of British industry in the post-war international economy; and a desire to lessen the rising levels of industrial unrest. That the NAEE initially stemmed in large part from concerns about reconstruction has been omitted in previous accounts.[14] Yet this is clear from the early meetings, both in London and elsewhere.

The initiative for the first meetings came from the Rt Hon. Frederick Huth Jackson (1863–1921), a leading banker. He had become the senior partner in the family accepting house of Frederick Huth and Co. in 1919, a member of the Court of the Bank of England from 1892 (circumstances preventing him from becoming Governor for the then customary two years in either 1909 or 1911), President of the Institute of Bankers 1909–11 and a Privy Councillor in 1911.[15] In the autumn of 1916 Huth Jackson and two

[13] Labour Research Department, *The Federation of British Industries* (London, 1923), pp. 7–15 and 43–47.

[14] For example, ibid. and S. White, 'Ideological Hegemony and Political Control: The Sociology of Anti-Bolshevism in Britain 1918–20', *Scottish Labour History Society Journal*, 9 (June 1975), pp. 3–20, which otherwise is a valuable survey.

[15] For all this his firm was in a shaky state and after his death was the subject of major rescue operations by the Bank of England well into the 1930s. R.S. Sayers, *The Bank of England, 1891–1944* (Cambridge, 1976), pp. 268–9 and 642. *Industrial Unity*, 1 (May 1918). *Who's Who 1919*.

other employers met with four leading trade unionists 'to consider the preparation which should be made by the government, and industry, for the absorption into civil employment of the men fighting . . . and the workers in munitions factories at home'. [16] The employers at this initial gathering were almost certainly leading lights of the Federation of British Industries, and one can surmise that two of Dudley Docker (its first president), Sir Vincent Caillard (its third president) and Sir Robert Hadfield are most likely to have been the others present. On the trade union side most probably all, or some, of Appleton, Hodge, Pugh and J.T. Brownlie, the chairman of the Amalgamated Society of Engineers (ASE), were present.

Huth Jackson's small informal gathering was followed by a larger conference held in London at the Hotel Cecil on 7 December 1916. At this there were twenty-five employers, including Docker, Caillard, Hadfield and Sir Algernon Firth, and fourteen trade unionists, including Appleton, Brownlie, Davis, O'Grady, George Roberts MP, Ben Tillett and J. Havelock Wilson. Again, this was held very specifically on the issue of organising the smooth reabsorption of those then in the armed forces or in munitions back into peacetime industry. Huth Jackson and his associates from the earlier meeting put to the conference, by means of a series of resolutions, a demobilisation scheme which involved the creation of a Central Statutory Board which would have complete powers to deal with the problem. A minimum of two-thirds of the board (and of local boards) was to be drawn in equal numbers from the nominees of employers' associations and trade unions, while the remaining members would come from government departments. The scheme also included one provision especially designed to meet the sensitivities of the craft unions:

> That where a trade union, by arrangement with an employers' association, is capable of placing its members in employment, it should be competent for the Central Board, if it deems it to be in the national interest, to delegate to the trade union in question the responsibility of dealing with the reinstatement of its own members. [17]

This was almost certainly pressed for by Brownlie on behalf of the ASE. For in November 1916 they had successfully pressed the government into

---

[16] NAEE, *Report, 1916–18*, p. 5. (copies of NAEE and NIA material are to be found in the Papers of the Engineering Employers' Federation, Iron and Steel Trades Confederation, the TUC and other collections).

[17] NAEE, *Report, 1916–18*, p. 6. *Industrial Peace*, 1, 2 (October 1917), pp. 24–46.

devolving on them some measure of control over the recruiting of their members for the armed forces under the 'trade card scheme' (whereby exemption cards were issued to their members, with the expectation that the union would help find men for skilled work in the army). [18]

The issue of arranging a smooth return of workers to peacetime employment at the end of the war was a very powerful one for gaining trade unionists' support for the NAEE. This is clear from the local meetings that were held to inaugurate area committees. At Swansea, on 6 May 1917, while others spoke of the merits of cooperation in industry and the need to improve the competitiveness of British industry, trade union speakers focused heavily on the problems of getting men back into peacetime employment. This was very much the case with Ivor Gwynne (general secretary of Tin and Steel Millmen's Association 1904–21), the main trade union speaker. It was even more the case with George Gunning of the National Sailors and Fireman's Union, who moved a vote of thanks to Huth Jackson and Appleton, the national speakers present at the meeting. Gunning bluntly declared that 'a good many of my comrades in the Labour movement', when he spoke to them of his involvement in the meeting, 'began to regard me as a sort of burglar trying to steal away the rights of the Labour movement'. But he added that he felt happy having heard what had been said at the meeting, commenting:

I think we ought to feel that those lads are entitled to say to us on their return home after peace is declared, 'What have our representatives done for us since we have been out fighting your battles? What machinery have you set up to put us back into our former position? What preparations have you made to get us work?' And if we have not done anything then I can see something happening to some of us. [19]

Cooperation with employers, when linked to this issue, was clearly hard to resist.

This may have been a major impulse in Ernest Bevin's involvement. Alan Bullock's classic biography of Bevin records Bevin's participation in

[18] C.J. Wrigley, *David Lloyd George and the British Labour Movement* (Hassocks, 1976), pp. 170–73.

[19] NAEE pamphlet, *Public Meeting at Swansea, May 6, 1917* (copy in the Iron and Steel Trades Confederation Papers, ISTC 36-N 39/2 at Modern Record Centre, University of Warwick). Gunning was to be Havelock Wilson's choice as assistant general secretary of the National Union of Seamen (holding the post 1926–37).

employer-employee meetings in the Bristol area, initiated in late 1916 by Arnold Rowntree (the Quaker cocoa industrialist, Liberal MP and a former member of the Reconstruction Committee), which led to him becoming a vice president of the Bristol Association for Industrial Reconstruction.[20] But it makes no mention of his involvement in the more controversial NAEE, of whose General Council he was a member. Bevin, in fact, was a member of the NAEE's General Council in a personal capacity, not as an official representative of his trade union. His attitude may be judged from his comments made at the inaugural meeting on 15 February 1918 of the national Industrial Reconstruction Council. There he was reported as saying, 'with much vigour', that 'rather than tolerate the awful poverty and brutally inhuman conditions imposed on his class he would deliberately organise revolt, but he was prepared to accept a reasonable alternative provided they started upon a purely equal basis'.[21]

In looking for 'a reasonable alternative' to industrial strife, Bevin was in line with much trade union opinion during the First World War. Arthur Henderson expressed well this mood for industrial cooperation in January 1917 when he aired his hope:

> . . . that the fellowship and comradeship which had been so marked a feature of our war experience might so continue that they would find expression in the removal of class distinctions, the lessening of glaring social and economic inequalities, the development of mutual confidence and closer co-operation between employers and employed, and the fuller and more complete recognition of community of interest and responsibility between the state and the people.[22]

The NAEE was based on this mood. Indeed, while demobilisation provided the important and unifying issue to bring employers and moderate trade unionists together, the broader possibilities of cooperation were important from the start. The NAEE's *Report, 1916–1918* noted of Huth Jackson's preliminary meeting that, while those present went on to draw up a demobilisation scheme, 'the main issue discussed was the need for a united effort on the part of employers and trade unions, on the basis of comradeship and goodwill, such as had never been realised hitherto, to

---

[20] A. Bullock, *The Life and Times of Ernest Bevin*, Vol. 1 (London, 1960), pp. 68–72.

[21] *The Times*, 16 February 1918.

[22] Wrigley, *Henderson*, p. 140.

deal with all problems of industry at the end of the war'. At the bigger gathering in December 1916 Dudley Docker and J.T. Brownlie moved as a preliminary resolution to those laying out the demobilisation scheme:

> That the cordial and whole-hearted co-operation of employers and employed will be the most important element in the success of any scheme for dealing with the reinstatement of the men of the forces and munitions in civil employment and the general redistribution of labour after the war, and for handling any subsequent problem of unemployment or labour dislocation.

This motion, with minor variations, was moved at the later meetings setting up area committees. With demobilisation problems always being seen as an issue limited to the fairly short term, the emphasis on broader spheres of cooperation grew stronger as time went by.

On the employers' side the underlying concern was to prepare British industry for post-war trade wars. Worries about serious industrial unrest were always present, but at most times were secondary to a determination to ensure British competitiveness in international markets. At the first provincial meeting, held at Central Hall, Birmingham on 20 January 1917 Huth Jackson declared that 'whatever excuses this country might have had for being unprepared for war, we must make it quite certain that we were prepared for peace'.[23] In a letter published in *The Times* on 2 April 1918 he outlined the difficulties facing industry during the transition from war to peace, including the reinstatement of workers and shortages of materials. He continued.:

> We shall have to face the fiercest possible international competition in our export trade, not only from our present enemies, but from neutral countries. Meanwhile we shall, as a nation, be much poorer than we were before the war, and shall have to carry the burden of a huge national debt.
>
> It is, therefore, essential that the productive capacity of this country should be developed to its fullest extent.

For him the precondition for this was the cooperation of employers and employed.

[23] *The Times*, 22 January 1917.

At the numerous NAEE meetings, nationally and locally, employers' representatives urged increased productivity as the greatest need. Thus, for example, at the Swansea meeting Frank Gilbertson (of the iron and steel firm Messrs W. Gilbertson and Co. Ltd and a member of the FBI's executive committee) urged:

> The whole future of this country depends . . . upon increasing the productivity of our brains and our labour. We want our workmen to be better educated; we want our managers and capitalists, among whom I include myself, to be better educated too. We want the fullest use of machinery and the fullest use of men's brains as well as their muscles for the common good.

At the same meeting Huth Jackson urged:

> Employers must . . . recognise that in certain trades workmen in the past have not received a proper portion of the profits of industry. They must be prepared . . . for the raising of the general standard of wages and of the standard of comfort. Men must be better housed and better educated as well as better clothed and better fed. On the other hand workmen must recognise that artificial restriction on output must cease; they must give a full day's work for a full day's wage. [24]

So, for the trade unions, what was on offer was higher wages and better conditions in return for a freeing of restrictions on the use of labour. The nature of the deal was very clearly understood by the major trade unionists involved. It appealed to the old style Liberal trade unionists such as Appleton who argued, 'If you spread efficiency over the whole population it will be less arduous for those who work than if you had inefficients, and it is obvious that workmen and employer combining can do things very much better than any government department can do it'. [25] Several pro-war Labour Party trade unionists saw the new political and industrial conditions stemming from the war as affording the opportunity to dump socialism and to follow the path of American trade unionism. Thus at a dinner organised

[24] On Gilbertson see G.M. Holmes, 'Francis William Gilbertson' in D.J. Jeremy (ed.), *Dictionary of Business Biography*, 2 (London, 1984), pp. 558–60. NAEE, *Public Meeting at Swansea, May 6, 1917*, p. 6.

[25] Ibid., p. 6.

in late May 1918 by the NAEE's sister organisation, the Industrial League, in honour of a pro-war Labour delegation that had just returned from the USA, G.H. Roberts (the trade unionist who succeeded Hodge in mid 1917 as Minister of Labour) was reported as declaring:

> The future of the Labour movement abided with the people who were represented there that night. The past was dead. The old cries, the old shibboleths had gone, never to be resuscitated. They could not allow mere sentimentalism to guide them. His purpose was work and wages for his own people. First of all he was going to be concerned with the prosperity of his own country.

While Charles Duncan, MP (general secretary of the Workers Union, 1900–28, and an executive committee member of the NAEE) who like Appleton had been a member of the delegation, was reported as commenting:

> He agreed with the attitude and policy displayed by the American Federation of Labour in regard to the Socialist movement. It had brought nothing but division within their ranks. The trade union movement was the greatest force in civilisation, and it was strong enough to fight its own corner successfully without the assistance of socialists. [26]

The fourth broad impulse behind first the creation of the NAEE and then, for a while, its success in gathering support was concern about levels of industrial unrest. Such concern, at least before the end of the war, was much more linked to anxiety about the competitiveness of British industry than with fears that the existing social order would be overturned. Huth Jackson, at the Swansea meeting, observed:

> There is an old saying: 'If you want to preserve peace, prepare for war'. I would like to suggest an alternative rendering for the present situation, namely: 'If you want to prepare for the economic war which will surely follow the military war, prepare for peace'.

[26] *The Times,* 30 May 1918.

The fundamental answer that the instigators of the NAEE had to industrial unrest became encapsulated in the reports of the Whitley Committee, which was an offshoot of Lloyd George's Reconstruction Committee (set up in early 1917). These reports, published in 1917 and 1918, urged that there should be joint committees set up in all well-organised industries and, where there was 'no adequate organisation of employers and employed, trade boards should be continued or established'. The reports envisaged that the joint councils (which would be in three layers – factory, district and national) should work to improve the economic performance of their industries and to improve working conditions for employees but should not get involved in matters of wages or hours of work. The Whitley Committee, chaired by J.H. Whitley, the Deputy Speaker of the House of Commons, included Allan Smith of the Engineering Employers' Federation (EEF), who found that some members of that federation did not share his enthusiasm for works committees, Sir Thomas Ratcliffe-Ellis of the Mining Association of Great Britain as well as Fred Button of the ASE, Robert Smillie of the Miners' Federation and J.R. Clynes.[27]

The NAEE, which was never backward in making large claims, stated that its own first success was the appointment of the Whitley Committee. It further observed that the Whitley Committee 'recommended the same co-operation, by joint councils and committees of employers and employed in each organised trade, as the Alliance six months before put forward in regard to the reinstatement in civil employment of men of the forces and munition works and the general distribution of labour after the war, and for handling any subsequent problem of unemployment or labour dislocation'.[28] In fact the war, and the prospect of post-war industrial competition, gave a boost to notions of industrial cooperation; as such it was a common source to first the NAEE and then to the Whitley proposals.[29]

The Whitley scheme, or variants on it, became attractive to more employers as they faced increased industrial unrest. Thus, in early December 1917, the National Employers' Federation, meeting in

[27] The Whitley Committee issued five reports (main and supplementary), signed between March 1917, 1917–18 *Cd.* 8606, *xviii,* 415 and July 1918, 1918 *Cd* 9153, *vii,* 629. For the EEF's divisions see E. Wigham, *The Power to Manage* (London, 1973), p. 102.

[28] NAEE, *Report, 1916–18*, p. 8

[29] For a survey of many who espoused the ideas of Whitleyism see P.B. Johnson, *Land Fit For Heroes* (Chicago, 1968), pp. 158–69.

Birmingham, supported a resolution urging 'the workers of the country to keep at work' until the Federation agreed with the trade unions a form of industrial representation based on the Whitley proposals. *The Times* reported, 'The idea is to establish works committees on thoroughly democratic lines, in the hope of finding a means of preventing the development of industrial strife'.[30] The government itself required the pressure of strikes to push it into action on the Whitley Reports. A *Times* editorial complained in June 1918:

> It was not until the end of October that the scheme was adopted as government policy, and not until after the remarkable strike at Coventry upon the shop stewards question [November 1917] that practical effect began to be given to it by the formation of a joint industrial council for the pottery trade.

The editorial went on to argue of the Whitley scheme, 'One of its merits is its elasticity and adaptability to varying conditions'.[31]

While the Whitley proposals owed much of their appeal to the prospect of lessening industrial unrest, at the same time they were also seen as offering assistance in improving the productivity of British industry. Indeed Christopher Addison, the Minister of Reconstruction, was explicit on this when speaking on 15 February 1918 at the inaugural meeting of the Industrial Reconstruction Council, a body set up 'to popularise the principle of industrial self-government and in particular to spread a knowledge of the recommendations of the Whitley Report', declaring:

> . . . the governing consideration in all reconstruction was the increased production of wealth. Unless we could so dispose of our national forces that all men, both employers and employed, could freely co-operate in an effort at increased wealth production distress must be our lot. The war had taught us . . . that we had in our people a capacity to produce which was quite unsuspected before, and by this same power and spirit, when the time arrived, we could rebuild our industries and increase and maintain our services for the benefit of all in the wide markets of the world. But unless

[30] *The Times,* 4 and 5 December, 1917. The NEF was based on the West Midlands engineering trades. In August 1918 it merged with the EEF.

[31] *The Times,* 21 June 1918.

we had industrial peace none of these things could be added unto us.[32]

With the apparent determination of the government to foster Whitley committees in British industry, the NAEE defined the role of its joint committees as being complementary to the Whitley ones. The Whitley committees dealt with wages and hours while the NAEE area committees were to provide a forum for 'all general questions to the industries in which no definite scheme has been adopted'. In practice they did take up a range of issues, the most important during the war being to press on local authorities and the Local Government Board 'local housing needs from the point of view of industry'. Other issues included pressing for adequate local train services, a more vigorous factory inspectorate, better fire precautions at work and at home, the improved position of women in industry and the provision of improved playing fields. In all this the NAEE prided itself for having gone 'a long way to achieve the recognition of industry as a national service in which the associates, Capital and Labour, hold the stewardship for the community at large'.[33]

In all this the NAEE's philosophy was not corporatist. It did not want partnership with the state and was emphatic that industrial matters were best left to industry to settle, hence the appeal to old style individualists like Appleton and Davis. *The Times* in its editorial on Whitley committees on 21 June 1918 pointed to the contrasting attitudes of the NAEE which 'cries "Hands Off!" to the government' and the Industrial Reconstruction Council which expected the government to lay down a uniform practice. The NAEE's viewpoint during the war was 'that the recent industrial unrest is largely due to the neglect of the principle of the regulation of industry by free discussion and agreement between employer and employed'. It therefore called on government not to interfere in industrial disputes without taking the advice of both sides of industry and 'until every form of direct negotiations has been exhausted'.[34] It was equally emphatic for the post-war period. A.H. Paterson, the NAEE's secretary, put this bluntly in a letter published in *The Times* on the same day as that editorial, in which he

---

[32] *The Times,* 16 February 1918.

[33] NAEE, *The Work An Area Committee Can Do* (n.d., but 1919), p. 4.

[34] Resolution moved by Pugh and Docker and approved at Special General Meeting of NAEE, 22 May 1917. Minutes, copy in ISTC 36, N 39/3.

deplored the government's lack of real commitment to Whitleyism and stated:

> . . . that after the war industry must have self-government, and that the basis of that self-government must and can be arrived at by the representatives of employers and employed working together with an equality of representation and free from outside interference. There are three parties concerned – capital, labour and the community. The role of the state must simply be that of a policeman guarding the interests of the community.

Home Rule For Industry included the maintenance of free collective bargaining. All involved in the NAEE were emphatic on that. For example, at Swansea Huth Jackson followed his glowing account of the benefits stemming from 'mutual goodwill' with the observation:

> But with all this masters must retain the right to declare a lock-out and men to strike; all we urge is that before such extreme measures are resorted to the representatives of both sides should meet and discuss their differences round a table.[35]

Moreover the NAEE was emphatic in its advice to its local committees that they must not interfere in collective bargaining or in an industrial dispute, except 'only if it is brought before them as an impartial authority by the parties engaged in the dispute'.[36]

Immediately after the war the NAEE was very much a propaganda organisation, even though it liked to claim otherwise.[37] At its peak immediately after the First World War, it was well funded and its influence was reaching into a range of industries, trade unions and trades councils. Yet in all this it was but one of several such bodies. Some of these were designed to operate among different groups, but others were near to

[35] NAEE, *Public Meeting at Swansea, May 6 1917*, p. 5. Also at Birmingham, *The Times*, 16 February 1918.

[36] NAEE, *The Work An Area Committee Can Do*, pp. 3–4.

[37] For example, 'The NAEE is *not* a propagandist body', NAEE memorandum, 'Details of the Education Scheme in Operation in Birmingham' (n.d. – but 1919 or early 1920), p. 2; copy in ISTC, N 39/28.

being duplicates, sponsored by other business groups and their client moderate trade unionists.

In 1921 the NAEE maintained a headquarters staff of seventeen and a regional organisation on a scale comparable to that of the Labour Party in 1990. The NAEE set up its formal organisation after holding successful meetings in Birmingham, Manchester and Cardiff in early 1917. At its meeting on 9 March 1917 the NAEE General Council agreed to raise a fund of £20,000, with immediate pledges being given of £500 from Dudley Docker, £500 from the FBI and £100 from Havelock Wilson on behalf of his National Sailors and Firemen's Union. Nearly a year later another fund was launched, specifically to pay for the NAEE's publicity campaign. This time there were guarantees of £500 each from Huth Jackson and Vincent Caillard and £100 from Sir Robert Hadfield.[38] The NAEE soon employed Arthur Paterson as its general secretary, Lieut. General Sir Edward Bethune as chief organiser on the employers' side, Harry Dubery as labour adviser, T. Ernest Jackson as trade union and labour organiser and H.R.S. Phillpott as director of its publicity department which was created in March 1918. In 1921 the NAEE was paying its headquarters' organisation staff £7,371 and its paid regional staff £3,950 per annum (excluding expenses or anything else paid to numerous honorary personnel).

Paterson was the chief officer, overlooking the whole of the NAEE's activities and working in tandem with the chairman ('with whom he is in daily communication'). This was at first Huth Jackson and then, from the autumn of 1920, Edward Manville, president of the Association of British Chambers of Commerce and Conservative MP for Coventry, He also worked closely with an emergency committee, made up of three employers and three trade unionists, whose responsibilities included vetting all publications before they received final approval by the executive committee. Paterson had a major role in determining 'the policy and the scope' of the NAEE's paper *Unity* and he was responsible for the development of a subsidiary movement, the League for the Commonweal. Bethune was 'primarily responsible for all communications with employers'. Jackson, soon succeeded by E.F. Leicester, was responsible for arranging all the local conferences with trade unionists. Phillpott, 'an experienced journalist', was the editor of *Unity* and drafted

---

[38] General Council minutes, 9 March 1917 and 21 February 1918; copies in ISTC 36, N 39/1 and 7.

all the material that was put into the press and secured articles from prominent sympathisers. By the end of 1918 his department was claiming to have placed some 2,000 pieces in over 200 newspapers. In July 1918 the NAEE also established a research department 'to collect, collate and supply information upon industrial and social problems' to its members.

Harry Dubery's role appears to have been deemed especially important. He had served on the trade union side of the NAEE's executive committee, representing the Federation of Post Office Supervising Trade Unions. By 1921, when Bethune's role had diminished, Dubery was receiving the then handsome salary of £1,000 per annum as labour director and adviser; this being second only to Paterson's £1,500 and well ahead of Captain F.N. Byron's £600 as publicity director (in succession to Phillpott) and Bethune's and others' £500. His job was described as follows:

> He addresses all meetings where it is necessary that an authoritative trade union and Labour point of view should be put forward on behalf of the Alliance. He is in communication with the War Office and other Departments regarding the Labour side of the Alliance work and propaganda. He is assistant editor of *Unity* and writes the Labour notes and some of the leading articles. He was the sole writer and editor of *Industrial Unity*. He is the founder of the League of the Commonweal and principal speaker at congregational meetings, and at public schools upon the new movement.[39]

The NAEE's programme, once the issues of demobilisation and reconversion of industry to peacetime work had passed in 1919, centred on 'the principle' that employers and employees interests 'are not antagonistic, but inter-dependent'. In pursuance of this, the NAEE put much of its efforts into creating joint area committees and then using these as a means of propagating its philosophy. Many had been set up during 1917 and 1918. In early 1919 the NAEE launched an intensive campaign

---

[39] NAEE, 'Report of Joint Sub-committee on Management, Branches and Honorary Officers', n.d. (but February 1919) and NAEE, 'Salaries and Organisation', n.d. (probably 1921); copies in ISTC 36, N 39/18a and 31. *Industrial Unity*, 1, 4 (August 1918), p. 28.

to create many more, and thereby to ensure a better coverage of the country. On the labour side, Jackson initially contacted trades councils. These usually proved amenable, at least at first. But some, like the Nottingham and the Loughborough trades councils, agreed to cooperate with the inaugural meetings but soon withdrew their support as many of their members became uneasy about the NAEE's underlying objectives.[40] Where trades councils proved hostile from the outset, as in early 1919 at Hereford, Kidderminster, Luton, Northampton and Stafford, Jackson by-passed them. He approached trade union branches direct, inviting them to send delegates to the initial conferences which usually were chaired by the mayor.[41]

Once local joint committees were set up they often took on a life of their own, pushing distinctive policies; but all thereby demonstrated the NAEE's overriding theme of both sides of industry's ability to work together. The NAEE's paid organisers were quick to warn during its campaign of early 1919 that those willing to be involved at local level emphasised that the area committees must be elected and that they must 'undertake definite constructive work' and not be merely bodies 'for passing pious resolutions and social purposes'. Early examples of distinctive area committee activities were at Newark, taking up the issues of housing, electrical power and transport; at Wellingborough, dealing with industrial education and housing; at Warrington, considering ways of improving workplace conditions; at Birmingham launching education schemes for trade unionists; and at Liverpool (in January 1919), successfully arbitrating and so avoiding a strike of coastwise workers.[42] Later, from 1920, the area committees became much involved in proposals to alleviate unemployment.

But the area committees prime role was to be in the front line of the NAEE's propaganda drive. In the autumn of 1918 the publicity department carried on an intensive campaign in thirty selected towns. From that May *Industrial Unity* was being put out in workplaces, having a print run of 10,000 by early 1919. After *Unity* was revamped in mid 1920 Paterson

---

[40] Nottingham Trades Council minutes, May to October 1918. Loughborough Trades Council minutes, 1918–1919. I am grateful to Richard Stevens for drawing my attention to the Nottingham case.

[41] NAEE, 'Report of Organisers on the Provincial Campaign, 28 January – 11 February 1919'; copy in ISTC 36, 39/16.

[42] Letter to the NAEE executive committee from Bethune, Dubery and Jackson, 5 February 1919. Executive committee and general council minutes, 28 January 1919. Copies in ISTC 36, N 39/11, 12 and 14.

could report that 'sales had increased considerably, large orders having been received from firms and associations, and that the editor had been obliged to refuse further advertisements for the coming issue owing to the numerous applications received'. The publicity department also provided detailed outline speeches on chosen themes for the NAEE's local speakers. In at least some areas a high level of activity was maintained during the war and in the three or four years after it. To take Hartlepool as an example, the regional NAEE's report on it for 1921 included:

> Throughout the whole year a steady average has been maintained of twenty-one open-air meetings a week, at factory gates during the dinner hour and in the streets of local industrial centres, to audiences totalling over 9,800 per week.
> The value of this work is emphasised by the fact that even when feeling ran highest during the coal dispute, and the subsequent unemployment crisis, no meeting was ever broken up, although on occasions Communist speakers who followed our meetings had to be rescued by the police, and this in spite of the fact that such subjects as 'Identity of Interests between Employers and Employed', 'Dangers of the Strike Weapon' and 'Conciliation *versus* Force in Industry' were amongst the subjects dealt with by the National Alliance speakers.[43]

The publicity department's sixteen specimen lectures for 1921 hammered away at a limited number of themes. Important among these was the message that industrial peace was essential to both sides of industry and to the wider community. The eighth lecture, 'Conciliation and Arbitration' (20 June 1921), warned that the disputes of the previous year were 'creating a feeling in favour of national arbitration'. It then suggested that the NAEE's voluntarist approach was preferable and that the adoption of either a cooling-off period or some form of conciliation would have avoided three-quarters of the recent strikes. A second theme of the specimen lectures, and of other NAEE publications, was the desirability of high production, with high wages but low unit costs. Wilson Dickens, the NAEE's West Midland organiser for labour, argued in one memorandum that this combination 'means high consuming power, with plenty of commodities at low rates and . . . must result in a diminution of unemployment'. But the NAEE also made repeated calls not just for wage costs to fall but for wage

[43] Executive committee report, 21 September 1920; ISTC 36, N 39. NAEE, *Report 1916–18*, p. 14. NAEE, *Annual Report 1921*, p. 3.

rates to fall along with profits and interest rates in order to get back to 1914 or 1896 price levels. Another variant on this was Harry Dubery's proposal that, instead of launching into futile strikes, the trade unions should accept wage cuts on a sliding scale which related such cuts to the fall in commodity prices, thereby offering some protection to real wages.[44]

Many of the NAEE's specimen lectures and other publications made much show of even-handedness between the merits and ills of both trade unions and employers. Thus, for example, the specimen lecture devoted to 'Ca' Canny and Waste' (late June 1921) included the argument 'that there is a type of ca' canny expressing itself in lack of initiative on the part of the employer, which is as dangerous to the community as the ca' canny expressed in lack of output by the workmen'. Yet while there clearly was an attempt to strike some balance, there was often an anti-trade unionism apparent in many publications stemming from the NAEE's publicity department. One can only wonder what the officials of the affiliated trade unions made of the specimen lecture 'Trade Unionism or Democracy' (4 July 1921), in which it was argued that one reason why the unions had moved away from their earlier, worthy, craft purposes was because union officials needed to find causes to give justification for keeping their jobs or because new aims provided a way for 'ambitious men . . . to climb to power'. In the case of a draft memorandum on the causes of unemployment, strikes and lock-outs were originally listed under political causes of unemployment, but this was changed after criticism by other committee members of the NAEE.[45]

Perhaps the tone of the NAEE's industrial message was best expressed in specimen lectures entitled 'Optimism in Industry' (mid July) and 'Message of May' (late April or early May 1921). In the former the prime requirement for economic recovery was deemed to be the creation of a state of optimism in industry. It asserted, 'Pessimism is naturally induced by a recrudescence of industrial trouble, and threats and hints of further trouble'; while optimism stemmed from 'the promise of industrial peace' and could be 'further induced by presumed reduction in taxation'. Overall both sides of industry needed to show 'that they intend to play the game'.

---

[44] These were issued between late April and 10 November. Copies of all but the first are in ISTC 36, N 39/25. G.W. Wilson Dickens, 'Production and Consumption in the Relationship to Unemployment' (n.d. but probably 1921). H. Dubery, 'Wages and the Falling Cost of Living' (n.d. but February 1921). Copies in ISTC 36, N 39/26 and 27.

[45] NAEE, 'The Causes of Unemployment' (n.d. but probably 1921), p. 18; copy in ISTC 36, U 8/7.

As for May Day the NAEE's disapproval was clear. The specimen lecture urged:

> Argue that the May Festival has been torn by continental extremists from its original idea. It was originally the Festival of the Spring, and was used to emphasise the bounteous character of Nature, and the fact that humanity, by hard work and combination with Nature, could product an abundant harvest . . .

> It is alleged that humanity, earlier in its history, was happier. If this is true it is because class warfare and class struggle were not preached. Emphasis was laid on the happier side of life, on the need for co-operation, not within a class but between the best people in all classes – peer and pauper, employer and employed, labourer, craftsman, brain-worker, organiser, statesman.

> The essential need in Great Britain today is to hark back to what . . . can be described as 'the good old times' and the good old principles.

The NAEE put much emphasis on education, especially adult education. The promotion of economic education was deemed to be a means of promoting industrial peace. For this trade unionists were to be instructed in 'all those standard works on economics by recognised authors which have stood the test of criticism' (by which they meant Adam Smith and the classical economists), plus 'the works of modern writers such as Clay, Marshall and Mill'. The NAEE's most advanced scheme was in Birmingham, where the area committee arranged for trade unionists to receive instruction from Birmingham University and the Workers' Education Association. When the area committee tried to raise £1,000 per annum to 'train not less than 100 selected trade unionists . . . as lecturers to their fellow-workers of the city and district', the objectives were declared to be to counter unrest in workshops and trade union lodges and 'to gradually build up a body of efficient open-air lecturers, who will be under the control of the executive committee of the NAEE'.[46]

In trying to mobilise moderate trade union leaders to help construct a body of opinion on the shop floor opposed to radical change, the NAEE

[46] Specimen Lecture 16, 'Economic Education as a Means of Promoting Industrial Peace' (10 November 1921). NAEE, 'Details of the Education Scheme in Operation in Birmingham'. Copies in ISTC 36, N 39/25 and 28.

soon found itself competing in a crowded market place. Its contribution was marked by its determination to exclude the state from industrial affairs as far as possible. In this it was even attempting to roll back current state activities. Thus in July 1917 the NAEE wanted local joint committees to control employment exchanges in order to ensure that men would be placed in civilian work after the end of the war 'with the necessary speed and efficiency'. In 1921 it seriously considered, before a majority decided it was impractical, getting the 1920 Unemployment Insurance Act repealed and putting in its place a scheme which would be independent of government funding and supervision.[47] In this, as well as in stressing the need for both sides of industry to come together, the NAEE was echoing its main founder, the FBI, which also then was advocating welfare measures to be run by both sides of industry in return for union help to achieve higher productivity.[48] In the area of housing, the FBI and NAEE jointly considered a scheme in 1918 to channel state funds through Public Utility Societies run by local employers, workpeople and others with specialist knowledge.[49]

Both bodies were ardent advocates of Whitleyism. Indeed the NAEE claimed not only to be the forerunner of the Whitley councils but also to be the initiator of the idea of the National Industrial Conference of February 1919 (attributing this idea to Phillpott). Whitleyism and the desire for a permanent National Industrial Conference remained major planks in the NAEE's platform. In 1935 a sub-committee rejected industrial proposals put forward by Harold Macmillan's Industrial Reorganisation League because they were not promoting 'joint bodies, but were to consist mainly, if not entirely, of those having an ownership interest' and instead urged that the government appoint a new committee to review Whitley's proposals 'and to report what modifications are necessary as a result of the experience which has since accumulated'.[50]

The promotion of Whitleyism was a notable feature of the years 1917–21. The body which in February 1918 ostensibly had been specifically set up to do this, the Industrial Reconstruction Council, had also a wider purpose.

---

[47] Minutes of General Council meeting, 26 July 1917. Major D.C. McLagan, 'Memorandum on Unemployment'. Minutes of Nineteenth Meeting of Sub-Committee on Unemployment, 6 March 1921. Copies in ISTC 36, N 29/6, U8/10.

[48] K. Middlemas, *Politics in Industrial Society* (London, 1979), p. 128.

[49] FBI, 'Second Report of Housing Committee' (n.d. but mid 1918). Minutes of Joint Housing Committee of FBI and NAEE, 17 December 1918; copies in ISTC 36, H 18/9 and 16.

[50] National Industrial Alliance, 'Reconstruction and Reorganisation of Industry' (December 1935); copy in ISTC 36, N 39/33.

The NAEE observed of it that 'while it advocates the formation of Whitley councils, [it] is principally concerned with the formation of an *esprit de corp* among all members of each trade, irrespective of their industrial position, for the general furtherance of the interests of the trade'.[51] Hence the Industrial Reconstruction Council had no difficulty in merging in early 1919 with the Industrial League for the Improvement of Relations between Employers and Employed. Whitley himself was prominent in both, becoming one of the joint presidents of the amalgamated body and devoting much energy in publicising his report (just as Beveridge was to do for his during the Second World War). The new amalgam, the Industrial League and Council, was much smaller than the NAEE, operating with just a general secretary, John Ames, and two typists. It also set up district councils, published the *Industrial League Journal* (from September 1918 to February 1922) and many leaflets, and organised many open air meetings. Its headed letter paper included a quotation from J.R. Clynes. Its other president (with Whitley) was G.H. Roberts and it attracted the support of such other right-wing trade union Labour MPs as G.J. Wardle and J.A. Seddon.[52] On the employer side it drew its support particularly from manufacturing, brewing, chemicals and metallurgy.[53] After abortive merger talks between January 1919 and February 1921, the Industrial League merged with the NAEE with effect from 9 July 1925, so forming the National Industrial Alliance. One major reason for the earlier failure to achieve amalgamation was to do with finance. The Industrial League was more modest in its activities and lived within its income, whereas by the autumn of 1920 the NAEE's finances were in deficit, it having spent, for that year, just over £16,000 of an intended £26,000 authorised on the grounds of 'the serious industrial situation'.[54]

If the NAEE, the Industrial League and the Industrial Reconstruction Council were somewhat similar bodies seeking to mobilise moderate trade

[51] NAEE, *Report, 1916–18*, p. 20.

[52] 'Report of Joint Sub-committee on Management, Branches and Honorary Officers' (n.d. but early 1919); copy in ISTC 36, N 39/18a. A note on the cover of the Industrial League's copy of the *Report of the Proceedings of the 50th Annual TUC, 1918* (now in the Working Class Library, Salford) drew attention to a report of a TUC delegation seeing Roberts about Whitley Councils and to the Parliamentary Committee subsequently recommending 'the desirability of a frank acceptance of the principles embodied in the Whitley Report'.

[53] White, pp. 6–8 and 13.

[54] Minutes of a joint meeting of the executive committees of both bodies, 29 September 1920; copy in ISTC 36, N 39/30.

union leaders, the British Commonwealth Union (BCU), the British Workers' League and even the National Party were others but of a different spectrum. The BCU was another organisation closely associated with the FBI, and with Dudley Docker and Sir Vincent Caillard in particular. It had begun in December 1916 as the 'London Imperialists', providing a vehicle for the Tariff Reform minded wing of the FBI to use to pursue political ends. In February 1918 Allan Smith of the Engineering Employers' Federation secured his colleagues' support for the BCU, by arguing that employers needed to take political action given the probable enlargement of the Parliamentary Labour Party. Subsequently the BCU backed both the British Workers' League and the National Party, and in the 1918 general election claimed to have had eighteen candidates returned to Parliament (under Coalition or British Workers' League banners).[55] Between 1918 and 1923 it spent some £50,000 engaging in similar propaganda activities to the NAEE as well as providing funds for 'patriotic' candidates and for amenable trade unionists.[56]

As for the British Workers' League and the National Party, they were seen as complementary bodies. Havelock Wilson appeared on both organisations' platforms. Indeed during and after the First World War he was ubiquitous as far as such bodies were concerned; being willing to support others such as the Industrial Peace Union (which published *Industrial Peace* between September 1917 and 1926) and the National Security Union.[57] The National Party in June 1920 adopted a report, *Industrial Unrest and Labour Policy*, which it deemed to be 'the practical alternative to that of nationalisation put forward by the Labour Party'. This included proposals to 'fix a date by which industries must be organised' and for those which were organised to join together in a National Industrial

---

[55] On the BCU see the valuable article by John Turner, 'The British Commonwealth Union and the general election of 1918', *English Historical Review*, 93 (1978), pp. 528–59. For the complexities of wartime business politics see also his 'The Politics of "Organised Business" in the First World War' in J. Turner (ed.), *Businessmen and Politics* (London, 1984), pp. 33–49.

[56] G.C. Webber, *The Ideology of the British Right, 1918–1939* (London, 1986), pp. 65–66.

[57] On the National Party see W.D. Rubinstein, 'Henry Page Croft and the National Party 1917–22', *Journal of Contemporary History*, 9 (1974), pp. 129–48 and C.J. Wrigley, '"In the Excess of their Patriotism": The National Party and Threats of Subversion' in C.J. Wrigley (ed.), *Warfare, Diplomacy and Politics* (London, 1986), pp. 93–119. On Havelock Wilson's non-political trade union activities see A. Marsh and V. Ryan, *The Seamen* (Oxford, 1989), pp. 96–130.

Council which would 'have drastic powers to deal with any industry which proved to be non-progressive or reactionary'. It also declared that 'there can be little hope of industrial peace unless [the workers] are well housed in a congenial environment and are provided with healthy, bright and inspiring opportunities for recreation and social life'.

The tariff reform minded leaders of the FBI busied themselves not only with the NAEE and the BCU. They became the backbone of National Propaganda, which stemmed from moves made by Lloyd George and his associates after the government's propaganda against the National Union of Railwaymen had been successfully countered by the Labour Research Department during the autumn 1919 railway strike.[58] National Propaganda had as its first chairman Sir Reginald Hall MP, who had been Director of Naval Intelligence at the Admiralty and who had played a leading role in the early attempts to merge the NAEE and Industrial League. His involvement was especially significant given that the building up of National Propaganda's files on 'subversives' was assisted by information from the Secret Services and from Special Branch. National Propaganda's constitution laid down its objects as:

(a) To diminish unrest, and by positive propaganda to correct economic and other misstatements, and impress upon Employer and Employed the vital necessity of increased production.
(b) To combat all activities directed against constitutional government, and
(c) To co-operate with and assist the activities of, other Non-Party organisations having the like or similar objects.

The NAEE was one such body with which, from very early on, it agreed cooperation and funding. National Propaganda itself was well funded by industry, and soon was working to set up eight area committees to cover the country. It also established Economic Study Clubs in London, Newcastle and Scotland to train speakers, and within its first year it claimed that thirty-one speakers had addressed 1,748 meetings, that 340,994 posters had gone up in urban centres, and that 2,736,500 leaflets had been distributed to urban homes as well as material being published in the press.[59] National Propaganda was

[58] Middlemas, pp. 131–2 and Wigham, p. 105.
[59] National Propaganda, *The Constitution*. Memorandum of interview in Sir Richard Vassar Smith's office, 9 February 1920. Copies in ISTC 36, N 39./21 and 22.

to become better known under its later name of the Economic League.[60]

For a short period before and after the end of the First World War many businessmen were as worried, perhaps even more worried, about industrial and social stability in Britain as they were about ensuring higher productivity in British industry. They were very aware of events in central and eastern Europe. These anxieties found one expression in the various anti-socialist organisations that sprang up between 1916 and 1921. Such bodies had policies which offered the stick if the carrot was rejected. Social concessions were available for those who would work within the pale of the constitution and who supported the free enterprise system, while tough measures were advocated for those deemed to be undermining the existing social order. The NAEE, one of the less aggressive these bodies, stated in a manifesto published in September 1918:

> We are convinced that the first essential is the definite and consistent government policy – a policy not of drift, but of prevention; one that shall be capable of direct and effective application before strikes occur, that will meet after-war conditions as well as present needs, and that shall either convert or destroy all the disruptive groups in the country. No government can of itself, or by its own instruments, do this. The policy of this alliance is to bring together in every conceivable way and in all industries the enlightened and progressive employer and the constructive evolutionary trade unionist, and, combining them with the seriously minded section of the public, to create a bulwark against the dangers ahead of us . . .[61]

The cooperation of a number of leading moderate trade unionists was crucial for the success of all these bodies. Accordingly the businessmen involved usually managed to involve selected trade unionists from their own industrial sectors. In the case of the NAEE, even with the falling away of trades council support to just thirteen, it also still managed to maintain a good spread of trade union support across British industry (though against the total number of trade union branches this support

---

[60] On this see A.J. McIvor, 'Political Blacklisting and Anti-Socialist Activity between the Wars', in Society for the Study of Labour History, *Bulletin*, 53, 1 (1988), pp. 18–22 and M. Hollingsworth and R. Norton-Taylor, *Blacklist* (London, 1988), especially pp. 144–50.

[61] *The Times*, 14 September 1918.

was small). In September 1921 the area committees of the NAEE included representatives from 1,858 trade union branches, as opposed to 1,118 in 1920 and 723 in 1919. These were distributed in 1921 across the following sectors (1919 figures in brackets): agriculture 50 (23); baking and confectionery 49 (14); boots, shoes, leather 61 (21); building trades 160 (86); clerical 92 (39); coalmining 42 (16); distributive trades 57 (31); engineering 201 (114); general workers 346 (89); glass workers 28 (7); metal workers 156 (82); printing 83 (28); teaching 49 (9); textiles 109 (43); transport 175 (91); and a further miscellaneous 200 (30).[62] The continued increase in numbers of affiliated trade union branches in 1921 owed much to trade unionists' greater desire for agreement with employers in a time of wage and job cuts.

Yet increasingly after the First World War for trade unionists to be enthusiastic for the NAEE itself (or its successor the NIA) was to place themselves outside of the mainstream of he British Labour movement. At trades council level, support rapidly dwindled for the NAEE. The 1925 Labour Party Conference accepted without opposition a motion moved by a delegate from Birkenhead Trades Council and Labour Party which suggested that support for the NAEE was inconsistent with membership of the Labour Party.[63] As for the leaders of the TUC, from the mid 1920s there was growing embarrassment that several members of its General Council were much involved in the NIAA. In 1932 Vincent Tewson wrote to the Staffordshire and District Trades Council observing that the TUC 'in no way officially recognised' the NIAA but listed the roles in the NIAA of T. Mallalieu, F.S. Button, J.B. Wilson, C.W. Bowerman, J. Varley, A. Dalgleish, H.H. Elvin and W.A. Appleton.[64] Whereas Fred Bramley, as secretary of the TUC, had been willing to be publicised as chairing a NIA meeting on 'The Power of the Press' (though in the event he sent his apologies, owing to 'a very important dispute in Manchester'), his successor, Walter Citrine, kept the organisation firmly at arm's length.[65] In 1936 Citrine advised his research department officers: 'Sir Walter will

[62] A. Paterson, *The Weapon of the Strike* (London, n.d.), p. 284. It was published in April 1922.

[63] Labour Party, *Report of 25th Annual Conference, 1925*, p. 302.

[64] V Tewson to R.C. Wallis, 16 September 1932; TUC Records (Modern Record Centre, Warwick) 292/202.1/5. (This file contains the TUC correspondence with the NIAA, 1924–42.)

[65] F. Bramley to J. Ames, 10 January 1924 and Citrine's secretary to Douglas Haigh, 21 December 1932; ibid.

never have any contact with this organisation'. The following year, when pressed to speak at one of the NIA's twenty-first anniversary meetings, he declined and at last bluntly informed the NIA's secretary: 'To be frank with you, I am not ready to take part in the work of the Alliance'. [66]

That such a moderate figure as Citrine should disapprove of the NIA from the mid 1920s onwards was not only due to the Labour Party's policy. The other roots of the TUC leadership's opposition to the NIA was summed up by W. Milne-Bailey of the TUC's Research Department: 'The objects of the Alliance can be . . . briefly summarised as industrial peace, and of course we have never lent ourselves to that sort of propaganda'. [67] Even when the NIA was more sympathetic to the viewpoint of labour on industrial reorganisation than the Political and Economic Planning group or those associated with Harold Macmillan the TUC leadership nevertheless felt it did not go far enough. George Woodcock observed:

> The policy of the TUC . . . and that of the National Industrial Alliance . . . differs broadly on two main points: (a) TUC views and policy almost invariably take into account the possibility of ultimate socialisation of an industry whilst the views and policy of the National Industrial Alliance do not; and (b) TUC views and policy are more comprehensive than those of the National Industrial Alliance in that they include more specific references to workshop and sectional organisation within an industry and consultative and supervisory machinery outside the particular industry. [68]

Nevertheless in 1916–21 the NAEE and the other bodies were working on a major strand of trade union thought, one which had been strong in some industries and in some areas of the country (such as the North-East and parts of the Midlands). Arthur Henderson was to continue to call for the reestablishment of the National Industrial Conference, or something like it, throughout the 1920s. He was also a leading figure in the Brotherhood Movement, which itself was seen by the NAEE as a potential conduit to earnest Christian working men. In late 1921 Henderson contributed a foreword to

[66] Memorandum from Citrine to F.E. MacDonald and G. Woodcock, 23 July 1936 and Citrine to D. Haigh, 3 December 1937; ibid.

[67] Memorandum by W. Milne-Bailey, 16 September 1932 (prepared for V. Tewson's letter of that date); ibid.

[68] Memorandum by George Woodcock, 27 July 1936; ibid.

Arthur Paterson's book, *The Weapon of the Strike*. In this Henderson urged:

> What is needed is a Parliament of Industry, representative of the organizations of employers and of organized workers in the field of Industry, and with such authority as would render it capable of expressing, after full and frank consultation and co-operative effort, the mind of Industry. Something more than a conciliation body is suggested, though it could perform such functions, but I should hope that the main work of the Parliament of Industry would be directed to the solution of those problems which give rise to conflict and render the use of the strike weapon necessary.[69]

This important conciliatory strand in British trade unionism played a major part in ensuring that the major social and industrial tensions of the later part of the First World War and of its aftermath did not have greater social consequences in Britain. It was more important than the efforts to mobilise it behind such bodies as the NAEE or the Industrial League. Nevertheless these anti-socialist bodies did play a part in counteracting radical and revolutionary sentiments in these years. Though the historian cannot go as far as Sir Ernest Benn did in 1925 when he observed of the NAEE and the Industrial League and Council:

> We have . . . seen a complete change of attitude towards the industrial problem – a revolution in thought, which . . . has saved us completely from the dangers of revolutions of other kinds. Men and women . . . who have learned to respect one another as individuals, even though they are unable to accept one another's opinions, are not willing to cut each other's throats or even to punch each other's noses. All this . . . is quite new and it is . . . due entirely to the work of the two organisations . . . It is to them that belongs the credit of having developed and promoted and spread these ideas.[70]

[69] Paterson, pp. 13–14.
[70] *Unity*, 5, 31 (July 1925), p. 6.

9

In Search of the Profiteer

Margaret Morris

The Profiteering Act (1919)[1] was the first attempt by a British Government this century to curb inflation by procedures aimed at determining whether prices were fair or excessive. The tribunals it set up can be seen as forerunners of the Prices Board of 1965–70 and the Prices Commission under the 1973 Counter Inflation Act. These bodies all operated on the expectation that market forces could be persuaded to give way to what was essentially a concept of fairness pre-dating the Industrial Revolution. An incentive to do so in the 1960s and 1970s was the linking of price restraint with wage restraint. This was not the case in 1919 nor did economists have any faith that the Profiteering Act would be in any way effective. Thus it was more a political propaganda exercise and less part of a serious economic policy than the later measures. For the Lloyd George government any measure to placate working-class unrest without conceding vital interests seemed worthwhile. It is in this context that the passing of the Profiteering Act 1919 repays examination.

Prices rose less sharply in Britain than on the continent during and after the First World War but the rate of increase was nevertheless very steep (see Table 2, p. 187). Inflation rapidly built up in the first few months of the war and mounted at the same fast rate throughout 1915, 1916, and the first six months of 1917. It then continued at a slightly more restrained pace as

[1] 9 & 10, Geo 5 cap 66 (1919).

Government measures to control it began to bite. The cumulative effect pushed up retail prices to an average of 120 per cent higher at the end of the war than at the beginning. Within this average there were big variations: food had risen slightly faster than the average and in December 1918 stood at 129 per cent above July 1914; clothing had risen much faster still and stood at no less than 260 per cent above July 1914; against this, fuel and light were only 90 per cent up; while rent and rates, due to the 1915 Rent Restriction Act, were only 2 per cent up and provided the biggest stabilising influence on the cost of living.[2] In the early years of the war wholesale prices moved more or less in line with retail ones but later began to move ahead, so that by 1918 average wholesale prices were 154 per cent higher than those prevailing before the war.

The end of hostilities was followed by six months of falling prices, although the fall was only modest and in July 1919 the upwards advance was resumed. In 1920 the cost of living index went up faster than in any year during the war. The peak was reached in November 1920 when retail prices were 176 per cent higher than immediately pre-war. Wholesale prices soared even more rapidly, reaching a peak in April 1920, when they were 225 per cent above the average for 1913, but they then began to fall. Well before the end of 1920 there was clear evidence of the approach of depression and during 1921 both retail and wholesale prices dropped sharply.

Despite the support evinced for the war by a majority of all sections of the population, such inflation was a threat to national unity. Hostility to rising prices was a feature of the early twentieth century. Prices had been either stable or falling during most of the nineteenth century so that when they began to rise after 1896 concern over falling living standards, both among the working class and those on fixed incomes, was allied to indignation and the conviction that such inflation, mild though it was by later standards, was abnormal and inherently wrong. It was associated by the trade unions with intensified exploitation due to the consolidation of industry, so helping to create the industrial militancy and heightening class antagonism of the years from 1911 to the outbreak of war.[3]

---

[2] Statistics are taken from *Labour Gazette* and *Parl. Papers* (1926), *xxix*, the eighteenth Abstract of Labour Statistics (Cmd. 2740).

[3] See Philip Bagwell, '*The Triple Industrial Alliance*', in *Essays in Labour History*, 1886–1923, ed. A. Briggs and J. Saville (London 1971)

Table 2

Retail Price Movements, July 1914–December 1922

	Food (per cent)	Cost of Living Index (per cent)
Jan. 1915 compared with July 1914	+18	+10–15
Dec. 1915 compared with Jan. 1915	+22	+20
Dec. 1916 compared with Dec. 1915	+28	+22
Dec. 1917 compared with Dec. 1916	+17	+12
Dec. 1918 compared with Dec. 1917	+12	+19
June 1919 compared with Dec. 1918	−11	−7
Dec. 1919 compared with June 1919	+15	+10
Nov. 1920 compared with Dec. 1919	+24	+23
Dec. 1921 compared with Nov. 1920	−33	−28
Dec. 1922 compared with Dec. 1921	− 9	−10

(a) Compiled from figures given in *the Labour Gazette* and *Parl Papers* (1926), xxix, 'The Eighteenth Abstract of Labour Statistics' (Cmd.2740).

(b) The original Ministry of Labour index used here has stood up well under examination by researchers. Its chief weakness was the overweighting of food (food was weighted 60 per cent, rent 16 per cent, clothing 12 per cent, fuel and light 8 per cent and other items 4 per cent).

In 1918–19, however, food prices increased more than was allowed for in the official index; as this offset the overweighting, there is a correlation for those years between the original and the revised indexes. See A.R. Prest, *Consumers Expenditure in the U.K., 1900–1919* (Cambridge, 1954), p. 7 and R. Stone and D.A. Rowe, *The Measurement of Consumers' Expenditure and Behaviour in the U.K., 1920–38* (Cambridge 1954 and 1966), ii, p. 114 and tables 49 and 55.

Resentment might have been muted if the Government had been able to show that the sharp upward movement in 1914 was solely attributable to the war, but it was widely believed that this was not so. Expert opinion at the Bank of England and the Treasury did indeed stress the effects of the dislocation of world trade and war-time shortages, together with the de facto abandonment of the gold standard and the multiplier effects on the expansion of credit and consequent depreciation of the currency brought about by the Government's use of budget deficits and bank loans to meet the costs of the war. Popular opinion, however, put the blame for inflation on profiteering. This was most firmly believed within the Labour movement but gradually gained more general acceptance.

The cartoonist of the left-wing *Daily Herald*, Will Dyson, created the prototype of 'The War Profiteer', who became a stock villain in cartoons in papers of almost all political complexions later in the war. He was portrayed as a grossly fat man, bulging out of his waistcoat in a flashy not very well-cut dress suit, wearing a top hat and smoking a cigar. He first appeared on 1 August 1914, before the war had even begun, and was shown with arms upraised to greet the gathering clouds: 'Even the war cloud has a silver lining for the Profiteer'. He reappeared frequently, sometimes as 'The Food Hog', 'Gunmaker to all the Crowned Heads of Europe' or 'Unscrupulous Contractor'; in the latter role he is shown saying to a soldier, 'A fair price, sir, when I can exact an unfair one! I hope I know my duty to my country better – "Business as usual" – and that's my usual way of doing business'.[4]

War provides opportunities for contractors to get rich and many people remembered the scandals exposed after the Boer War.[5] In the autumn of 1914 the radical liberal paper, *The Daily Chronicle*, ran a series of articles about over-priced or poor quality goods supplied to the army. Inside Parliament a Unionist back-bencher, B. Douglas Hall, called for a select committee to examine Government contracts with power to revise the prices after the war if they were found to have been unduly profitable to contractors.[6] By mid January 1915 *The Daily Express*, then a rather dull Conservative paper, not yet the property of Sir Max Aitken, was carrying almost daily stories of rising prices; it laid the main blame on over charging by shipowners. Thus even early in the war there was considerable criticism of profiteering outside as well as within the Labour movement, although it was the need to win the cooperation of the trade unions which finally moved Asquith, the Prime Minister, from his position that no Government action was necessary. In March 1915, in return for the engineers' signature on the Treasury agreements, in which the trade unions agreed to give up strikes and restrictive practices, the Government undertook to limit prices and profits on war work in engineering.[7]

It was easier to concede the principle than to put it into effect. As shown

[4] *The Herald*, 14 Nov. 1914 (*Daily Herald* shrank to a weekly from October 1914–March 1919).

[5] See Parl. papers (1906), vii, 'War Stores in South Africa' (Cd. 3127); see also G.R. Searle, *Corruption in British Politics* (Oxford, 1987), pp. 52–79.

[6] *Parl.Debates*, H. of C., 26 Nov. 1914

[7] C.J. Wrigley, *David Lloyd George and the British Labour Movement* (Hassocks, 1976), pp. 86–90; 106–7.

in Table 2, the rate of inflation was not checked until the last two years of the war and, even then, was only held back a little. By this time the Government had switched to a policy of increasing the proportion of the costs of the war borne by taxation; it was also raising a substantial part of its borrowing requirements on the market in the form of War Loan instead of from the banks. Even more important was direct control: by 1918 the Government controlled all major aspects of the economy and could employ a whole armoury of devices to hold down prices and profits. The most effective were the application of cost-accounting techniques to the negotiation of war contracts, Excess Profits Duty, rent restriction, the setting up of the National Factories, Government purchase and marketing of food and raw materials, and subsidies on bread, coal and railway transport.

There were inherent difficulties in administering most of these measures. For example, it was difficult to assess a price for Government contracts which could be deemed 'fair' to both the Government and the manufacturer. The initial problem was vividly described by Christopher Addison, who was first Under Secretary and later Minister of Munitions: 'The astounding thing', he recorded in August 1915, is that nobody seems to be able to tell us what things cost to make'. He brought in a team of businessmen and cost-accountants to find out. He was soon singing their praises: 'many and ingenious were the shifts and devices by which they helped to defeat to some extent the rapacity of some of the metal corporations'.[8]

A constant problem, both in negotiating contracts and in purchasing food or raw materials, was that the Government needed all the supplies it could obtain, even those from the least efficient firms. The dilemma facing the ministry is well illustrated by the negotiations over the price of soap in September 1916. Addison wrote, 'It is a ticklish business we stand to be accused either of depriving the householder of cheaper soap or allowing a large number of the smaller glycerine makers to be thrown out of business, which we cannot afford as we must have the glycerine'.

The limitations of price and profit control were made clear by the cheaper costs achieved by the National Factories compared with even the most carefully scrutinised contracts with private firms. An example is given by

---

[8] C. Addison, *Four and a Half Years* (London 1934), pp. 116 and 241. For a full account of the problems of war contracts see the unpublished 'History of the Ministry of Munitions', iii, P.R.O. MUN 5.

Addison: in April 1917 National T.N.T. Factories were set up at a capital cost of £1.5m and running costs to the end of the war were £3.5m, a total of £5m, as against a cost of £6m for the same quantity of T.N.T. under the revised contracts.[9] Winston Churchill, who took over from Addison at the Ministry of Munitions, claimed that its achievements 'constitute the greatest argument for State Socialism that has ever been produced'.[10]

The most controversial measure was Excess Profits Duty (EPD) When originally introduced by Reginald McKenna in September 1915 as part of the supplementary war budget, it was fixed at 50 per cent of the difference between pre-war and war-time profits. This was raised to 80 per cent in the 1917 budget. Despite many loop-holes in collection, EPD provided a quarter of all money raised by taxation during the war.[11] The tax was very unpopular with businessmen, who argued that it tempted their competitors (never of course, themselves) to raise prices more than necessary.

Sir Jessie Boot (of Boots the Chemist), described the way firms could get round the tax:

> I asked an expert in these matters how we could make a profit on it (a government contract). You may find his reply illuminating: For every shilling of profit you need, you must charge the Department 5s. Then the Government will get back 4s. from you in taxation.[12]

It was also claimed that firms added to their renovating and reequipping costs in order to avoid the tax; and Sir Stephenson Kent, director of the Department of Labour Supply, pointed out to the Cabinet that employers were becoming 'over-ready' to give wage increases because these could be offset against E.P.D. There was undoubtedly some truth in the argument that E.P.D. encouraged high prices, although the sustained outcry by businessmen against the tax suggests that it bit hard into profits, while the fact that it reduced the Government's reliance on borrowing served to stem inflation.

The failure to make a bigger impact on inflation during the war reflected both the inherent difficulties of the task and the correctness of the assessments made by expert opinion of its underlying causes.

[9] C. Addison, *Politics from Within* (London 1924), p. 107

[10] Quoted in P.B. Johnson, *Land Fit for Heroes* (Chicago, 1968), p. 400.

[11] See J.R. Hicks, U.K. Hicks and L. Rostas, *The Taxation of War Wealth* (Oxford 1941), p. 71.

[12] *The New Statesman*, 18 Jan. 1919.

The British record compared favourably with that of her chief ally, France. Nevertheless, dissatisfaction over the rising cost of living was as widespread at the end of the war as during the early months and profiteering was more than ever seen as the chief culprit.

One manifestation of the deep-seated conviction that the profiteers were doing well out of the war was the appeal of the 'Conscription of Riches' campaign. The invention of this phrase with its obvious emotional appeal is credited to Ben Tillett of the Transport and General Workers Union. It was taken up by the War Emergency Workers National Committee (WEWNC) and became a rallying cry for the whole Labour movement. As argued by Professor Royden Harrison, this campaign helped to prepare the way for the introduction of the new Labour Party constitution with its commitment to socialist aims.[13] Although H.M. Hyndman of the British Socialist Party and others tried to define it as a call for the outright nationalisation of industry, in immediate practical politics it became narrowed down to the more widely acceptable demand for heavier taxation of the rich. When in November 1917 the WEWNC, the TUC, the Labour Party Executive and the Miners' Federation of Great Britain sent a joint deputation to Bonar Law to press for the conscription of riches, what they actually asked for was a capital levy. The Conservative leader promised to consider the proposal but argued that it was impractical in wartime, as it would frighten businessmen and undermine the Government's ability to borrow money. Nevertheless, the idea gained support: the Asquithian Liberals as well as the Labour Party adopted it as part of their 1918 election programme and a number of economists, most notably Professor Pigou, argued in favour of a levy.

Everyone at the end of the war was eager to condemn profiteering and to disassociate themselves from it. In the debate on the King's address in February 1919 Bonar Law, the Conservative leader declared: 'I do not suggest for a moment that there was not a great deal of it and there may be a great deal of it now, but I do say with absolute certainty that there was never in the world's history such determined efforts as we made to put down profiteering of all kinds in the country'.

What was not agreed was who exactly were the profiteers. Many of the debates about high prices were interwoven with the old and thorny

---

[13] Royden Harrison, 'The War Emergency Workers' National Committee, 1914–20' in *Essays in Labour History*, op. cit., pp. 219,247–52; See also, R.C. Whiting, 'The Labour Party, capitalism and the national debt' in P.J. Waller (ed) *Politics and Social Change in Modern Britain* (Brighton, 1987), pp. 140–60.

controversy over free trade versus tariff reform and with discussions on the role of the state in economic matters. Free traders, whatever their party allegiance, generally wanted to scrap controls and believed that they kept prices high. This view was put forward consistently by the Asquithian Liberals, a solidly free-trade group, who accused the Government of preventing imports in order to keep up prices. F.D. Acland claimed: 'The Government is perhaps so much a profiteer itself that it has a certain fellow feeling with other profiteers'.[14]

Later in the year Keynes criticised the European governments for directing resentment for rising prices against the entrepreneur class, 'the active and constructive element in capitalist society', and said it was endangering the continuance of the social and economic order.[15] Members of the Government and back-bench Conservative MPs saw this danger and did their best to point out that business men who profiteered were the exception. Several of the new MPs with a business background felt obliged to explain to the House how they had sacrificed making money to help the country's war effort. A refreshing exception was Mr Remer, M.P., an owner of saw mills, who in his maiden speech, announced that he had entered Parliament because he thought it vital that the views of employers of labour should be heard there and stated, 'Personally I do not mind admitting that I have made good profits during the war'.

There was a tendency to blame retailers and small men as the key profiteers. Many tales were told of upstart butchers who were said to be buying cars and attending Ascot, or haberdashers who were said to be buying country estates of several hundred acres. When the President of the Board of Trade, Sir Auckland Geddes, was asked to admit that wholesalers and manufacturers were the worst offenders he replied that this was not the Government's view: 'We believe in the retailer, where there is profiteering, being on the average the more persistent and incorrigible profiteer'.[16] The propaganda battle over who were the profiteers was extended to the pages of *Punch* with a cartoon in July 1919 showing a character very similar in appearance to the Will Dyson 'War Profiteer' but with the added twist that the captions showed him dropping his aitches to make clear that he was not an established member of the capitalist class.

[14] *The Times* 3 Jan. 1919.
[15] J.M. Keynes, *The Economic Consequences of the Peace* (London 1919).
[16] 'Select Committee on High Prices and Profits', *Parl.Papers* (1919) v. pp. 296f.

Labour spokesmen in Parliament refused to be deflected by easy Government reassurances. For example, J.H. Thomas challenged the Conservative view that only a minority of businessmen profiteered: 'Does Bonar Law suggest by his definition that profiteering such as I have indicated was the exception and not the rule, because I desire to point out that taking shipping, steel, coal, railways and cotton, there was an increase, and a substantial increase amounting in the main to 100 per cent on the dividends, as a whole, and not isolated cases'.[17]

Both the Sankey Commission and the Committee on Trusts seemed to provide evidence to reinforce the convictions of those who saw profiteering as an intrinsic feature of capitalism, while the sale of Government assets early in 1919 and the April 1919 Budget confirmed the suspicions of those who saw the Lloyd George Government as the champion of the profiteers.

The Royal Commission on the Coal Mines under the chairmanship of Mr Justice Sankey provided ample evidence both of the coal owners' wartime profits, which amounted to more than the pre-war capital of the industry, and of the inefficiency of the industry under private enterprise.[18] The whole proceedings, which were widely reported, were highly dramatic. Beatrice Webb described them as 'like those of a revolutionary tribunal, sitting in judgement on the capitalist owners and organisers of the nation's industries'.[19] All but the coal owners' representatives on the commission were convinced of the need for fundamental change.

The debate on profiteering was further widened by the publication in April of the report of the Ministry of Reconstruction Committee on Trusts.[20] Profiteering had usually been discussed as a war time problem which would disappear once the economic system was back to normal. Making high profits would then be evidence of efficiency and of being ahead in the market, and prices would be regulated by the self-adjusting laws of supply and demand. The Committee on Trusts challenged this view: 'There is in every important branch of industry in the United Kingdom an increasing tendency to the formation of trade associations, having for their purpose the restriction of competition and the control of prices'. They concluded that, 'a system which creates virtual monopolies and controls

---

[17] *Parl.Debates*, H. of C., 13 February 1919.

[18] *Parl.Papers*, 1919, Minutes of Evidence to the Royal Commission on the Coal Industry, 1st Stage (Cmd. 359).

[19] *Beatrice Webb's Diaries, 1912–24*, ed. M. Cole (London 1925), pp. 152–53

[20] *Parl.Papers*, (1919), xiii (Cd. 9236).

prices is always in danger of abuse' and recommended that permanent machinery should be set up to investigate and control monopolies and trusts.

The trend of Government policy, however, was by then clearly against the maintenance of controls and there had been a retreat from earlier proposals for state-managed reconstruction.[21] The Labour movement was deeply alarmed at this trend and accused the Government of promoting the interests of businessmen at the expense of the community. In particular, they attacked the decision to sell off the National Factories, Ships and Shipyards, and suspected that these national assets were being virtually given away to private enterprise. The Cabinet decided to sell by tender in some cases, at a price to be determined by an independent arbitrator in others and, in the case of ships under construction, by private arrangement at prices which the Shipping Controller told the Cabinet would show comparatively little, if any, loss to the Government, but which a bitter article in the *New Statesman* described as a 'handsome donation to the Coalition fund for the relief of distressed ship-owners'.[22] It was the injustice of profiteering rather than high prices in themselves which aroused the bitterest anger and class feeling in the Labour movement in these months. Many companies issued free or very cheap bonus shares during 1919 and both the *New Statesman* and the *Daily Herald* made a point of listing these. The Directorate of Intelligence in one of its weekly reports on revolutionary organisations warned that the watering of capital and distribution of bonuses was causing bitter comment, and that stories of profiteering were a cause of general unrest.[23]

The first post-war Budget was seen as yet further evidence of the Government's lack of will to tackle profiteering. The absence of a coherent economic policy had made the task of the Chancellor of the Exchequer, Austen Chamberlain, extremely difficult. He would have liked to follow the orthodox recommendations of the Cunliffe Committee but a return to the Gold Standard was ruled out as deflationary. He opened his Budget statement with a *cri de coeur*: 'I am called upon at one and the same time to remit or repeal the taxation which was imposed, and to remedy all the grievances which have been cheerfully endured in these years of stress and strain, and not merely to resume the civil expenditure which was

---

[21] See P. B. Johnson, op. cit. pp. 306–37; and R. H. Tawney; 'The Abolition of Economic Controls, 1918–20', *Econ. Hist. Review*, xiii (1943), pp. 1–30.

[22] *The New Statesman* 1st March 1919.

[23] P.R.O. CAB 24/83, GT 7671, 10 July 1919.

interrupted under the stress of war, but to provide the means for creating within a few months or a few years a new heaven and a new earth; and the same people who call upon me for fresh and large expenditure in every special field expect me at the same time to accomplish vast reductions in expenditure. I can work no such marvel.'[24] Nor did he.

The economic purists criticised the Chancellor for still budgeting for a deficit. Others thought social expenditure too low. The *Daily Herald* immediately labelled it 'A Profiteers' Budget' and commented, 'the war profiteers, the capitalists and the financial reactionaries need not have been afraid . . . they had told Mr Chamberlain what to do, and he could be trusted to do it'. This attack was provoked by the reduction of EPD from 80 per cent to 40 per cent Chamberlain said this was to encourage businessmen to invest, but the *Daily Herald* saw the issue differently: 'The reduction in E.P.D. is an almost incredible instance of concession to the capitalists who pull the strings of the parliamentary puppet. There never was a juster . . . nor a more lucrative tax.'

The 1919 Budget marked the end of the period when Government policy was dominated by fear of impending depression. This had been both a reason and an excuse for lack of action on prices or profiteering, despite mounting public feeling and growing class antagonism. By May the economic prospect was beginning to look brighter as industry settled down to satisfy the backlog of consumer demand left behind by the war. The excess of demand over supply for many domestic goods, world shortages and the food crisis in Central Europe all acted to reverse the small downward trend of prices. The renewal of inflation was foreseen in May and in July prices started off on a fresh upwards spiral.

The expectation that a boom was on the way created a new context for making political and economic decisions. It meant that the problems of inflation and profiteering would not resolve themselves, nor would time alone alleviate the political and social tensions which they aroused. Something had to be done, yet Lloyd George's policy options were curtailed by the new economic outlook. The boom, coupled with his own success in handling Labour unrest during the spring, greatly strengthened the confidence of businessmen both inside and outside Parliament and made them very impatient of legislative curbs on their activities. It also hardened their opposition to any part of the economy being taken out of the private sector.

---

[24] *Parl.Debates*, H. of C., 30 April 1919.

A few days after the final Sankey Reports came out Bonar Law was confronted by a militant gathering of 150 backbenchers led by W. Joynson-Hicks: they demanded assurances that the government had not accepted nationalisation of the mines or the railways. Bonar Law gave them such assurances.[25] As a result, Lloyd George, always a realist, gave up nationalisation as one of his options, although he realised that this would alienate the Labour movement. He thought, however, that he could handle the situation and told the cabinet that if the refusal to nationalise the mines led to a strike, it would be better to have it in August than later.[26]

This decision gave Lloyd George a compelling need to find some new way to placate the Labour movement. Could anything be done about inflation and discontent over profiteering? The full implementation of the recommendations of the Committee on Trusts or a return to a full system of controls as operated during the war would certainly please the Labour Party but would not be accepted by the Unionist backbenchers. Yet the new upsurge in prices meant that the issue of controls required urgent attention. Some controls had already been scrapped and others were expected to go soon. Respect for the regulations was diminishing and the bodies for enforcing them were reluctant to prosecute.

The problem began to take up an inordinate amount of Cabinet time. One issue alone, the price and shortage of beer, together with stories of brewers watering it to produce 'wash', its taxation and accusations of profiteering by the brewers, was discussed by the Cabinet on five occasions between 22nd May and 23rd June. On the last occasion the beer problem, which was seen as an emotive issue in relations with the working class, took up the whole agenda. It was decided to raise gravity but not to increase the taxes paid by the brewers.

Nothing placated the electorate and the barrage of criticism continued. On the continent the situation was even more acute with mass protests in France and Belgium; in Italy goods had been seized by force and sold at half-price.[27] The *Daily Herald* predicted that there would be similar outbreaks of violence in Britain. Consequently the government announced that the Ministry of Food, previously scheduled for abolition, would be retained over the winter. The decision did little to increase the Government's popularity.

---

25 *The Times*, 8 July 1919.
26 P.R.O., CAB 23/11 23 July 1919.
27 *The Times* 8th July 1919.

Trade union militancy during the period following the Armistice had resulted in wage rates in the main industries catching up with the retail price index. In addition, hours of work had in many cases been reduced. The real position in relation to working class living standards, however, was not so favourable. During the war, although wage rates had lagged behind price increases, this had been partly offset by overtime earnings, piecework bonuses, the availability of work for women and dependants' allowances for soldiers' families. No reliable earnings statistics were collected nor were the factors which counterbalanced low wage rate quantified, but an enquiry into standards of living in the summer of 1918 had concluded that the working class as a whole could afford to eat as well as in 1914 and the unskilled were better off; there were fewer undernourished children in the schools and pauperism was down by a third.[28] Against this, standards of living were always in jeopardy as prices rose so that there was never any sense of security.

With the ending of the war, overtime, piecework and women's work all began to disappear. In order to consolidate existing standards of living, it became vital for wage-earners to win increases in basic rates. This explains some of the militancy over wages in the first half of 1919. Even the Government felt it necessary, where it was in direct control, as in the coal industry, to authorise substantial increases. In general employers were receptive to wage demands in early 1919, but by the time prices began to rise again they were more resistant, with the result that despite the many strikes of 1919–20, it was not until halfway through 1920 that wage rates again caught up with the cost of living. By that time a press campaign had been launched blaming wage increases for inflation.

In the summer of 1919, however, high prices were still generally blamed for inflation so that when Lloyd George needed a sop to offer the Labour Movement before announcing his decision not to implement the Report of the Sankey Commission, action against profiteering seemed a possible way out. The Cabinet found it difficult to agree what this should be. Sir Auckland Geddes proposed the setting up of tribunals to hear complaints from the public against retailers, with the Board of Trade investigating complaints against manufacturers and wholesalers,[29] but the Cabinet were not convinced this would be effective. A select committee was therefore

---

[28] *Parl.Papers* (1918), vii. 'Report of the Committee on the Cost of Living' (Cd. 8980).
[29] P.R.O. CAB 24/83 GT. 7685, 'Memorandum by the President of the Board of Trade on the Prevention of Profiteering', 12 July 1919.

appointed, 'to inquire how far the present high prices of articles of general consumption are due to excessive profits on the part of any persons concerned in their production, transport or distribution, and to advise action'.[30]

The committee did not hold its first meeting until 5 August and spent that day questioning G.H. Roberts, the Food Controller. He explained that in most cases food control had been complete with the ministry itself owning the supplies, fixing prices and margins at all stages and regulating distribution: 'It is no exaggeration to say that profiteering in the sense in which it is understood by the general public as something exceptional, attributable to undue speculation, and that like, is excluded'. He added that the chief problem in operating controls fairly, was the wide variation in costs of production (Addison's old problem see above, p.189). Some bakers could turn a sack of flour into bread at a cost of less than 10s. while others required 30s. or 35s. and the Ministry allowed an average of 23s. This meant that the more efficient firms made very big profits. One member of the committee, Vernon Hartshorn, a miners' MP, suggested that such firms were profiteering and ought to be compelled to pass the benefit of their cheaper costs to the consumer, but Roberts said that it would be impossible to compel them to charge less than the regulated price. This led to a very complex and inconclusive discussion of what was meant by the term a 'fair' or 'reasonable' price and by profiteering. The committee was unable to pursue its attempts at definition because the next day Sir Auckland Geddes announced that the Government had decided to go ahead and introduce a Bill without waiting for the committee's report.

It seems probable that the pressure to go ahead came from Lloyd George himself.[31] The Cabinet did not discuss the matter between 14 July, when they examined Sir Auckland Geddes' memorandum, and 6 August, when it was announced that a Bill was to be introduced. The earlier discussion had certainly not shown much enthusiasm among the Cabinet for taking action nor belief that what was proposed would be in any way effective against inflation. Even Sir Auckland did not like his own proposals but thought tribunals were better than extending direct controls. Bonar Law thought that tribunals would be overwhelmed with work and would give no satisfaction. The Home Secretary said that if profiteering was to be made a criminal offence the term 'reasonable price' was not an acceptable

[30] *Parl. Papers* (1919), v (166). Select Committee on High Prices and Profits.

[31] See C.J. Wrigley, *Lloyd George and the Challenge of Labour* (Hemel Hempstead 1990), pp. 233f.

definition. Sir Eric Geddes thought tribunals would not be competent to fix prices. Austen Chamberlain thought it would be better to test prices of staple products and announce what was fair and leave it to public opinion to deal with any manufacturer or retailer shown to be making undue profits. Only Sir Robert Horne and Charles McCurdy showed any real support for the proposals and their concern was limited to measures curbing trusts and monopolies.

Most of the ministers present were just as sceptical when the Bill was finalised between the 6 and 8 August. Churchill said the Bill embodied an extraordinary principle: 'it was apparently intended to treat every business transaction as if it were conducted by a usurious moneylender'. Sir Walter Long doubted if Parliament would accept it. Roberts thought that the use of tribunals to deal with vaguely defined profiteering would prove unworkable. Addison was only enthusiastic about the proposals to give Local Authorities power to trade and so provide an alternative price level. Auckland Geddes was worried about regional disparities and his brother about the impartiality of locally constituted tribunals. Nevertheless the Bill went ahead. The second reading took place on 11 August and the Act was placed on the Statute Book on 29 August.

The main clauses of the Act provided for the Board of Trade to have power to investigate prices, costs and profit at all stages of production or distribution; to fix maximum prices; to investigate complaints of unreasonable profits; to dismiss complaints or fix a new price with the seller repaying the excess to the complainant; and to take summary proceedings where unreasonable prices were found, the maximum penalty to be a £200 fine or three months' imprisonment. It was laid down that a profit should not be deemed 'unreasonable' if it did not exceed the fair average rate earned upon the sale of similar articles before the war. The second part of the Act gave the Board of Trade power to set up local committees or authorise Local Authorities to do so and to delegate to them any of their powers under the Act except the power to fix prices. The third section dealt with trusts: the Board of Trade was to obtain all possible information as to the nature, extent and development of trusts and arrangements having for their purpose the regulation of prices or output. The fourth section gave Local Authorities power to purchase and sell any articles of common use, provided they did so on a commercial basis and not by way of subsidy at the expense of the ratepayers. The Act was to run initially for six months; it was later extended unaltered for another three months.

Reaction to the Act was lukewarm both in Parliament and the press. *The Times* commented that by trying to please everyone it would end up by pleasing noone. Retailers were alarmed at the powers given to Local Authorities to trade, although they need not have worried as this section of the Act remained dormant. Housewives would have preferred some direct action to bring prices down, although the tribunals would provide a safety valve for extreme indignation over individual purchases. Lloyd George may have hoped to please the Unionist bank-benchers by not extending direct controls, but they would have preferred no legislation at all. The Labour Party and Asquithian Liberals were meant to be pleased by the clauses dealing with trusts, but they both wanted positive steps to be taken and Lloyd George was merely offering them the collection of more information. Clynes called the Act, 'a half-hearted device', and said it would be useless in curbing the big firms.[32] The Labour movement, in any case, would not agree to be distracted. Militant trade unionists remained convinced, as *the Daily Herald* had said in July, that: 'Under all this talk and all the writing about prices and profiteers, food and shortages, coal and the consumer, there is only one basic issue facing the nation at the moment. That is the issue of nationalisation.'[33] Nor were moderate members of the Labour movement any more impressed.

Scepticism about the Act became widespread in the autumn and winter because, despite the setting up of nearly 2,000 local committees and the opening of investigations by the central committee over a whole range of products, prices rose rapidly. The most that could be claimed for the Act was that it had a deterrent effect, although even that was doubtful. When it became due for renewal in May 1920, it was reported that 4,000 complaints had been investigated; in 934 cases it was held that the prices charged had been unreasonable and 200 prosecutions had been initiated.[34] A proposal was put forward to amend the Act by the insertion of a clause giving the Board of Trade power to accept schemes submitted by a substantial proportion of those engaged in a particular industry for limiting the profits allowed. The acceptance of such a scheme would carry with it clearance of the charge of profiteering and freedom from the operation of the rest of the Act. This clause infuriated the Asquithian Liberals, who saw it as an encouragement of monopoly, and they submitted a motion against the Act's renewal.

The Labour MPs took little part in the debate: they considered the Act irrelevant and argued that the only effective form of price control was total

[32] *Parl. Debates*, H. of C., 11 August 1919.
[33] *Daily Herald*, 14 July 1919.
[34] *Parl. Debates*, H. of C. 29 April 1920.

control of prices at all stages of manufacture and distribution. Not even the Government spokesmen claimed very much for the Act. Nevertheless, it was renewed as amended for a further twelve months.

The reports of the Central Committee began to be published in June 1920. The first to come out was on the biscuit trade and it set the pattern for all the reports in its conclusion that the profits earned in the industry were 'not unreasonable'. Ben Turner, the textile workers' leader, put in a reservation: 'I agree that they are not very unreasonable judged by the present day standard of profits, but that this increase in such standards of profits is the wicked vicious circle the country is suffering from'.[35] These reports completely failed to assuage the indignation of the Labour movement over inflation and high profits. Labour resentment had been given a new impetus by the publicity surrounding the Dock Inquiry in March 1920, in which Ernest Bevin so brilliantly contrasted the high profits and luxurious living of the dock owners with the low pay and hard life of the dockers.[36]

The Government had been inclined to underestimate the militancy of the Labour movement after the announcement of the decision not to nationalise the coal mines had passed off without a strike, but the railway strike of autumn 1919 cut short any complacency. The ineffectiveness of the Profiteering Act led Lloyd George to look for other ways to propitiate the Labour movement. The National Industrial Conference of February to April 1919 had been of limited long-term value to either side, its message of joint consultation being challenged by the constitutionalism of the Labour Party leaders. The political situation remained volatile throughout 1919 and 1920, but it was mainly the acute difficulty of managing the National Debt rather than political calculation, which prompted the government to give attention to another of the proposals put forward for dealing with profiteering: the imposition of a capital levy.

By the summer of 1919 pressure on the Chancellor to reduce Government expenditure was already considerable. He was also having great problems in managing the floating debt as it came up for renewal, despite the partial success of a new public loan in July. The Financial Secretary to the Treasury, Stanley Baldwin, was so moved by his chief's difficulties and the burden of the National Debt, that he gave a gift to the nation of a fifth of his increased wealth since before the war. (Baldwins Ltd.

---

[35] *Parl. Papers* 1920 xxiii (Cmd. 856).
[36] A. Bullock, *Life of Ernest Bevin*, (London, 1960) pp. 124f.

had issued free bonus shares in February 1919 on the basis of one share for each four held.)[37] He appealed through *The Times* to other public – spirited men to follow his example. Unfortunately, only about £500,000 was raised by this voluntary effort, whereas the National Debt at the end of the war was not far short of £7,500m., of which a quarter was floating debt, which all the experts urged should be funded as soon as possible. A compulsory levy was, therefore, seriously considered. Although a Select Committee on Increases in War Wealth was set up in the autumn of 1919[38] Conservative opposition rapidly mounted.

Meanwhile the 1920 Budget increased EPD, which provoked an outcry among businessmen and the rare event of support for the Government by the *Daily Herald*. The committee eventually reported in May 1920. It said that the collection of a capital levy on war wealth to yield about £500m was practicable and would not damage the economy. Although it would be fiercely resisted by the financial and commercial world, it would fall on individuals who could best afford to pay and would be seen by the public as 'a just and necessary attempt to equalise the losses suffered during the war'. It would help to relieve the problems caused by the large national debt.

The Cabinet met to decide their policy on 2 June. Austen Chamberlain, though he wanted the revenue and had agreed to the inquiry, admitted that he had all along hoped the committee would turn the tax down: 'I have felt throughout the danger of the present position of capital. We have for the first time a great political party organised on an anti-capitalist basis.' Lloyd George, who was originally inclined to support a capital levy, rapidly back-tracked. He said that he was worried about the signs already appearing of a trade recession and thought this a good reason not to proceed. The burial of the proposal marks the end of Government attempts to moderate inflation or lessen its redistributive effect in favour of the owners of capital. It is true that the Profiteering Act continued in operation until May 1921, when it was allowed to lapse, but it was the least effective of all the measures introduced during the whole period of inflation from 1914 to 1920. Compared with war-time controls and costings or with E.P.D. all of which had some partial success in achieving their declared purpose, the Profiteering Act was a public relations exercise. The fact that so shrewd a politician as Lloyd George had felt impelled to bother with such an Act illustrates the problems of his political position.

[37] *The New Statesman*, 1 February 1919.
[38] *Parl. Papers* (1920), vii. Select Committee on Increases in War Wealth (102).

The Parliamentary Labour Party was weak in numbers and conciliatory in spirit, but the militancy of the working class outside Parliament forced the Government to take into account working-class aspirations, even if this meant displeasing the Conservative backbenchers. Lloyd George undoubtedly played upon Conservative fears of Bolshevism in order to strengthen his position within the Coalition. It is unlikely that he ever feared revolution, although his powers were taxed to the full to prevent a major industrial show-down. But he could not be content with merely containing unrest: he needed to maintain his popularity with working class voters. He also had to consider the reception which Government policies would receive among both groups of Liberals. The prolongation of the war-time consensus, even in an attenuated form, was essential to him and would enable him to keep his options open until he could find a solution to his isolation from the existing party machines and so end his dependence on Bonar Law. The dropping of the proposal to impose a capital levy, on the other hand, indicated the hardening of the resolve of the Conservative Party to defeat not propitiate the Labour Party and trade unions. It marked a step towards the dissolution of the Coalition in 1922 and the banishment of Lloyd George.

10

Labour and the Trade Unions: George Lansbury, Ernest Bevin and the Leadership Crisis of 1935

John Shepherd

On 30 September 1935 delegates assembling for the Labour Party Conference in the Dome at Brighton received the official programme containing an appeal by the party leader, George Lansbury, to support the Victoria House Printing Press, the official party printers. However, opposite the photograph of Lansbury, the advertisement for the League of Nations Union pamphlet on the Italo-Abyssinian dispute provided a grim, albeit unintentioned, portent of the subject which was to dominate the proceedings of the thirty-fifth annual conference and occasion the downfall of the most popular leader in Labour Party history.[1]

By the early 1930s the expansionist aggression of the Fascist dictatorships of Germany, Italy and Japan on the international scene destroyed the efforts of World Disarmament Conference and menaced the role of the League of Nations as a supranational peacekeeping organisation. With the advent of Hitler and Mussolini, how far socialist principles could still be applied in foreign policy to achieve world peace and disarmament became the crucial issue facing the Labour Party, led by the veteran pacifist George Lansbury. Against the background of the gathering international storm clouds of the Italo-Abyssinian crisis in East Africa, the delegates in Brighton in 1935 witnessed the longest and most emotional debate to take

---

[1] Labour Party Conference, *Brighton 1935: Diary for the Week* (1935), pp. 2–3.

place at an annual party conference. On 1 October Hugh Dalton moved the resolution on behalf of the National Executive Committee (NEC) of the Labour Party that:

> The Conference pledges its firm support of any action consistent with the principles and statutes of the League [of Nations] to restrain the Italian Government and to uphold the authority of the League in enforcing peace.[2]

As an absolute Christian pacifist Lansbury judged his personal position as party leader untenable if the NEC motion was endorsed. Unconditional support for the League might mean the use of armed force and war. In this way the Italian invasion of Abyssinia (which took place on 3 October) precipitated the leadership crisis at the Labour Party Conference at Brighton. On the morning of the crucial debate the *Daily Herald*'s front page headlines, 'Labour Votes for Sanctions Today', 'Majority for the Party's Policy is Certain' and, in particular, 'Mr Bevin and Mr Lansbury Wind Up Dramatic Whole-Day Debate at Conference', described the scene of the dramatic confrontation between the elected and greatly revered party leader and the most powerful trade union boss of the inter-war years.[3]

In a passionate speech outlining his Christian principles and life-long opposition to the use of force, George Lansbury explained to the conference delegates why he was unable to support the National Executive Committee resolution. He was immediately followed to the platform by Ernest Bevin, whose savage denunciation of Lansbury's position turned the mood of the party conference against its leader. At the end of the debate Lansbury and his small band of pacifist supporters were comprehensively defeated, as the NEC resolution was carried overwhelmingly by 2,168,000 to 102,000 votes. As a result, a few days later, George Lansbury met the Labour members of the parliamentary party and resigned the leadership.

At the time, Bevin's savage attack on Lansbury drew considerable comment in the press, particularly as the Labour leader had tried immediately, without success, to reply to his critic and as no member of the NEC had come to his assistance during the debate. The *Morning*

---

[2] Labour Party, *Report of the 35th Annual Conference* (1935) [hereafter cited as 1935 Report], p. 153.

[3] *Daily Herald*, 2 October 1935.

Post reported that only twenty minutes before Bevin's speech Lansbury had been the hero of the conference but that the tussle between 'bellicose Trade Unionism' and 'die-hard Pacifism' had ended in an 'astonishing scene'. According to the newspaper, 'with the Chairman on his feet, Mr Lansbury gripped the microphone and shouted unheard remarks against hoots, shouts and clamour from the assembled delegates'.[4]

The mainly Tory press believed that Lansbury had no alternative to resigning the party leadership. The next day the *News Chronicle* carried the headline 'Lansbury will be Forced to End Leadership', which soon turned into a 'Lansbury Must Go' campaign.[5] The result of this conference vote was seen as having greater significance for the future of the Labour Party than simply the grave doubts expressed about Lansbury's leadership. *The Times* devoted a long editorial to the problems of the Labour Party. The newspaper commented that, though the outcome of the debate was a pledge of loyalty by the annual conference to the League of Nations, serious divisions still existed within the party between the trade union and political wings:

> Of greater moment than a change in the Parliamentary leadership of Labour is the cleavage – narrow at the moment but deep – between the trade union and the purely political sections of the labour movement . . . The size of the majority for the official policy does not hide the gravity of the internal dissensions . . . There was never a doubt of the issue of the debate, and the size of the majority could almost have been measured in advance. The serious side for the Labour party is that the difference occurs between the leaders. On a foremost issue of the day the leaders are hopelessly divided.[6]

After the conference, therefore, Lansbury's resignation was no surprise as his position as the Labour leader had become impossible. According to a local paper in his parliamentary constituency, he had become the politician holding fast to unrealistic ideals in a modern international world:

> There are still some things in this world worth fighting for, and in his love of peace the dear old member for Bow and Bromley has gone

---

[4] *Morning Post*, 2 October 1935.
[5] *News Chronicle*, 2 and 3 October 1935.
[6] *The Times*, 3 October 1935.

sadly astray as a political leader whose dreams are as delightful as castles in the air at night time but which dissolve in the grey light of morning . . .[7]

Since his public defeat and humiliation at the Brighton Conference in 1935, historians in the main have written about George Lansbury's downfall in similar vein. In his account of modern British political parties, Robert Mackenzie regarded Bevin's slaying of Lansbury at Brighton in 1935 as the most decisive dismissal of a British leader, made infamous by 'one of the bitterest remarks in the history of labour party polemics': Bevin accused Lansbury of publicly parading his pacifist conscience and betraying the trade union movement by not supporting the agreed Labour policy in the 'War and Peace' document. Bevin's unexpected and furious attack was the turning point of the conference.[8] In retrospect, one delegate told Bevin's biographer: 'He [Bevin] compelled a naturally sentimental body to see an issue in larger than personal terms. He had to attack Lansbury to make the issue clearer. But it was not the personal attack, but the sense of responsibility of the issue itself that gave force to his speech and carried the conference'.[9]

Some accounts have been more sympathetic to Lansbury's position as a party leader who found his loyalty to conscience in conflict with a major issue of public and political importance. In 1951 Lansbury's official biographer, Raymond Postgate, recalled his father-in-law's difficult situation as leader and his offers to resign before the party conference.[10] Reviewing Postgate's book, Robert Blake provided a perhaps more lasting, albeit inaccurate, portrayal of Lansbury as the elderly socialist, hopelessly out of date in the 1930s in the world of the Fascist dictators, whose vacillating pacifist conscience enraged Ernest Bevin:

George Lansbury is remembered today for the years of his dotage; remembered as the elderly pacifist driven from the leadership of the socialist party . . . Lansbury remained at heart a Victorian Radical. He was perhaps the last of our political leaders to believe in peace, progress and the perfectibility of man . . . but in fact Lansbury lived

---

[7] *City and East London Observer*, 5 October 1935.

[8] Robert Mackenzie, *British Political Parties* (2nd edition, 1964), pp. 381–83.

[9] M.A. Hamilton to A. Bullock, 17 December 1956, quoted in Alan Bullock, *The Life and Times of Ernest Bevin, 1, Trade Union Leader, 1881–1940* (1960), p. 569.

[10] Raymond Postgate, *The Life of George Lansbury* (1951), pp. 298–301.

on from the days of Queen Victoria into the dark age of Hitler and Stalin. It was his tragedy that he failed to realise this change.[11]

At the 1935 Labour Party Conference the Transport and General Workers with four other major unions, the Miners Federation, the National Union of Railwaymen, the Municipal Workers and the Textile Workers, together controlled nearly 2,000,000 of the votes cast at Brighton. As a result, there was no doubt that the NEC's resolution would be overwhelmingly supported and Lansbury would be defeated. October 1935 was one of the few occasions when foreign affairs dominated the proceedings of the party conference. Up to that point the major concerns of the Labour Party, faced by the seemingly impregnable domination of British politics by the National Government, had been mass unemployment, the control of the economy and related domestic issues. After the electoral débâcle of 1931, one of the major achievements of Lansbury's leadership had been to hold the decimated Parliamentary Labour Party together as an effective official opposition in the House of Commons. At the same time the veteran socialist remained an inspirational and universally popular figure, addressing meetings and rallies of the Labour movement throughout the country. Despite this, in October 1935, with a forthcoming general election close at hand, George Lansbury was dismissed in a storm of bitter public humiliation. Over fifty years on, it is worth examining again the circumstances surrounding the remarkable events at Brighton Conference. In 1935 the leadership crisis at the Brighton Conference represented a clash of political faith, policy and personality whose prehistory can be traced in the characters and in the political philosophies of the main protagonists, as well as in the history of the political party in which they had both served.

In 1931, four years before the Brighton Conference, the seventy year old George Lansbury was not only the sole surviving Cabinet minister in the Labour ranks in the House of Commons, but was also the most famous and popular left-wing politician in the country after a lifetime in the labour movement preaching the socialist faith. Lansbury's socialism, feminism, pacifism and internationalism derived from a devout but simple Christian faith and direct experience of the hardships of working-class life in the

---

[11] Robert Blake, 'The Tragic Dreamer', *Evening Standard*, 12 November 1951. For a sympathetic appraisal of Lansbury's role in the 1930s, see Michael Foot, 'The Pacifist who Lost the Peace' in *The Guardian*, 8 November 1990.

East End of London. A tireless supporter of a host of minority causes and organisations, Lansbury was renowned as a great humanitarian with a burning passion for social justice and a deep compassion for suffering. His active political career had included serving on the Royal Commission on the Poor Laws (1905–190); resigning his parliamentary seat to fight the 1912 Bow and Bromley by-election on the women's suffrage cause (after which he said he had learnt 'Never Resign!'); editing of the *Daily Herald* as a crusading newspaper; and leading the Poplar Rates Rebellion of 1921.[12]

Originally an unskilled labourer who had risen through the ranks of the Dockers' Union, Ernest Bevin had built a reputation within the trade union movement since the period of the labour unrest before the First World War as a forceful, rugged and at times ruthless union organiser. His leadership, administrative skills and powerful personality helped to establish the General Council of the TUC and created the massive amalgamation of the Transport and General Workers Union (TGWU), the largest trade union in the world, out of fifty unions. The measure of Bevin's growing reputation in industrial relations and his stature in the labour movement can be seen by 1928 in the building of Transport House, the headquarters of the TGWU, which also housed the Labour Party and the TUC as tenants.[13] While, as general secretary of the TGWU, Bevin had his new offices close to Westminster and Whitehall, as yet he had made no sustained attempt to enter politics. By contrast Lansbury had been an elected guardian, councillor, county councillor, MP and Cabinet Minister.

Though their careers represented the two trade union and political wings of the labour movement, the two men had much in common: their Christian background and upbringing; early contact with Social Democratic Federation politics; and leadership of the right-to-work campaigns of the unemployed in the Edwardian years. Bevin had become one of the trade union directors of the *Daily Herald*, established by Lansbury as a mass

---

[12] For George Lansbury, see Margaret Cole, 'George Lansbury (1859–1940): Socialist, Pacifist and Labour Leader' in Joyce M. Bellamy and John Saville (ed.), *Dictionary of Labour Biography ii* (1974), pp. 214–23, which includes a detailed bibliography. Mike Lewis, 'George Lansbury and the Labour Party 1931–1935: Transition and Opposition' (unpublished dissertation, Colgate University, 1974). Two recent studies are Bob Holman, *Good Old George: The Life of George Lansbury* (1990) and Jonathan Schneer, *George Lansbury* (Manchester, 1990).

[13] For Ernest Bevin see the authoritative biography, Alan Bullock, *The Life and Times of Ernest Bevin, i, Trade Union Leader, 1881–1940* (1960). Two shorter accounts are Trevor Evans, *Bevin* (1946); Mark Stephens, *Ernest Bevin: Unskilled Labourer and World Statesman, 1881–1951* (Stevenage, 1985).

circulation left-wing newspaper and supporter of trade union, pacifist and feminist causes. During the years of Lansbury's editorship, and afterwards, Bevin was instrumental in securing finance from the trade union and labour movement which maintained the *Daily Herald* as a prominent daily Labour newspaper. In 1929 he negotiated the agreement with Odhams Press which provided the resources to develop the paper into the first daily in the world to reach a circulation of two million copies.[14] Both men were critics of MacDonald's leadership of the Labour Party, especially after the failure of the first Labour Government in 1924. Bevin saw the Labour Party as the creature of the trade unions and was distrustful of left-wing socialist intellectuals in the labour movement. Lansbury had always opposed MacDonald's gradualist approach to politics from the time he had resigned his parliamentary seat, without official party approval, over the women's suffrage cause in 1912. In the mid 1920s his new venture in journalism, *Lansbury's Labour Weekly*, was also a vehicle for left-wing ideas and often highly critical attacks on MacDonald's moderate and cautious leadership. In 1931 Lansbury led the minority in MacDonald's Second Cabinet who resolutely opposed the 10 per cent cut in unemployment insurance, also condemned by Bevin and the General Council of the TUC.

Between 1931–35 Lansbury's leadership of the Labour Party represented an important period of reexamination of policy and strategy, in the aftermath of the collapse of the Second Labour Government and the formation of the National Government with Ramsay MacDonald as Prime Minister. In the 1931 general election the National Government's overwhelming victory with 554 MPs left an annihilated parliamentary opposition of only forty-six Labour members in the House of Commons. As the only former Cabinet minister to survive at the polls, Lansbury became leader of the parliamentary rump of mainly right-wing trade union MPs.[15] As leader, Lansbury was supported by two other middle-class socialists, Clement Attlee and Stafford Cripps, who had held junior office in the second MacDonald government. Although the triumvirate of Lansbury, Attlee and Cripps was in general to the left of the party, these years saw an emerging concordat between the moderates in the political and industrial wings of the labour movement. In particular, the growing influence of the

[14] For Lansbury's editorship of the *Daily Herald,* see George Lansbury, *The Miracle of Fleet Street: The Story of the Daily Herald* (1925).

[15] Outside parliament Arthur Henderson, who had been defeated at the 1931 general election, was Leader of the Labour Party until Lansbury took over in 1932.

trade unions in Labour circles on domestic and international questions was characterised by the personalities and stance on political issues of Ernest Bevin and Walter Citrine, General Secretary of the TUC.

After the defection of MacDonald and Snowden to the National Government, Bevin, Citrine and other trade union leaders displayed a strong distrust of the parliamentary intellectuals within the Labour Party and blamed the failure of the Second Labour Government on its lack of effective policy on domestic questions.[16] As a result there were determined efforts to strengthen trade union influence within the organisation of the Labour Party. Citrine's memorandum of TUC's views (January 1932) led to greater cooperation on electoral and party matters, in which the TUC gained increased authority within the NEC and the PLP. A reinvigorated National Joint Council (NJC), composed of the chairman and members of the General Council of the TUC, the NEC and Parliamentary Labour Party (PLP), met monthly to decide a common approach on matters of national importance. From 1934 the NJC was renamed the National Council of Labour (NCL). In the 1930s both joint bodies became important sources of policy pronouncements on defence, foreign policy and relations with the Communist Party.

In particular, the developing collaboration between the TUC and the Labour Party in the early 1930s was seen in the work of the newly-established Policy Committee of the NEC, created in December 1931 to discuss policy matters before consideration by the full NEC. Half of the membership of the Policy Commiittee consisted of trade union representatives. In re-examining economic policy and bringing forward proposals on the reorganisation of industry, finance, local government and social services, its four sub-committees provided opportunities for growing cooperation and consensus between the political moderates, such as Hugh Dalton, Herbert Morrison and the trade union leaders. This collaboration was strengthened by dual exchanges between the NEC Policy Committee and the TUC Economic Committee.[17]

As a result Bevin, Citrine and other trade union leaders developed strong views on the content and style of the programmes to be adopted by a future Labour Government. At the same time suspicions of left-wing intellectuals

16 Bullock, *Life and Times of Ernest Bevin*, i, pp. 531–32.

17 For a discussion of the growing trade union influence in the formation of Labour Party policy, see David Howell, *British Social Democracy* (1980), pp. 48–62; for the role of Dalton and Morrison, see Ben Pimlott, *Hugh Dalton* (1985). pp. 203–24; B. Donaghue and G. W. Jones, *Herbert Morrison: Portrait of a Politician* (1973), pp. 186ff.

persisted, especially, for example, in relation to Stafford Cripps and the activities of the Socialist League in their attempts to influence the direction of party policy firmly leftwards.[18] At the National Council and in speaking out against the Left at the Annual Party Conference, Bevin enjoyed a degree of political independence, since he was not a member of the NEC nor an MP. At the 1932 Leicester Conference, where the main policy recommendations of the NPC for the future party programme were received, Bevin strongly opposed the Socialist League's amendments to nationalise the joint-stock banks. One year later, at Hastings, Bevin challenged the attempt by Cripps to pledge the next Labour Government to take emergency powers to secure a programme of socialist legislation. On a different tack, a small incident is indicative of Bevin's character and manner in his dealings with the National Executive at this time. In July 1933 Bevin, in an outburst of anger about lack of consultation, withheld his union's party membership fees after the former Labour leader, Arthur Henderson, had been selected for the by-election at the safe seat of Clay Cross instead of the TGWU candidate. A few months earlier Bevin had criticised Lansbury for speaking at a Socialist League meeting at the Albert Hall without the permission of the NCL. In reply Lansbury maintained:

> Whenever I feel it is impossible to state the Party's own view I shall of course resign, not merely from the leadership, but from membership; but I do maintain my right to put the Party's case . . . wherever an opportunity occurs, and I do not think I am called upon to ask permission from anybody to do this – and certainly have no intention of doing this.[19]

While opening a Labour Party fête in Gainsborough Town Hall on 9 December 1933 the now seventy-four year old George Lansbury broke his thigh in a serious fall on a balcony step. After an operation, he was in the Manor House Hospital in London for seven months. His accident was one of a number of personal tragedies which beset him during this period. Earlier in the year, on 23 March 1933, Lansbury had suffered the grievous loss of his wife, Bessie, with whom he had had a close and loving relationship during over fifty years of marriage. Bessie had been a devoted and life-time supporter of her husband's political work for socialism and the

---

[18] Bullock, op. cit, pp. 528–33.
[19] Quoted in Postgate, op. cit., p. 288.

labour movement. Their large family of sons and daughters had from their earliest days been politically conscious and active in feminist and socialist causes.[20] Shortly after Lansbury's return to the Labour leadership, his forty-eight-year-old son Edgar died of cancer. Edgar and George Lansbury had been extremely close personally and politically: both, for example, going to prison together during the Poplar Rates Rebellion of 1921.[21]

During his enforced stay in hospital, George Lansbury reflected deeply on his life and political philosophy. He clearly felt his religious faith reaffirmed and renewed and that he had been spared for the particular purpose of continuing his long career as a propagandist and speaker for the labour movement. In a moving account on leaving hospital he declared, 'it is also with a profound sense of gratitude for my recovery and with the conviction that I have been spared only because there is still work for me to do'. Lansbury's specific mission was to devote the remainder of his life to an unremitting fight to achieve democracy through socialism and to secure the abolition of fascism, imperialism and war.[22] At the same time he felt that he had an important contribution to make in influencing the Christian churches to undertake a crusade to eradicate social evils and build a just and fair society.[23]

By the early 1930s the horror of the First World War was an ever more powerful memory and was reflected in an almost universal desire for peace and general resistance to war in this country. In February 1933

[20] In 1913, as a result of their political activities, at least six members of the Lansbury family were in prison or had narrowly avoided imprisonment, George Lansbury, *Looking Backwards and Forwards* (1935), p. 110.

[21] Raymond Postgate, *The Life of George Lansbury* (1951), pp. 289–90, 299; for the Lansburys' family life, see Edgar Lansbury, *My Father* (1934); Daisy Postgate,' A Child in George Lansbury's House', *Fortnightly* 164 (November 1948), pp. 315–22 and (December 1948), pp. 390–94. For the Poplar Rates Rebellion of 1921, see Noreen Branson, *Poplarism, 1919–1925: George Lansbury and the Councillors' Revolt* (1979). I am grateful to members of the Lansbury family: Angela Lansbury and Peter Thurtle gave me interviews about their grandfather and, in particular, Esmé Whiskin, who gave me considerable help and support with this research.

[22] In the late 1930s Lansbury was a prominent member of the Peace Pledge Union and was elected President following the death of its founder, the Rev Dick Sheppard in October 1937. After his resignation as Party Leader, Lansbury undertook a major peace campaign, touring the USA and Europe, including visits to Hitler and Mussolini. For details, see Sybil Morrison, *I Renounce War: The Story of the Peace Pledge Union* (1962); George Lansbury, *My Quest For Peace* (1938). I am grateful to Lord Soper for an interview about his recollections of George Lansbury.

[23] *Daily Herald*, 4 June 1934.

the Oxford University Union had passed the celebrated resolution, 'That this House will in no Circumstances Fight for its King and Country'. A few months later, on 25 October 1933, in the East Fulham by-election, in which Lansbury, Dalton, Morrison and other Labour leaders all campaigned, the pacifist candidate John Wilmot (who was to participate in the debate at Brighton), turned a Conservative majority of 14,521 into a Labour victory of 4,840. At the time, only two weeks after Hitler had broken away from the League and from the Disarmament Conference, this electoral upset was attributed to the voters' overwhelming desire for international peace and disarmament.[24] In June 1935 the League of Nations Union published the results of its private Peace Ballot in this country, the largest opinion poll evertaken by a British peace movement, which demonstrated overwhelming public support for international peace through the collective security of the League of Nations.[25]

Up to the mid 1930s the main aims of Labour Party foreign policy had been to abolish the interrelated evils of capitalism, imperialism and war and to achieve world peace and socialism. There was broad agreement within the party that these could be accomplished through the rejection of secret diplomacy and alliances; by resistance to militarism and rearmament; and by support for the League of Nations to provide international security and achieve general disarmament. Yet by 1933–35 the serious deterioration in the international situation threatened the post-war order based on internationalism and collective security through the League of Nations and exposed the weakness of the League as a peacekeeping organisation. In September 1931 Japan, using bomber seaplanes, beseiged Mukden and began the invasion of Manchuria. Two years later the demise of the Weimar Republic and Hitler's rise to power resulted in German rearmament and the withdrawal of Germany from the League of Nations and from the World Disarmament Conference, which collapsed shortly afterwards.

[24] Tom Stannage, *Baldwin Thwarts the Opposition: The British General Election of 1935* (1980), pp. 69–70. For a detailed analysis of the East Fulham by-election issues, see Martin Ceadel, 'Interpreting East Fulham' in Chris Cook and John Ramsden (ed.), *By-Elections in British Politics* (1978), pp. 118–19.

[25] The Peace Ballot polled over 11.6 million people between the autumn of 1934 and the summer of 1935 asking their opinions on British membership of the League, multilateral disarmament, the private manufacture and sale of armaments, and the abolition of national military and naval aircraft. Nearly 90 per cent of those polled supported economic sanctions against aggressor states, though less than 60 per cent were prepared to approve military measures. James Hinton, *Protests and Visions: Peace Politics in 20th-Century Britain* (1989), pp. 94–99.

During this time the Labour Party foreign policy went through a period of re-examination of pacifism and rearmament, in which the trade union leadership of Bevin and Citrine played a key role with moderates such as Hugh Dalton. While in the main the overall aims of achieving world peace and socialism were maintained, the division in views within the labour movement centred on whether the new fascist regimes should and could be opposed through pacifism and disarmament or whether it would be necessary to resist their aggressive imperialism by economic sanctions backed, if necessary, by the use of military force.[26] Lansbury's return to active political duty coincided with these developments and changes in policy. His pacifist convictions, deepened by his experience during the First World War in pacifist societies such as the No Conscription Fellowship, were no longer shared by large sections of the labour movement and Labour Party.

The differences in part can be explained by the changes in the use of the term 'pacifism'. In the late nineteenth century the longer and etymologically correct version of the term was *pacificism*, which meant opposition to militarism and the attempt to achieve peace through the arbitration and the settlement of international disputes. By the 1930s the shortened form of pacifism was in common usage: it embraced not only pacificism but, in its absolute form, the belief that any resort to war and the use of force *in any circumstances* was morally indefensible and wrong. At the same time, as definitions developed and altered, people's sympathies also changed on this question. By 1935 the proposer of the NEC resolution at Brighton, Dalton, for example, no longer held those views displayed by his membership of the pacifist No More War Movement in the late 1920s.[27]

Against this background, for almost the first time, foreign policy became an important concern of the Labour Party at the the annual party conference. Although the Japanese attack on Manchuria in 1931 received relatively little attention within the Labour ranks, by 1933 the delegates at the Hastings Conference carried Charles Trevelyan's anti-war resolution including the proposition of a general strike by the working-class against international conflict in the future. The Hastings Conference was the first skirmish between the Labour Left and the trade union leaders.

---

[26] John W. Young, 'Idealism and Realism in the History of Labour's Foreign Policy', *Bulletin of the Society for the Study of Labour History*, 50, (Spring 1985), pp. 14–19.

[27] Martin Ceadel, *Pacifism in Britain, 1914–1945: The Defining of a Faith* (Oxford, 1980), pp. 2–6.

Bevin opposed Trevelyan's resolution on the grounds of 'Who and What is there to oppose?', since the fascists had wiped out organised trade unionism in Germany and Italy.

By the summer of 1934 the Labour leadership had renounced Trevelyan's pacifist resolution, in favour of resisting aggression through the collective peace system of the League of Nations. After the 'Three Executives' (the General Council of the TUC, the National Executive Committee and the Parliamentary Labour Party) had discussed the matter, the former Foreign Secretary Arthur Henderson, who remained Secretary of the Labour Party but who had given up the leadership of the Labour Party to Lansbury in October 1932 to devote his time to being President of the World Disarmament Conference, produced the memorandum 'War and Peace' for the National Executive Committee. From his considerable experience of international affairs and his management of the party machine Henderson was able to establish a workable consensus on foreign policy between the TUC and the Labour Party, which rejected a workers' general strike against war for the collective peacekeeping machinery of the League. As a result, this stance became party policy in the document 'For Socialism and Peace' at the Southport Conference in 1934 where, despite his failing health, Henderson made one of the longest speeches delivered at a party conference. In opening the War and Peace debate, he declared:

> I am asking Conference to begin this discussion with the full recognition that in this Conference there is no fundamental difference as to the objective at which we are aiming. May I make it clear that the executive is not putting forward a new policy . . . We are restating Labour's aims and Labour's policy, and indicating the method by which we hope that policy may be applied.[28]

Henderson's speech provided a comprehensive and detailed commentary on the responsibilities and obligations of British membership of the League of Nations. Labour's policy was to work through the collective security system of the League to abolish war, to support international peacekeeping and to promote the peaceful settlement of disputes. Article X of the League Covenant pledged member states were to refrain from aggression against

---

[28] Labour Party, *Report of the 34th Annual Conference* (1934), pp. 153–58. For two recent studies of Henderson, see F. M. Leventhal, *Arthur Henderson* (Manchester, 1990) and Chris Wrigley, *Arthur Henderson* (Cardiff, 1990).

fellow members. Under Article XI the League was bound to take any action to safeguard the peace of nations. Members of the League had to fulfil all the obligations including those of sanctions. By this provision, if the member states comprising its council agreed, the League could impose economic sanctions and take military action following Italy's invasion of the territory of a fellow member of the League, Abysinnia.[29]

'For Socialism and Peace' in 1934 was the final outcome of meetings of the 'Three Executives'. The policy was also put to, and endorsed by, the Annual Congress of the TUC, which met the month before the Labour Party Annual Conference. While 'For Socialism and Peace' was being written Lansbury was ill in hospital. He did attend the 1934 Southport Conference shortly after his return but made no direct contribution to the debate. Shortly before the conference, in a personal letter to the new Labour Party Secretary, Jim Middleton, Lansbury explained his views on international policy:

I feel strongly that those who have drafted the chapters (of 'For Socialism and Peace') should be in charge and will be quite satisfied if the whole thing is taken up without me . . . I think we have been all wrong for centuries. The only path to peace is *not* to fight . . . our people must give up all *right* to hold any other country, renounce all Imperialism and stand unarmed before the world. She will then become the strongest nation in the world, fully armed by justice and love.[30]

At the Brighton Conference, and since then, one of the criticisms made of his leadership was that he kept silent about his position in relation to this latest policy document. Lansbury in fact agreed with Labour Party policy, except for the obligation to support military sanctions under the Covenant of the League of Nations: from the beginning of his leadership, his views as a convinced pacifist against all forms of violence and war were well known. In the months leading up to the Brighton Conference, Lansbury made his position clear on many speaking engagements throughout the country. At Stafford in March 1935, for example, Lansbury urged the churches to act for peace in resisting preparations for war. Two days later,

---

[29] For an analysis of the weakness of the League of Nations as an international peacekeeping organisation, see P. Raffo, *The League of Nations* (1974).

[30] Lansbury to Middleton, 9 August 1934, Middleton Papers, MID 54.

at the Norwich by-election, he revealed his plans for a world economic conference as a preliminary step towards disarmament and peace. The following month Lansbury addressed a gathering of over 3,000 in a 'Victory for Socialism' campaign at Ipswich, where he admitted: 'If I had my way I would stand up before the world unarmed. But that I am told and I know is impracticable. The maintenance of order in a community and in the world is not the result of a show of force but because of the spirit of good behaviour which is in the heart of everyone'.[31]

Prior to the Brighton Conference there was little doubt about the personal position of George Lansbury as party leader. On 19 August Lansbury had written to the *The Times* in a famous letter entitled 'Mr Lansbury's Plea for a Truce of God', in which he called on the Pope and the Archbishops of Canterbury and York to summon a convocation in the Holy Land of all religions to seek world peace through a 'Truce of God'. While expressing sympathy with the spirit behind Lansbury's Christian action in calling for this initiative, the Archbishop of Canterbury urged Christians to support their government in taking such action as would give support to the Covenant of the League. The next day Lansbury responded with a statement to the Press Association in which he claimed that his call for a world economic conference had not been understood: 'Let us remove the causes which lead to armaments'. On 9 September, speaking in a critical by-election in Dumfries, Lansbury made his position clear on the international crisis. At the same time in a press interview he explained:

> During the whole period I have been serving as leader of the Labour party I have made it quite clear that under no circumstances could I support the use of armed force, either by the League of Nations or by individual nations. However anomalous the position may appear to be, it has been accepted by the Parliamentary Party and by the National Executive of the Labour Party.[32]

Lansbury's statement sums up the dilemma he faced, especially in the weeks before the Brighton Conference, when two of his closest friends and supporters made clear their attitude to Labour policy. During September the pacifist Arthur Ponsonby, who had been a long standing associate with Lansbury in the peace movement in the interwar years, gave up

---

[31] *Daily Herald*, 11 and 13 March, 6 April 1935.
[32] *Manchester Guardian*, 9 September 1935.

the leadership of the Labour peers in Parliament.[33] Ponsonby wrote to Lansbury: 'I cannot wait any longer – so here goes. After careful consideration I have thought it best to make the move *before* Brighton. I am sending a copy of my letter to the press'.[34] At the same time Stafford Cripps decided to resign from the NEC. At the meeting which discussed Cripps' resignation, Lansbury raised his own position as leader in relation to the Labour Party's attitude towards the Italo-Abyssinian dispute. He was told that it was a matter for the Parliamentary Party, but that 'in the opinion of the National Executive Committee, *there is no reason why he should tender his resignation*'[35] [emphasis added]

Only a few days before Lansbury had been compelled to attend the TUC Congress at Margate as the fraternal delegate of the Labour Party. There, before the Congress, Lansbury was present at the meeting of the 'Three Executives' which agreed a joint declaration condemning Italian aggression and supporting any action by the League to enforce peace. At the Congress Lansbury was distressed to hear Walter Citrine, the General Secretary of the TUC, tell the delegates that to reject the joint resolution 'will be turning down the deliberate and considered policy of this movement . . . *It will mean turning down George Lansbury*' (*emphasis added*). After this, Citrine had great difficulty in persuading Lansbury, who was by now suffering from a grave crisis of conscience, to address the Congress as party leader without dissenting from official policy.[36] Afterwards, no longer able to reconcile his conscience with his political position, in a private letter to the new Party Secretary, J.S. Middleton, Lansbury appealed:

This note is to say the position at conferences and meetings . . . is quite impossible . . . the question of possible war and preparations for war cannot be dodged or avoided and so we are forced to contradict each other in friendly though painful way. Someone should break the circle. Everybody publicly and . . . privately urges me to continue. My own mind never wavers I should resign . . . cannot they (the NLC) pass a friendly resolution saying the situation is one which must be

33 For Lansbury's support of Ponsonby's Peace Letter in 1926, see Raymond A. Jones, *Arthur Ponsonby: The Politics of Life* (Bromley, 1989), pp. 165–66.

34 Ponsonby to Lansbury, 17 September, *Lansbury Papers*, vol. 28.

35 National Executive Committee, *Minutes*, 19 September 1935.

36 For Citrine's speech and for Lansbury's fraternal address, in which he repeated his call for a world economic conference to settle the Italo-Abysinnian dispute, see *Report of Proceedings at the 67th Annual Trades Union Congress*, 1935.

resolved the party cannot go into a general election with a leader who disagrees with them on so fundamental a question of policy. I should take action myself were it not for the request at meetings and from my colleagues to remain.[37]

Lansbury also told Middleton that he was going to call a meeting of the PLP at the annual conference to settle his position. At this point, the Party Leader made his views clear to the press on military sanctions and prepared to speak out about party policy at the Brighton Conference.[38]

Hugh Dalton opened the morning session of the Italy and Abysinnia debate by moving the five-paragraph resolution of the National Executive Committee. It is worth examining this resolution in some detail, since its main provision of support for *any kind of action* by the League of Nations, was at the heart of the leadership crisis at Brighton. First, the resolution condemned the Italian fascist imperial aggression towards Abysinnia and Mussolini's defiance of the League of Nations. In its third and main paragraph it called on the British Government and other nations 'to use all the necessary measures provided by the Covenant (of the League of Nations) to prevent Italy's unjust and rapacious attack upon the territory of a fellow member of the League'.[39] Firm support by the Brighton Conference was pledged for 'any action consistent with the principles and statutes of the League to restrain the Italian Government and to uphold the authority of the League in enforcing Peace'. In addition, in an attempt to eradicate economic causes of world war generated by imperialism and capitalism, the resolution also proposed that the League should summon a world economic conference to discuss the international control of the sources and supply of raw materials and their more equitable use for all nations.

In speaking in support of the resolution, Dalton pointed out that world attention was focused on the outcome of the proceedings at the Brighton Conference. Aware of the divisions over foreign policy within the Labour leadership, which the debate was to reveal, Dalton paid tribute to the work of both Lansbury and Bevin in pioneering the proposal for a world

[37] Lansbury to Middleton, n.d. September 1935, *Middleton Papers*, MID 54.

[38] For a private memorandum on his position, see 'A Page of History by GL', *Lansbury Papers*, vol. 28.

[39] All quotations from the speeches of Dalton and the other delegates at the Brighton Conference are drawn from Labour Party, *Report of the 35th Annual Conference* (1935).

economic conference. Socialists and trade unionists in other countries were standing firm behind the League of Nations. Above all, Dalton reminded the delegates, support for collective security through the League of Nations was a long-standing tenet of Labour foreign policy: a position which had been recently endorsed by Lansbury and Stafford Cripps. According to Dalton, only a few weeks before, Lansbury had declared in the House of Commons:

> The Labour party will support the Government by every means in its power so long as the Government stand quite firmly by their obligation under the Covenant of the League . . . ever since the League was formed the Labour Party has pinned its faith to the League for the preservation of peace and law and order.

Dalton finished his speech by interpreting the League of Nations Union Peace Ballot as a popular mandate for the Labour Party's foreign policy on the collective security of the League of Nations. By contrast he accused the National Government over its conduct of foreign affairs, in particular over the failure of Ramsay MacDonald and Sir John Simon to take the necessary initiatives at the World Disarmament Conference and at the Stresa Meeting with Mussolini on the reduction of armaments and on the settlement of the Abyssinian question.

Dalton was followed by Stafford Cripps who argued that the successful endorsement of the NEC resolution by the Brighton Conference would only strengthen their opponents in the Conservative Party who dominated the National Government:

> To me the central factor in our decision must turn, not so much upon what we as a country should, or should not, do but who is in control of our actions. I cannot rid my mind of the sordid history of capitalist deception. The empty and hollow excuses of 1914, which I was fool enough to believe, echo through the arguments today, the 'War to End War', the need to fight to save democracy, the cry to crush the foul autocracy of Prussian militarism, all have their counterparts in todays arguments . . . Can we trust the Conservative Party whose criminal record has been so admirably painted by Hugh Dalton, backed by the great industrialists and capitalists who today control the National Government – can we trust them with the lives of the British workers?

For Cripps war was the direct product of the economic conflict generated by international capitalism and imperialism which could only be resisted by the unity and cooperation of socialists throughout the world. As a result, at the Brighton Conference Cripps, who had originally supported the concept of the League of Nations, argued that the organisation was the creation of capitalist governments and an integral part of capitalism and imperialism. Any support for economic or military sanctions by the League against Italy would only commit workers in different countries to a capitalist war machine. Cripps defended the change of views which had brought about his resignation from the National Executive Committee:

> I have been accused of changing my views on this topic. I have changed them, because events have satisfied me that now the League of Nations, with three major Powers outside, has become nothing but *the tool of the satiated imperialist powers*. [emphasis added]

In this way, Cripps clearly told the conference that the endorsement of the NEC resolution would only put the weapon of sanctions in the hands of imperialist governments over which the working class had no control. Even if the Italian fascist dictator was defeated by this strategy, he believed that 'in all probability Mussolini will drive a satisfactory bargain with his fellow-members of the international burglar's union even though they had momentarily turned policemen'. Instead Cripps could only advocate that the labour movement channel its efforts into replacing the National Government with a British Socialist Government.[40]

By this time, the scene was set for the two sides in the debate to present their arguments for and against the NEC resolution. John Marchbank, of the National Union of Railwaymen, noted that Cripps had presented an eloquent critique of capitalism and imperialism which bore little reality to current events in international affairs. Marchbank argued that, from the foundation of the League of Nations, British support for the League Covenant and the public enforcement of sanctions always carried the possibility of the use of armed force and war. In making this point he demonstrated that, two years before, Cripps had advocated the use of sanctions against Japan over the invasion of China. He also quoted the following from Lansbury at that time: 'Some people may think that Great Britain signed the Covenant of the League and did not mean it. I think

[40] For Cripps, see Colin Cooke, *The Life of Richard Stafford Cripps* (1957).

222

we did mean it. If we did not mean that we were going to use these means of stopping or preventing war, I do not know why we signed the Covenant.'

The National Executive position was supported by several other speakers: trade union leaders, Charles Dukes (National Union of General and Municipal Workers), Rhys J. Davies (Distributive and Allied Workers) and John Williams (Miners Federation of Great Britain); as well as Charles Trevelyan and Clement Attlee, who had deputised for Lansbury during his illness. Trevelyan admitted that the obligation to support sanctions against Mussolini was the inescapable outcome of membership of the League and might entail war. Speaking directly for the National Executive and its policy of support for collective security through the machinery of the League, Attlee argued that in the final analysis maintenance of the rule of law in a civilised society depended on the use of force. Aware that Lansbury was still to speak, he added:

I have the greatest respect for Christian pacifists and their ideal. I was very greatly impressed by what Dr Salter said, but in his everyday life he does not practise that. All governments rest in the last resort on the use of force . . . the peace propaganda of Lord Ponsonby goes on in safety because there is force behind it which enforces the rule of law. Miss Lucy Cox is able to preach pacifism because somebody's boy is there, if need be to enforce peace . . . we are in favour of the proper use of force for ensuring the the rule of law. Non-resistance is not a political attitude, it is a personal attitude. I do not believe it is a possible policy for people with responsibility.

In his speech, Attlee referred to the main speakers who had presented the pacifist case before Lansbury addressed the conference. Dr Salter, MP for Bermondsey, proposed the application of Christian pacifist principles of non-resistance and moral persuasion as an alternative to the futility of force and violence. Instead of sanctions Salter suggested that the British Government offered to surrender immediately its colonial possessions to an international regime, as a concrete demonstration to Italy of the peaceful method of settling imperialist disputes. In a classic defence of pacifism he told the Brighton delegates:

The Executive's policy means almost certain and inevitable war . . . You start to fight Italy, and before you know where you are you may be in the middle of a general European, or even a World War . . . and if that happens . . . this Labour Party will have part responsibility if you commit yourself to military sanctions.

At the Brighton Conference only three women had the opportunity to participate in the debate: Dorothy Woodman of the Wood Green and Southgate Labour Party, Lucy Cox and Helen Bentwich who were the prospective parliamentary candidates for Pudsey and Otley and for Harrow. Woodman emphasised that pacifist principles could no longer be applied in a world changed by the rise of the fascist dictators. Instead support for the League of Nations and sanctions provided an excellent opportunity for the Labour Party to campaign for international solidarity with socialists throughout the world. Bentwich took up this theme: three weeks before she had been present in Geneva at the League when the British Foreign Secretary, Sir Samuel Hoare, had made his famous speech committing the Conservative-dominated National Government to the League of Nations, which, she declared, not only stole Labour's policy but was the best piece of electioneering propaganda any government could have. On the other side, in opposing the Executive policy, Cox poured scorn on the notion that Mussolini was a megalomaniac. Instead she saw the dispute as an economic problem associated with capitalism and the effects of the First World War:

> Those of us who represent the pacifist point of view at this conference ask now that we should take the opportunity of using the League of Nations to solve those economic questions that are not only the question of Japan or the question of Italy; but are questions of the whole world.

Late on the Tuesday afternoon, to the accompaniment of loud and prolonged applause and the singing of 'For he's a Jolly Good Fellow', George Lansbury addressed the conference with an impassioned and open-hearted speech on his dilemma as a Christian pacifist and Leader of the Labour Party. From the outset he admitted his difficulties on a major and fundamental point of policy. Lansbury readily agreed that, in these circumstances, his deeply held convictions were irreconcilable with his position as party leader:

> My only difficulty, and it is a real one, is my relationships with the Party . . . I agree with the position of those of my friends

who think that it is quite intolerable that you should have a man speaking as Leader who disagrees fundamentally on an issue of this kind . . . And I want to say that I should not consider an expression of opinion [by the Brighton Conference] hostile to my continuance as Leader as anything more than natural and perfectly friendly. I hope that statement will make it absolutely clear where I stand . . .

Lansbury also dealt directly with his 'Jekyll and Hyde position', explaining that he had always attempted to represent the views of the party when speaking as Leader, as for example, to the Foreign Secretary, Sir Samuel Hoare. The remainder of his speech was a clear statement of the pacifist views he had held since boyhood. He found it morally indefensible to advocate peaceful methods to the labour movement in domestic politics but to support the use of force in foreign affairs: 'I believe that force never has and never will bring permanent peace and permanent goodwill in the world . . . I have no right to preach pacifism to starving people in this country and preach something else in relation to people elsewhere'.

As an absolute Christian pacifist, Lansbury gave as his reasons that his religion taught that those 'who lived by the sword, shall perish by the sword'. His experience demonstrated that the First World War and the Treaty of Versailles had not ended the horror of total war conflict nor made the world safe for democracy by the reduction of the level of armaments. As an alternative, to serve as a moral example of practical Christian values to the rest of the world, Lansbury brought forward his remarkable proposition that, as well disarming unilaterally, this country should renounce imperialism by placing its colonial resources under the control of an international commission:

I would go to them [at Geneva] and say . . . that Great Britain – the great imperialist race – led by the common people of our race were [sic] finished with imperialism, that we were willing that all the peoples under our flag, wherever you can establish Government, should be free to establish their own Governments . . . that the whole of our resources . . . should be pooled for the service of mankind . . . under the positive control of an International Commission.

In this respect Lansbury clearly answered the critics who claimed he was inconsistent in his views. Inside and outside Parliament, he had always

225

been passionately anti-imperialist, supporting nationalist causes in Ireland, Egypt, India and elsewhere in the world against the tyranny of colonialism. In announcing the programme he was to campaign on following his return to the leadership, he had emphasised to the British people: 'There must be no mistake about this [the abolition of imperialism]. If we are to have peace in the world Imperialism must go and be replaced by a Commonwealth of brothers'.[41]

At Brighton Lansbury stressed to his audience the essential connection between the ending of imperialism and the securing of world peace. He also suggested that his days were numbered as Party Leader: 'It may be that I shall not meet you on this platform any more. [cries of "No"] . . . It may well be that in carrying out your policy I shall be in your way'. Finally Lansbury answered the charge that he had acted irresponsibly as Party Leader, in the line he had taken, by a simple restatement of his Christian pacifism:

> If mine were the only voice in the conference, I would say, in the name of the faith I hold, the belief that God intends us to live peacefully and quietly with one another. If some people do not allow us to do so, I am ready to stand as the early Christians did, and say, "This is our faith, this is where we stand, and, if necessary, this is where we will die'.

Immediately after Lansbury had finished, Bevin, who always sat with his trade union delegation in the main body of the conference hall, walked directly to the platform. The *New Statesman and Nation* noted that his bulky figure and aggressive manner had long made him a conspicuous personality at Labour Party conferences. His reply was in stark contrast to Lansbury's speech, which Bevin could see had been received in the Dome with great popularity at the end of the day.[42] He immediately launched into Lansbury's conflict of loyalties between personal conscience and political party by accusing him of betrayal. In one of most infamous and cruel taunts heard by delegates at an annual party conference Bevin raged in anger: 'It is placing the Executive and the Movement in an absolutely wrong position to be *taking your conscience*

41 *Daily Herald*, 4 June 1934.
42 *The New Statesman and Nation*, 5 October 1935.

round from body to body asking to be told what you ought to do with it'.[43]

Behind this invective was Bevin's seething sense of outrage of a man who had spent a lifetime in the labour movement fighting for, and keeping, agreements. He thundered angrily that the trade unions had been betrayed by the leadership shown by Lansbury in not abiding by decisions in the policy document 'For Socialism and Peace' but had, late in the day, publicly declared his dissent directly to the Press Association: 'When you work on a Committee and you have to take collective responsibility, there is a standard in the Trade Union Movement which we all follow. In this world loyalty to a decision gives less publicity than disloyalty under certain circumstances'.

Bevin explained how the policy on war and peace had been the product of joint collaboration in the NCL between the TUC and the Labour Party and endorsed by the meeting of the 'Three Executives' at Margate, but at no point had unilateral disarmament been mentioned. He chided those who had opposed the NEC resolution at Brighton for not speaking out the previous year at the Southport Conference. In this respect, a key part of Bevin's attack was directed at Stafford Cripps, whom he castigated for failing to turn up at the main meeting of the 'Three Executives' at Margate and for resigning just before the conference:

People have been on this platform talking about the destruction of capitalism. The middle classes are not doing too badly as a whole under capitalism and Fascism. The thing that is being wiped out is the Trade Union Movement . . . It is we who are being wiped out and who will be wiped out if Fascism comes here . . . All the speeches that have been made against this resolution ought to have been made last

---

[43] *1935 Report*, p. 178. In some accounts Bevin accused Lansbury of '*hawking his conscience*'; see, for example, J. T. Murphy, *Labour's Big Three* (1946), p. 184. At the time, where the accusation was directly reported, most of the daily newspapers printed a similar version to the official report, except for the *Observer* on the following weekend which used 'hawking'; see *Observer*, 6 October 1935. Esmé Whiskin, Lansbury's granddaughter, who was at the Brighton Conference, in interviews with the author in 1989–90 recalled that Bevin may have used the term '*carting* his conscience'. Bevin's colleague, Citrine (who was not at the conference but on a visit to Russia), accurately summed up the charge of 'hawking his conscience': 'It was a cruel . . . unnecessarily brutal assault on a man who was certainly no hypocrite and had served the Labour movement well'. Lord Citrine, *Men and Work* (1964), p. 352.

year at Southport, and the people who oppose this resolution ought to have had the courage of their convictions and tabled a resolution at this Conference to the effect that we should withdraw from the League of Nations.

Bevin's speech went to the heart of the historic relationship between the trade union and labour movement and the political leadership of the Labour Party. Since its foundation, as the Labour Representation Committee (LRC), the Labour Party had always been a broad church but it had been essentially a trade union party which socialists joined. In a famous, often-quoted remark, Bevin reminded the delegates of this: 'I want to say this to our friends who have joined us in this political movement, that our predecessors formed this party. It was not Keir Hardie who formed it, it grew out of the bowels of the Trades Union Congress'.

Bevin ended his speech on the theme of loyalty, by recalling the contribution of the TUC in serving on the NCL. By contrast he linked the actions of Lansbury, Cripps and the other dissenters to that of Ramsay MacDonald in 1931 and urged the delegates to give an almost unanimous vote for the NEC resolution on the next day. Lansbury tried to respond but, with the microphones switched off, could only shout a few brief points. No member of the NEC went to Lansbury's rescue; only Morrison sympathetically (according to Lansbury's biographer) said to him on leaving the platform, 'Stand by your beliefs, George'.[44]

The strength and tone of Bevin's speech had effectively ended the debate. Although several delegates participated on the second day, which included an impressive speech by Philip Noel Baker, the parliamentary candidate for Coventry, it was left to Herbert Morrison to wind up for the NEC with a conciliatory speech, in which he revealed that he had opposed the First World War. Morrison was, however, no different to virtually every delegate who had supported the NEC resolution, which was carried overwhelmingly at the end of the two-day debate. Nearly all had previously held some kind of pacifist position, either in the First World War or in the years before the Brighton Conference. Only Lansbury and his small group of supporters, who shared his views on war and peace, had not altered their position by the mid 1930s. The following week Lansbury offered his resignation at the meeting of the Parliamentary Labour Party

[44] Postgate, op. cit., p. 304.

that he had called before the Brighton Conference. Remarkably, even then, as Parliament reassembled for the new session, his fellow MPs refused at first to allow him to relinquish the leadership by thirty eight votes to seven with five abstentions, until Lansbury finally insisted.

Lansbury's resignation did not bring to an end his long and eventful political career. He remained an active politician identified with the peace movement inside and outside parliament. As a prominent member of the Peace Pledge Union Lansbury was elected president following the death in 1937 of its founder, Dick Sheppard. Though nearly eighty years of age he devoted himself in his last years to a major international crusade to prevent the outbreak of war by peace journeys to the USA and Europe, including personal visits to Hitler and Mussolini.[45] Nor did the Brighton Conference immediately settle the matter of the Labour leadership or difficulties within the party over defence and foreign policy. Fifteen days later, Stanley Baldwin seized the opportunity to call the 1935 General Election, which the Labour Party fought with Attlee as a caretaker leader. At Bow and Bromley Lansbury achieved a resounding victory, polling 19,064 votes to his Conservative opponent's 5,707. In the new House of Commons the Labour Opposition to the Conservative dominated National Government increased to 154 MPs, including the return of prominent individuals, such as Dalton, Morrrison and Clynes. In the ensuing election contest between Attlee, Morrison and Greenwood, Attlee finally won on the second ballot.[46] Yet while the Labour Party had elected a new leader it was still bedevilled by policy divisions, especially in its attitude to rearmament. New threats to international peace were posed by Hitler's remilitarisation of the Rhineland and the outbreak of the Spanish Civil War. The Brighton Conference had given unambiguous and clear support to the League of Nations, including the use of military force if necessary, but the Parliamentary Labour Party continued to oppose Conservative arms estimates in the Commons. Not till July 1937 did the Parliamentary Labour Party, by a narrow majority of forty-five votes to thirty-nine, decide to abstain on the arms estimates. At the Labour Party Conference at Bournemouth Lansbury was again part of a small minority who opposed the statement *International Policy and Defence*, prepared by Dalton for the National

[45] Lansbury wrote regularly on peace issues in the *Tribune* newspaper during most of 1937. For his account of his two peace journeys to Hitler and Mussolini, see *Tribune*, 30 April, 23 July 1937.

[46] Kenneth Harris, *Attlee* (1982), pp. 120–22.

Council of Labour and endorsed both by the TUC and by 1937 Labour Party Conference. By this vote, the Labour Party finally gave a clear signal that it supported a policy of rearmament to face the threat of war in Europe.[47]

[47] For the role of Dalton and Bevin in changing Labour policy on rearmament, see Ben Pimlott, *Hugh Dalton* (1985), pp. 234–35, 241–42; Henry Pelling, *A Short History of the Labour Party* (1972), pp. 81–82. For the influence of the Spanish Civil War on Labour Party foreign policy, see Michael Foot, *Aneurin Bevan, 1879–1945* (1982), pp. 220–38, 252–56. I am grateful to Michael Foot for an interview about George Lansbury.

11

The Intercity Bus and its Competitors in the United States in the Mid Twentieth Century

Margaret Walsh

In 1976 Charles A. Webb, president of the National Association of Motor Bus Owners (NAMBO), reported in his decennial message to members of his trade association that the intercity bus industry was losing out in the American transportation network. The bus industry would soon be crippled because Amtrak, the rail corporation recently subsidised by the federal government, was able not only to alter its fares without government permission, but could also maintain these fares at very low levels. The message was familiar. Since the start of Amtrak's operations in 1971 the bus industry had been well aware that its livelihood, not only on routes in direct competition with Amtrak trains but also throughout the country, was threatened. NAMBO thus campaigned against the continuing multi-billion dollar subsidisation of a declining form of transportation which was not essential other than in a few areas. [1]

[1] National Association of Motor Bus Owners (formerly National Association of Motor Bus Operators) [hereafter NAMBO], *1926–1976: One Half Century of Service to America* (Washington D.C., 1976), pp. 6–10; *Bus Ride*, 8, 2 (1972), pp. 23–26; U.S. Department of Transportation, *1974 National Transportation Report* (Washington D.C., 1975), pp. 306–9. Acknowledgements: I should like to thank the Nuffield Foundation and the School of Social Sciences, University of Birmingham for their financial support in undertaking research for this article. I should also like to thank George A. Rossman for allowing me access to Laurence A. Rossman's papers, Louis N. Zelle and Charles A. Zelle for access to Edgar F. Zelle's papers and William A. Luke for access to his collection of bus materials. These private collections of materials have been essential in extending my knowledge of the bus industry in the United States.

Some fifty years earlier, when NAMBO was founded in 1926, carriers were also complaining about unfair competition. This time the railroads voiced their opinions about the indirect subsidies received by motor carriers in the form of lack of regulation and inadequate taxation. Having emerged from the First World War as the only viable form of long-distance transport for passengers and freight and being accustomed to their centrality in the nation's transport system they felt threatened by the sudden presence of both buses and trucks which were already cutting into their local and regional traffic. *Railway Age*, the railroad trade journal, frequently voiced the opinions of irate rail officials as they called for government assistance. The comparative novelty of highway traffic was then responsible for the highly defensive position of the railroads in the mid 1920s.[2]

The continuing uneasy relationship between the railroads and the buses, and then after the Second World War between these two public carriers and the airlines, reflected more than the competitive nature of commercial passenger transport in a free enterprise economy. It revealed the marked preference of Americans to drive their own automobiles and the hesitancy of the federal government to establish a national transportation policy. Caught between these cross currents neither of the earlier forms of passenger transport, the railroads or the buses, was able to enter the last quarter of the twentieth century in a healthy position. Though both had shown initiative and enterprise in obtaining and retaining passengers and had even ventured into some cooperative schemes, they both carried only a meagre fraction of the travelling public by 1976. The middle years of the twentieth century witnessed the decline of commercial surface transport in the United States.[3]

The statistics of the intercity passenger service provide essential background for understanding the competitive travel patterns of the United States. In 1910 railroad statistics were the only figures worthy of note. With 240,831 miles of railroad track in operation rails provided a network capable of bringing the nation together. In the second decade of the century, however, the automobile, now being mass produced, became

[2] *Railway Age* [hereafter *RA*], 74–81 (1923–26).

[3] For historical surveys of the individual transport modes see J.B. Rae, *The Road and the Car in American Life* (Cambridge, Mass., 1971); B.B. Crandall, *The Growth of the Intercity Bus Industry* (Syracuse, N.Y., 1954); J.F. Stover, *American Railroads* (Chicago, 1961); R.E. Bilstein, *Flight in America* (Baltimore, 1984). For a survey which covers all aspects of transport see D.P. Locklin, *Economics of Transportation* (Homewood, Ill., 7th ed., 1972).

more readily available; in the 1920s it became almost commonplace with one car per 6.6 persons. By this time two of the car's hybrids, the bus and the truck, had emerged as vehicles in their own right and even the plane was offering some pioneering passenger service. By 1929 when figures for the distribution of intercity travel become available, the train had already lost out to the automobile, though it retained its dominance in the public service sector. (See Table 3) For the next forty-five years, except during the petrol shortage of the Second World War, the private car accounted for over 80 per cent of domestic intercity travel. By 1976 the once mighty train was reduced to 0.7 per cent, its surface rival the bus claiming 1.7 per cent, while their joint rival the aeroplane had climbed to 10.5 per cent. Most Americans preferred to or chose to travel by land and here the individualistic car was paramount. Even when considering the public sector by itself, travelling Americans soon moved to the airlines when the faster and more comfortable jet plane became available. Trains and buses had a limited and often captive market.[4]

Railroad and bus operators were well aware of the advantages of alternative modes of transport as well as of their own strengths and weaknesses. Yet they were not always free to choose how best to run their businesses. Despite Americans' loud and vigorous defence of laissez-faire, or since the 1930s, of a modified laissez-faire policy, the twentieth century has been marked by large-scale and continuing government intervention in the economy. The transportation sector has been no exception. Already at the turn of the century the railroads were subject to federal regulation. The emergency of the First World War brought government operation of the railroads in the name of efficiency. They were subsequently returned to private ownership, but still subject to regulation. Yet by then railroads no longer held a monopoly over long-distance movement of either passengers or freight. The advent of motor vehicles brought vigorous competition, but these vehicles were not yet subject to federal government regulation. Moreover they and the new airlines were receiving developmental subsidies in the shape of federal highway grants and airmail contracts. Even after motor vehicles and airlines became subject to federal regulation in 1935 and 1938, federal money continued to be poured into creating an interstate road system and a skyway of marked

[4] B.J. Wattenburg, Intro., *The Statistical History of the United States: From Colonial Times to the Present* (New York, 1976), Chapter Q 'Transportation', pp. 703–74; Frank A. Smith, comp., *Transportation in America: Historical Compendium, 1939–1985* (Washington D.C., 1986), pp. 8–15.

Table 3

Intercity Travel in the United States by Mode
(Billions of Passenger Miles, 1929–1976)

| YEAR | TOTAL INTERCITY TRAVEL | | PRIVATE CARRIER | | | | | | PUBLIC CARRIER | | | | | | | |
| | | | TOTAL (1) | | AUTOMOBILE | | AIR | | TOTAL (1) | | RAILROADS | | BUSES | | AIRLINES | |
	AMOUNT	%	AMOUNT	%	AMOUNT	%	AMOUNT	%	AMOUNT	%(2)	AMOUNT	%	AMOUNT	%	AMOUNT	%
1929	216	100	175	81.1	175	81.1	–	–	40.9	18.9	32.5	15.0	7.1	3.3	–	–
1934	219	100	191	87.2	191	87.2	–	–	27.5	12.7	18.8	8.6	7.4	3.4	0.2	0.1
1939	310	100	275.4	88.8	275.4	88.8	–	–	35.4	11.0	23.7	7.7	9.5	3.1	0.7	0.2
1944	311	100	181.4	58.3	181.4	58.3	–	–	129.4	41.4	97.7	31.4	27.3	8.8	2.2	0.7
1949	478	100	410.2	85.8	409.4	85.6	0.8	0.2	68.7	14.2	36.0	7.5	24.0	5.0	7.3	1.5
1954	669	100	598.5	89.6	597.1	89.4	1.4	0.2	71.1	10.4	29.5	4.4	22.0	3.3	17.9	2.7
1959	764	100	689.5	90.4	687.4	90.1	2.1	0.3	75.2	9.6	22.4	2.9	20.4	2.7	30.4	4.0
1964	895	100	805.5	90.2	801.8	89.8	3.7	0.4	89.4	9.8	18.4	2.1	22.7	2.5	45.5	5.1
1969	1,134	100	985.8	86.9	977.0	86.1	8.8	0.8	148.3	13.1	12.3	1.1	24.9	2.2	111.1	9.8
1974	1,307	100	1,133.1	86.7	1,121.9	85.9	11.2	0.9	173.6	13.3	10.5	0.8	27.7	2.1	135.4	10.4
1976	1,460	100	1,271.7	87.1	1,259.6	86.3	12.1	0.8	187.9	12.9	10.5	0.7	25.1	1.7	152.3	10.5

Source: National Association of Motor Bus Operators, *Bus Facts*, xxxiv (1966), p. 6, 8 and Frank A. Smith, *Transportation in America, Historical Compendium 1939–1985* (Washington D.C., 1986), p. 12.

(1) Percentage do not always sum to 100 because of rounding up. (2) Includes Waterways as well as Railroads, Buses and Airlines.

routes with adequate airports. Though recognising that the alternative modes of transport were receiving differential treatment the federal government was slow to consider a national policy which could reflect each of their inherent advantages and serve the public interest. Even when such policy was discussed it was subject to both political and economic pressure groups and remained more an an illusion than a reality. Facing both government intervention, and on some issues lack of intervention, buses and their main commercial rival, trains, fared less well as the century progressed.[5]

There was little if any thought given to federal regulation when bus service first emerged in the decade 1910–20. Then numerous entrepreneurs all over the country were seizing the opportunity to participate in an exciting new venture with low entry costs. Having acquired an automobile sedan they took passengers to work or to visit, loading on the streets or at a hotel or store. There were no definite routes or schedules until a payload was established and then an advertisement in the local newspaper or store was sufficient. Gradually individual or family enterprises took root. Though lacking experience in the transport business, the more ambitious entrepreneurs set up longer and more regular services, either undercutting or amalgamating with nearby competitors. Having made enough money to buy more reliable, comfortable and purpose-built vehicles, they were poised to move into regional operations. As early as 1924 the trade journal *Bus Transportation* proclaimed that the bus industry had emerged from its infancy to reach adolescence.[6]

These developments had not gone unnoticed by the railroads. While most rail managers were preoccupied with their own problems of rising operating costs, increased taxes, regulatory interference and a shortage of capital to invest, they recognised the threat of increased financial problems if the buses took away from their passenger revenue. The new motor competition was regarded as unfair. Bus operators did not maintain their own highways,

[5] For a general survey of government intervention see B.L. Jones, 'Government Management of the Economy', in *Encyclopedia of American Economic History* ed. G. Porter (New York, 1980), 2, pp. 808–31. For specific government intervention in the transport sector see Locklin, pp. 222–337; H.S. Norton, *Modern Transportation Economics* (Columbus, Ohio, 1963), pp. 179–380; J.C. Nelson, *Railroad Transportation and Public Policy* (Washington D.C., 1959), pp. 67–110.

[6] M. Walsh, 'The Early Growth of Long-Distance Bus Transport in the United States', in *The Economic and Social Effects of the Spread of Motor Vehicles* ed. T.C. Barker (London, 1987), pp. 81–87; *Bus Transportation*, [hereafter *BT*] 3, 1 (1924), pp. 6–8.

they paid small licence fees and were free to set whatever fares the market would bear. With low entry costs and relatively few operating costs, other than the acquisition of vehicles, their rates were frequently lower than those of the railroads. What could or should the railroads do?[7]

Externally they could press for state government regulation or more stringent state regulation. Already by the mid 1920s some state governments witnessing the rapid increase in highway transport, particularly by automobiles, had recognised the need to finance improved roads and to establish some basic guidelines for their use. Early general laws licensing vehicles and requiring driver insurance and competence were strengthened by more specific and stringent legislation which encompassed economic issues such as competition and fares. Nineteen states had motor bus regulation by 1922. Three years later there were thirty-six, including all the most heavily populated states. Regulations varied widely, but most state governments insisted that buses as public utilities should be subject to laws protecting passengers from unnecessary and inefficient lines, high charges, unsafe vehicles and inexperienced drivers. Ironically newly established bus operators themselves often supported legislation because it protected their businesses from being undercut by 'fly-by-night' venturers.[8]

Railroads did more than lobby for more effective legislation and regulation. Internally they offered improved facilities and cut rail fares. Improvements included increased speeds, changes in scheduling to meet the new road competition and more comfortable rail coaches. Passengers might then prefer to travel by train when given the choice. Even more passengers might stay on the trains if the fares dropped. While it proved difficult to reduce regular scheduled fares, it was possible to offer special fares: excursion rates to resort areas, weekend round trips or cut rates to suit specific groups of workers. There might also be some temporary general reductions as an incentive to stay on the rails. Such positive efforts did have a small impact on the immediate declining revenues of the railroads, but could not prevent net passenger revenue from falling over a longer period.[9]

[7] 'Great Northern Railway Manuscript', Ralph and Muriel Hidy Papers (James J. Hill Library, St Paul, Minnesota), II, 7, pp. 2–3; *RA*, 81, 13 (1926), pp. 599–601.

[8] M. Walsh, 'The Motor Carrier Act of 1935: The Origins and Establishment of Federal Regulation of the Inter-State Bus Industry in the United States', *The Journal of Transport History*, 3rd ser. 8 (1987), pp. 66–73.

[9] Great Northern Railway Manuscript, II, 7, pp. 4–8; Interstate Commerce Commission [hereafter ICC] 'Co-ordination of Motor Transportation', *Report*, 182, (1932), p. 330; R. W. Hidy et. al., *The Great Northern Railway* (Boston, Mass., 1988), pp. 176–77.

Taking a more negative and defensive stance railroads also moved to obstruct the development of independent bus companies. Most of the new state regulations governing motor carriers came under the jurisdiction of either the Public Utilities Board or the Railroad Commission, who now set up a Motor Carrier or an Auto Transportation Company Division, often staffed by officials who were used to thinking like railroad men. It could become difficult for bus companies to obtain operating certificates. In Iowa, for example, the Red Ball Transportation Company faced the opposition of four railroads and two interurban railways before obtaining a licence. Though this case was famous because the company was run by a woman, Helen Schultz, the 'Iowa Bus Queen', this was not an isolated incident.[10] In the 1920s the Iowa Board of Railroad Commissioners frequently heard objections from railroads like the Rock Island and the Chicago, Milwaukee and St Paul to the establishment or extension of a bus line. In neighbouring Minnesota the Railroad and Warehouse Commission also heard written and verbal objections from major railroads with tracks in the state.[11]

It was not surprising that legal representation should be made about the new competition which the railroads deemed unnecessary. This the bus operators expected. What was more difficult to counteract was the continuing pressure which was placed on state officials to favour the railroads. Again in Iowa, the head of the Highway Commission, an old Northwestern Railroad man, is said to have done much to hinder the growth of truck and bus companies by promoting curved roads and narrow bridges.[12] Rail lobbyists there frequently plied their local state representatives and the chairmen of important committees with information about the unfairness of their operating costs and taxes in comparison to those of the buses and trucks, who neither built roads nor maintained them nor held property and had earnings on which they were taxed. Due to this powerful railroad influence it seems at times that

[10] *BT*, 3, 12 (1924), p. 573; 4, 7 (1925), p. 358; *Mason City Globe Gazette*, 13 June 1930, *Des Moines Tribune*, 13 June 1930, *Sioux City Tribune*, 14 June 1930 (Clippings File, E.F. Zelle Collection, Jefferson Lines, Minneapolis). Zelle was president of the Jefferson Transportation Company and a major figure in the national bus industry.

[11] *Waterloo Tribune*, 13 February 1930, (Clippings File, Zelle Collection); Minnesota Railroad and Warehouse Commission, Auto Transportation Company Division, *Biennial Report*, 1926.

[12] Interview with L. N. Zelle, former president of Jefferson Lines Inc., by M. Walsh, Minneapolis, 8 October 1990.

some motor taxation was imposed for reasons of competition rather than for raising essential revenue.[13]

Not all railroads were negative about their bus competitors. Some company presidents realised that the real threat to their declining passenger revenue was the automobile. After all in 1929 there were 23 million cars registered in the United States in contrast to 48,000 buses in common carrier service. Many ex-rail passengers were driving their own cars. Yet even here the new road transport had beneficial effects on rail revenues. The automotive industries were responsible for a large increase in freight revenue, to the tune of some 3.6 million carloads in 1929. As for the buses themselves, these rail men recognised that they were a different form of transport having particular advantages of low capital costs, economy of operation and flexibility of route. Bus companies had, to a certain extent, created their own new business rather than taking it away from the railroads. They had not only found passengers in those areas where there were no rail tracks, but had also stimulated more people to travel nationwide. Futhermore buses could even be an asset to railroads facing problems of unprofitable local services which they were required to maintain. Some railroad managers saw they could cut losses on local passenger trains, which had previously been cross-subsidised by the more profitable long-distance services, if they substituted buses run at a fifth of the cost of the local train.[14]

Seeing the potential of the motor bus, constructive managers of major railroads like the New Haven, New York and Hartford, the Pennsylvania, the Boston and Maine or the Great Northern moved to coordinate transport by establishing bus subsidiaries. While only three railroads were engaged in bus transport at the beginning of 1925, a year later thirty-one companies operated nearly 350 buses and forty-two more railroads had plans to follow suit. Some of these railroads established bus routes paralleling their rail lines, some substituted buses for rail service on branch lines while some used buses as feeders through territory not served by rails. Bus subsidiaries could be useful revenue savers for railroads facing mounting operating costs. Indeed

[13] 'Iowa Legislative Data relating to Bus Tax Reduction, 1933, Iowa Motor Passenger Carrier Correspondence, 1933, (Zelle Collection); *BT*, 10, 3 (1931), pp. 135–38; L.A. Rossman, "Why Pay Tribute to the Railroads?" (An Address subsequently published as a booklet) (Grand Rapids, Minnesota, 1932) (L.A. Rossman Collection, Grand Rapids, Minnesota). Rossman was a newspaper editor and a consultant to the bus industry.

[14] *BT*, 3, 2 (1924), pp. 64–66; 5, 5 (1926), pp. 277–79; L.A. Rossman, 'Motor Bus Transportation' (Typescript, 26 February 1930), pp. 1–19 and L.A. Rossman, 'Rail and Motor Coach Transportation' (Proof copy of a booklet, Grand Rapids, Minnesota, 1935), p. 11 (Rossman Collection).

by 1929 sixty-two steam railroad companies ran 1,256 buses over 16,793 miles of route.[15]

While some railroad managers might see bus subsidiaries as a blessing, their independent bus rivals saw them as a heavy-handed means of retaining railroad dominance in intercity pasenger service. The bare statistics do not support the bus men's fears in that railroads only owned 3.4 per cent of the buses in operation and only controlled 5.48 per cent of bus route miles at the beginning of 1929. Nevertheless bus men reasoned that railroads were able to inject capital, personnel and transport expertise into a fledgling industry which they would then take over and use as an adjunct to their existing business. Bus entrepreneurs preferred their industry to remain a separate entity which made good use of the highways and offered convenience, economy, comfort and safety as well as tapping a new leisure market. The bus was not destined to be a substitute or a subsidiary.[16] 'It is part of a great system of transportation, a unit, a definite independent, growing sound element in national life.'[17]

Reacting to both the antagonism of the railroads and the establishment of bus subsidiaries as well as envisaging a variety of opportunities within their own industry, bus entrepreneurs consolidated lines in the late 1920s and sought to build up a regional network and then a national bus network. When in 1928 a transcontinental bus service was pieced together a new threshold was attainable. The following year the future of long-distance bus travel looked even more promising. Then the Motor Transit Company, soon to be called the Greyhound Corporation, amalgamated several companies with routes in forty-one out of the forty-eight states. The presence of the Greyhound Corporation became a stabilising element in the growth of the motor bus industry into young adulthood. The new company set high standards and helped establish some advanced practices of management, accounting, traffic-flow analysis and technical efficiency.[18] It also foreshadowed the future structure of the intercity industry in terms of a core of one or two large operations surrounded by numerous small scale carriers.

[15] *BT*, 4, 7 (1925), pp. 357–78; 4, 9 (1925), pp. 462–63; 4, 10 (1925), pp. 482–84; *RA*, 80, 25 (1926), pp. 1401–4; 86, 17 (1929), p. 998; 87, 8 (1929), pp. 492–97; 88, 25 (1930), pp. 1509–13; *Bus Facts* for 1927, p. 7; *Bus Facts* for 1929, p. 5.

[16] *BT*, 8, 2 (1929), p. 82; Rossman, 'Motor Bus Transportation', p. 17.

[17] The Greyhound Lines, 'Motor Bus Transportation' (Chicago, n.d.), p. 13 (Rossman Collection).

[18] Walsh, 'The Early Growth of Long-Distance Bus Transport', pp. 86–87; L.A. Rossman, 'Memorandum Concerning some Financial Aspects of Intercity Motor Bus Transportation' (Grand Rapids, Minnesota, 24 December 1938), pp. 11–13 (Rossman Collection).

Railroads faced the challenge of the burgeoning long-distance national bus industry in some of the worst years the American economy experienced. Business conditions in the 1930s were abysmal. Already in serious difficulties the railroads could not afford to let this new challenge go without fighting to preserve their share of the commercial passenger trade. Yet their tactics of the 1920s had not proved to be very successful. While train travel was faster and more comfortable than bus travel, it was more expensive and in a depression the cost of a fare became much more important when deciding how to move. Railroads needed some means of offering more competitive prices. They thus looked for further subsidies for their passenger operations from their freight earnings.[19] Between 1931 and 1937 the railroads cut their fares by more than one-third, dropping them from 3.06 cents per mile to 1.95 cents per mile. This sharp reduction was meant not just to embarrass competing modes of transport, but to destroy them. Bus operators responded in kind. Given the diversified nature of the bus industry in its early years there are no average figures for fares. However, evidence from a large diversified bus operation, whose prices fell from 2.52 cents per passenger mile in 1931 to 1.54 cents in 1937, indicates substantial price competition.[20] Bus operators were not about to be driven out of business by railroads.

How did they survive competition in the midst of a major depression? Many small carriers collapsed when their revenues fell because fewer people could afford to travel. The number of bus companies fell from 3,140 in 1931 to a low of 1,790 in 1937 and bus miles fell from 1.02 billion to 0.9 billion in the same years. But passenger miles did not show the same decline, dropping from the 6.7 billion of 1931 in the two years immediately following and then increasing to reach 10.0 billion in 1937. Reductions in fares did not destroy highway transportation. Rather the industry experienced a painful reorganisation which eventually left it in a better condition to compete. The stronger companies improved maintenence, facilities and equipment and sought out new business, taking care to advertise their services in the local and national media. They modernised their operating procedures and even adopted some new marketing strategies. The smaller companies attempted to stay in business by searching out non-competitive markets.[21] With the economy in poor condition the buses were able to take some passengers

[19] L. A. Rossman, 'Rail and Motor Coach Transportation' (Proof Copy of Booklet, Grand Rapids, Minnesota, 1 July 1935), pp. 1–17 (Rossman Collection); L. S. Lyon, V. Abramson and Associates, *Government and Economic Life* (Washington D. C., 1940), 2, pp. 835–38.

[20] Rossman, 'Memorandum Concerning some Financial Aspects', p. 5.

[21] Walsh, 'The Early Growth of Long-Distance Bus Transport', pp. 87–88; Crandall, pp. 280–82.

away from the trains and to provide a service for those Americans who could not afford to run a car.

Railroad and bus companies did not compete for passengers in a vacuum. The federal government watched their contest and eventually intervened. Concern for the decline in rail revenues not only from passenger trade, but also more importantly from freight traffic, had alarmed the federal government from the late 1920s. For over forty years interstate railroads had been subject to federal regulation which was concerned primarily with protecting the public from discriminatory rates. Following the First World War a more flexible approach was adopted to railroad structure and to rates, but the financial position of the industry was not healthy. The slump of the early 1930s struck at the very foundations of the railroads; the federal government had to step in with financial assistance and to alter existing policies on rates. It also finally regulated the motor carrier industry in 1935. Following ten years of lengthy House and Senate discussions, two major hearings by the Interstate Commerce Commission (ICC) and the initial findings of the newly appointed Federal Co-ordinator of Transportation, Congress passed the Motor Carrier Act. This legislation provided for regulation of both trucks and buses along lines similar to those enacted for the railroads. Not content with this move, a now more interventionist Congress, apparently desiring a comprehensive system of transportation, moved to regulate the fledgling airlines with the Civil Aeronautics Act of 1938 and the older water carriers in the Transportation Act of 1940. This latter act also included a statement of national policy in which the federal government attempted to recognise the interrelationship of the alternative modes of transport.[22]

Recognition, however, did not bring decisive action. Subsequent transport legislation, congressional hearings and government reports of the post-war years were as much expressions of intent and hope as of actual comprehensive policy. This lack of a national transportation policy subsequently brought frequent overlap and conflict of views which resulted in specific decisions about individual transportation modes. There was little coordination. The very establishment of separate regulatory agencies aided this fragmentation. The ICC regulating the railroads, the Motor Carrier Bureau (MCB), a separate division of the ICC, regulating motor transport and the Civil Aeronautics Board (CAB), an indepedent body regulating the airlines, all had separate control over entry of firms, rates and fares and CAB was also directed to promote transportation. Decisions and rulings were

---

[22] Walsh, 'The Motor Carrier Act of 1935', p. 69–74; Norton, pp. 179–203; Stover, passim.

not always compatible. The notion that the government might establish guidelines and targets suitable to the national interest was never realised given the competitive ethos of the country and the political pressures of interest groups.[23]

Yet in the mid 1930s when buses and railroads were the main competitors for the available commercial intercity passenger traffic, federal regulation suggested some coordination. Early decisions of the MCB tended towards regulated competition. Within the bus industry the Greyhound Corporation was the dominant organisation controlling some 14 per cent of the national route mileage in 1935. Aware of its monopoly or virtual monopoly in certain parts of the country, the MCB encouraged the formation of an amalgamation of independent carriers, Trailways, as some type of intra-industry competition. On an inter-industry basis bus subsidiaries of railroads could not acquire competing independent bus companies in order to eliminate these rivals. Choice should be available to passengers if there was sufficient business for two carriers. Only in some sparsely populated parts of the West and South, where traffic volume was light was a single carrier certificated for a given route. Motor subsidiaries, however, could establish uneconomic routes provided that the parent railroad company absorbed the losses and the subsidiary became part of a system competing with Greyhound. There was to be both competition and coordination.[24]

The setting of bus fares now lay in the hands of the MCB but it is difficult to establish whether or not this government agency actively encouraged price competition between the trains and the buses, given the different cost patterns of the two modes. Many bus operators had set their rates according to their estimates of what the local market would bear or on the basis of existing rail rates. But they had done this without any formal accounting system. There was thus no uniform rate in the bus industry. The one general rule of thumb was that bus rates were lower than those of the railroads, which continued to fall in the late 1930s from 2.18 cents per passenger mile in 1935 to 1.84 cents in 1939. Early federal regulation of different types of carriers was still in an experimental phase when the outbreak of the Second World War changed transport patterns.[25]

[23] Locklin, pp. 282–310, 844–93; Norton, pp. 204–35, 406–47; D.V. Harper, *Transportation in America: Users, Carriers, Government,* (Englewood Cliffs, N.J., 1978), pp. 537–72.

[24] Crandall, pp. 166–220.

[25] Norton, pp. 351–53; Rossman, 'Memorandum Concerning Financial Aspects', p. 5; L.A. Rossman, 'A Memorandum Concerning the Losses Incurred by the Railroads in their Operation of Passsenger Trains' (Typescript, Grand Rapids, Minnesota, March 1955), p. 2 (Rossman Collection).

War and the general upturn in the American economy brought full business and increased revenues to both the railroads and the buses. The need to move both military personnel and civilian workers combined with a petrol and parts shortages, which curtailed the use of automobiles, forced Americans onto public transport whether they liked it or not. Seats were filled to capacity and there was standing room only. Railroad passenger miles of service increased from 26.5 billion in 1941 to 88.1 billion in 1945 and for the intercity buses the figures for the same years were 13.6 billion and 26.9 billion respectively. Fares increased only slightly despite rising operating costs. Nevertheless both modes of transport enjoyed substantial net operating revenues which contributed to greatly increased earnings. Though subject to restrictions imposed by the Office of Defense Transportation, some of which, such as the speed limitations, were opposed by the bus industry, there was ample business and good profits. These were the 'halcyon days'.[26]

On the return to normal peacetime conditions intercity passenger transport declined, but not as rapidly as many operators feared. Railroad passenger miles in 1948 were still 38 per cent of their peak of 1944 while buses still retained 87 per cent capacity of their peak performance of 1943 in 1948. The mobile American population was anxious to return to the freedom of their cars, but new vehicle and parts production could not satisfy demand. The drift away from public transport was thus gradual. For those who remained on the trains and the buses, whether by choice or default, buses were the preferred mode, carrying 63 per cent more passengers than the trains in 1948 and 78 per cent more in 1949. The fall in revenue thus showed more rapidly on the railroads with deficits on passenger service running at $649,627,000 in 1949. Such bad news had already been anticipated in government discussions. As early as 1946 official hearings and reports on national transportation were in process, raising such questions as intermodal competition, the role of the regulatory agencies, the advisability of consolidations and the nature of capital costs.[27]

---

[26] NAMBO, *Intercity Buses at War*, (Washington D.C., 1944); NAMBO, *The Intercity Bus Industry at War* (Washington D.C., 1943); *Bus Facts*, 19 (1949), pp. 6–7; Rossman, 'A Memorandum Concerning the Losses', p. 2; L.A. Rossman, 'Greyhound, the Motor Bus and Modern Highway Transportation' (Draft Booklet, Grand Rapids, Minnesota 28 October, 1946), p. 15.

[27] *Bus Facts*, 19 (1949), p. 6; U.S. Congress, House, Special Subcommittee on Transportation of the Committee on Interstate and Foreign Commerce, *National Transportation Inquiry* (79 Cong. 2 Sess., 1946), H. Rept. 2735; Rossman, 'A Memorandum Concerning the Losses', p. 4.

In the immediate post-war years the transport advantage lay with motor vehicles. The popularity of the car was easily visible in the increase of registrations from 25.8 million in 1945 to 40.3 million in 1950. Car ownership aided by the commercial success of both buses and trucks had stimulated the construction and extension of modern highways. Already in the interwar years there had been a boom in road building. Federal legislation helped this process not only by providing financial aid, but by stimulating well-organised state highway departments. After the war more money was invested in roads and the 1950s saw the start of Interstate Highways, making road travel not only faster, but more comfortable and cheaper. Commercial aviation was still in its childhood. Though flight became more popular for long-distance middle and upper income passengers in the 1950s, mass air transport awaited the widespread use of jet planes in the 1960s.[28]

Motor bus operators were well aware of their potential for growth, given Americans' love affair with the road. They were also well aware that they needed to resolve many problems if they were to capitalise on this romance. Larger and more comfortable buses might attract passengers away from both car and train provided that state regulations on sizes and weights of motor vehicles were altered. Such improved vehicles would need to be supported with better terminal facilities. The travelling public could be informed of these changes through advertising and publicity. The tax structure also required changing so that companies should only pay one state vehicle registration to be duly apportioned between other user states. Furthermore bus operators needed more flexibility in regulations so that firms could respond to differing local and regional markets, especially when establishing fares.[29]

The problem of fares and adequate earnings emerged as the first and highest priority in bus entrepreneurs' quest for economic viability and a better competitive position than their main commercial rival, the railroad. This issue was soon raised, not by the motor bus operators but officially by the ICC, which in July 1946 instituted a nationwide investigation of bus fares. Concern had been expressed about the profit margins of the intercity

[28] *The Statistical History of the United States*, p. 716; B.E. Seely, *Building the American Highway System: Engineers as Policy Makers* (Philadelphia, 1987), passim; C A. Taff, *Commercial Motor Transportation* (Centreville, Maryland, 6th ed. 1980), pp. 15–55; Bilstein, pp. 169–78, 227–39, 257–66.

[29] NAMBO, *Proceedings*, 17 (1946), pp. 12–14; 18 (1947), pp. 10–11, 93–99, 142–44; *BT*, 24, 8 (1945), pp. 46–48; 25, 5 (1946), pp. 39–40, 42–44; L.A. Rossman, 'Modern Highways' (Chicago, April, 1946), pp. 9–16; 'Unpublished Confidential Statement of NAMBO Responding to the U. S. House Committee Request for Information for "National Transportation Inquiry"', Washington, D.C., December 1945, pp. 13–17 (Greyhound Collection, Collection 3191, American Heritage Center, University of Wyoming, Laramie, Wyoming).

bus This issue was soon raised, not by the motor bus operators but officially by the ICC, which in July 1946 instituted a nationwide investigation of bus fares. Concern had been expressed about the profit margins of the intercity bus industry during and after the war and about the lack of uniform bus fares. The ICC thus decided to make the first comprehensive study of intercity bus fares and charges in order to establish a fair rate structure. The ensuing hearings established that existing fares were just and reasonable. They also agreed that fares charged by intercity bus companies should generally taper with distance thereby making the bus competitive with both the car over short distances and the train over longer distances. Clearly the train still had advantages of higher speeds and luxury service in the shape of dining cars, lounge cars and freedom of movement while in motion. Any theory, or practice, of competition would thus require bus fares to be lower than corresponding rail fares. Indeed such competition generally imposed an effective ceiling on bus fares. This situation had not changed significantly from the 1930s. But if the buses now kept their fares low in the late 1940s they too, like the railroads of the earlier years, would run into financial deficits. Increasing operating expenses in the post-war years threatened the ability of bus companies to run a cheap service and still remain profitable.[30]

Why had bus operating expenses increased? Unfair taxes were one part of the answer. The other parts involved a quest to modernise the bus industry and increased labour costs in a period of inflation. With the expansion of long-distance and thus interstate travel, bus companies found that they had to pay a larger number of state registration and motor fuel taxes as well as federal excise taxes. They were very anxious to have state taxes apportioned between the various states rather than paying to each state through which their buses travelled. A programme of better buses, new and improved terminals, garages and restaurants, involved high capital investment. Greater attention to safety and accident prevention, publicity and advertising and the introduction of both 'through buses' and luxury buses on certain routes all involved more expenditure than in the early years of growth. The item which caused most bus companies most worry, however, was increased wages. As the cost of living rose after the war, workers generally insisted on higher wages. In the bus industry in particular greater productivity brought claims for more increases and the unions also bargained for better working conditions. Wages doubled between 1939 and

---

[30] ICC, 'Investigation of Bus Fares', Docket No MC-C-550, 1, *Brief of Respondents* (Washington D.C., 1950) (Collection BMC-C-550, 23, Washington National Records Center, Suitland, Maryland).

1949 causing a disproportionate rise in bus company payrolls. To meet some of these costs bus fares were increased by 26 per cent in the 1940s. Buses still offered lower fares than trains, namely 1.84 cents per passenger mile in 1949 to the train's 2.45 cents in the same year, but it was becoming more difficult to make profits.[31]

While bus travel was becoming more expensive, rail travel was becoming uneconomic for railroad companies. Other than the four years of heavy wartime traffic, passenger and allied services had showed losses since 1927. Various explanations were offered for these losses including the inability of express and postal revenues to cover their costs, duplication of service between railroads, inadequate fares and too much regulation. But what was different in the generally prosperous post-war years and what became critical was the inability of the railroads to continue subsidising their rail passengers from their freight revenues. The railroads still shipped large amounts of bulky low-rated goods like cereals and minerals, which were difficult to move by alternative means on land, and they carried freight from three to four times as cheaply as trucks. Nevertheless their share of intercity freight traffic dropped from 66.61 per cent of the nation's total in 1946 to 48.22 per cent a decade later. With declining earnings and increasing expenditures for capital equipment, including diesel-electric trains, containerised wagons and computer-operated yards and terminals, the railroads were facing crises rather than problems. These crises brought some lines into bankruptcy and others into consolidations.[32]

Even if the railroads increased their freight rates, as indeed they did during and after the Second World War, their operating expenses were so high that returns on investment were unsatisfactory. In the modern era of freight competition they could not afford to subsidise a passenger service. What could be done? They could not work together with, rather than competing with, other carriers. The Motor Carrier Act of 1935 ensured limited railroad intervention in bus and truck operation either through direct ownership or subsidiaries. The Civil Aeronautics Act of 1938 prevented railroads and other

---

[31] *Bus Facts*, 19 (1949), pp. 38–45; 21 (1952), pp. 34–39; Rossman, 'A Memorandum Concerning the Losses', p. 9; L.A. Rossman, 'Intercity Motor Bus Transportation: The Greyhound Lines and the Public' (Proof Copy of Booklet, Grand Rapids, Minnesota, December 1951), p. 9 (Rossman Collection); Greyhound Corporation, *Annual Reports* (1941–1951) (Greyhound Collection); *BT*, 25–29 (1946–50).

[32] U.S. Congress, Senate, Committee on Interstate and Foreign Commerce, *National Transportation Policy*, Committee Print (87th Cong., 1st Sess., 1961), pp. 47–81; Hidy et. al., pp. 238–45; Stover, pp. 210–45; Nelson, pp. 8–13.

surface carriers from entering air transportation unless such services were auxiliary and supplementary to existing operations.[33]

A solution or partial solution seemed to lie in abandoning distinctly unprofitable passenger services. By the late 1940s and early 1950s American society clearly had alternative means of both commercial and private movement and no longer depended primarily on railroads for intercity travel. Discontinuance of passenger trains started under the control of state commissions: between 1951 and 1956 they approved 981 applications involving savings of 33.3 million train miles. This process, however, was slow, cumbersome and subject to the influence of local pressure groups. By 1957 the passenger deficit was still equal to 44 per cent of net rail operating income from freight. When the Transportation Act of 1958 granted the ICC jurisdiction over discontinuance of service the railroads were able to gain more relief. Annual passenger train mileage shrank from 275 million in 1957 to just over 180 million in 1964. By 1965 there was no passenger service on over half of the country's rail network and on the routes where trains still ran their frequency had declined, even in the densely populated Northeastern corridor.[34]

With railroad passenger services in trouble, did the bus industry seize its opportunity to capture a large or larger share of the intercity passenger travel market? There were certainly many innovations and changes. Larger buses with diesel power, air suspension and air conditioning offered more comfortable and enjoyable rides and, given the better condition of roads, a faster journey. Terminal construction and expansion brought improved waiting facilities, ticket purchase, access to information and better baggage handling. Many of these terminals had restaurants or dining counters not only for the convenience of passengers but also for use by the general public. Bus operators were attempting to rival not only the railroads but also the airlines in their standards and conditions of service. They also offered the advantage of a more flexible and cheaper service running into the heart of major cities and through most communities in the United States.[35]

---

[33] Locklin, pp. 371–72, 651, 860–71; Crandall, pp. 166–220; D.M. Itzkoff, *Off The Track: The Decline of the Intercity Passenger Train in the United States* (Westport, Conn., 1985), p. 49.

[34] Nelson, pp. 311–16; Stover, p. 239; Itzkoff, p. 58; G.W. Hilton, *The Transportation Act of 1958: A Decade of Experience* (Bloomington, Indiana, 1969), pp. 35–38.

[35] *BT*, 29–35 (1950–56); *Fleet Owner*, 52–55 (1957–60) contain many articles on improvements in the bus industry.

Such business enterprise was not reflected in the statistics. Passenger miles on intercity buses dropped from 24.0 billion in 1949 to 20.4 billion in 1959 or from 5.0 per cent of the national intercity mileage to 2.7 per cent. While improvements to the bus service retained a high proportion of existing passengers, the industry was unable to capitalise on being the only means of public 'intercity transportation to and from an estimated 40,000 communities throughout the country.'[36] Management seemed to lack both the initiative and the aggression necessary to introduce new ideas and ways of operating. More significantly, perhaps, in the age of high mass consumption, new approaches to marketing and selling their industry were necessary. With the older bus pioneers or their successors still frequently in control, there was perhaps a lack of skill and training. Talented newcomers often found their way blocked. Clearly it was very difficult to persuade Americans to abandon their automobiles, of which there were 61.9 million in 1960 or one per 2.9 persons. Yet the airlines were marketing an increasingly attractive and more frequent service to those passengers who were abandoning the Pullman and sleeper rail service and to new customers who now believed that they should travel long distances for business or pleasure. Certainly airlines had the advantage of speed, but they had to sell their mode in terms of cost, flexibility and easy access. Bus companies seemed to be content with a smaller share of an expanding travel market.[37]

The same general comment was applicable to the 1960s. Despite an increase in revenue pasengers of 11 per cent from 336 million to 396 million during the decade and an increase in total bus miles of 5.6 billion, the industry's share of the national intercity total fell from 2.5 per cent to 2.2 per cent. Different interpretations were placed on such figures. Reacting positively to changing trends in the travel market bus operators proudly noted their ability to keep passengers. By contrast intercity passengers on the railroads fell from 122.7 million to 87.8 million between 1960 and 1969. Buses were also important means of transport for particular parts of the travelling public, especially those who for financial or age reasons could not own and drive automobiles. Yet these Americans who rode the buses on regular scheduled routes often did so by default rather than by choice. They were a captive market, albeit one which was likely to remain. More potential lay in the local and middle-distance charter and the special markets.

[36] *Bus Facts*, 29 (1959), p. 5.

[37] Interview with W. A. Luke, editor, *Bus Ride*, by M. Walsh, Spokane, Washington, 22 October 1990; *Greyhound News* 14, 7 (1955), pp. 8–9, 14; *BT*, 34, 11 (1955), p. 54; 35, 4 (1956), p. 24; 35, 5 (1956), pp. 42–43.

Here bus operators catered to groups who wished to go together to sports events, on educational trips, on holidays or even on military manouevres. Indeed by 1970 intercity buses carried some 19 million charter passengers who comprised 10.9 per cent of their total traffic. Yet even with room for expansion in the leisure market the bus was unlikely to make a significant impact on the nature and structure of passenger transport. Most Americans who travelled commercially did so for work purposes and the introduction and spread of the jet plane boosted the position of airlines in the intercity mileage patterns despite their relatively high price. Meanwhile the popularity of the car continued unabated, with 89.3 million registered in 1970 or one vehicle per 2.3 persons.[38]

The strategy for survival and perhaps growth within the intercity bus industry lay, as Charles A. Webb, then a member of the ICC, remarked 'not in reducing fares below the present reasonable levels, but in providing faster, safer, more comfortable service'.[39] The bus was already the cheapest means of travel. It could also become a more popular means by marketing itself as a full-service, high-quality industry. Resolving the problems internal to the industry such as apportionment of licence and fuel taxes, the liberalisation of legislation on size and weights of buses, improved baggage handling and high labour costs was a constructive and effective way forward. Reckoning that a drop of one per cent in intercity car travel meant 9.5 billion passenger miles to commercial carriers NAMBO wanted to target the car drivers who could be persuaded to travel by public transport. They thus advertised that the bus was very convenient, comfortable and safe. It was also getting faster given the improvements in the highway system. Thinking positively, bus operators could look forward to expanding their business as the 1960s drew to a close.[40]

Yet there were already indicators that the national bus companies were looking to alternative ways of retaining or expanding their position. The largest carrier, Greyhound, which had over 50 per cent of the intercity bus traffic in the late 1960s, had started to diversify its interests in 1961. While the scheduled intercity routes remained an essential part of operations, the Greyhound Corporation looked increasingly to other bus activities like sightseeing tours, charter operations, services such as to and from major airports and an expanded package handling capacity as sources of income. Seeking to broaden its base further and to attract new sources of capital

[38] *Transportation in America*, pp. 12–15; *National Transportation Policy*, p. 277; ICC, *The Intercity Bus Industry* (Washington D. C., 1978), pp. 53–55.

[39] NAMBO, *Proceedings*, 33 (1962), p. 77.

[40] NAMBO, *Proceedings*, 36 (1965), p. 19; 37 (1966), pp. 53–54.

Greyhound moved into other areas such as van lines, leasing industrial equipment and computers, insurance and food services. Diversification was a general business strategy of the 1960s which the major intercity bus company was quick to follow. Indeed by 1969 their slogan 'Greyhound's got more going for you than buses' was being beamed into millions of houses in a new televised advertising campaign. Three years later the Greyhound conglomerate, with its new corporate headquarters 'Greyhound Tower' in Phoenix, Arizona, was important enough to be ranked as the twenty-ninth largest industrial concern in the United States by *Fortune* magazine. Trailways, the other national and second largest intercity bus company, was also part of a corporate body with broader interests though these frequently provided services for the carrier.[41]

The regional and local intercity bus carriers tended to remain in transportation services. Their larger operators provided scheduled service, usually of an interstate basis with charter and special service as a backup. Firms like the Jefferson Lines Inc., which became the eighth largest firm after its acquisition of Crown Coach Company in 1966, operated in Minnesota, Iowa, Missouri and Arkansas. Peter Pan Bus Lines Inc. worked on this basis in Massachussets, Connecticut and New York. The smaller operators, like Badger Coaches in Madison and Milwaukee, Wisconsin, or Wolf's Bus Line of York Spring, Pennsylvania, had a considerable amount of charter and special work often within a 200 mile radius and when involved in regular scheduled business plied intrastate routes.[42] There was much variety among the operating patterns of the regional and local companies nationwide, not only in terms of their size, but also in terms of revenues and methods. Indeed there was no single bus industry. There was rather a group of individual carriers each serving their particular markets.[43]

Flexibility was a prime factor in enabling bus operators to retain and increase their passengers and in trying to hold their position within the intercity travel market. Those operators located in the Northeastern coastal

---

[41] *Go Greyhound*, 4, 1 (1969), pp. 9–10, 12–13; 4, 3 (1969), p. 16; *Greyhound West*, 2, 1 (1972), pp. 1–3 (W.A. Luke Collection, Spokane, Washington); G.H. Trautman, 'Greyhound, Yesterday, Today and Tomorrow' (Chicago, 1968), pp. 1-12 (Greyhound Collection); *The Intercity Bus Industry*, pp. 86–87.

[42] *Corporate Report*, January, 1978, p. 47 (Luke Collection); *Bus Ride* 7, 5 (1971), pp. 17–19; 24, 2 (1988), pp. 50–51; *Motor Coach Age*, 21, 9 (1969), pp. 4–6; 35, 4 (1983), pp. 8, 11–12.

[43] *The Intercity Bus Industry*, p. 59; *Bus Facts*, 34 (1966), pp. 5,7; National Transportation Policy Study Commission, *Intercity Bus Transportation* (Iowa City, Iowa, 1979), p. 12.

section of the United States in particular needed to draw on their flexibility when faced with the new challenge of government-subsidised rail travel in the early and mid 1970s. In order to reduce congestion on the highways and in the skyways of certain high density corridors, and also to stimulate modern, fast, comfortable and efficient rail service, the federal government established and subsidised Amtrak, a national railroad passenger corporation. With Amtrak, rail fares were reduced and were unregulated. Competition with buses became intense. Bus companies requested permission from the ICC to make fare adjustments at short notice and introduced special 'high quality' service. It was important for the major bus carriers to maintain income from the high density areas because these helped cross-subsidise the unprofitable lightly travelled rural routes and thereby maintained a national network. Yet declining earnings and rising capital replacement costs made the future of these companies look bleak. With about a third of Amtrak's service being paid for by the passenger and the remainder by the general taxpayer, it was the bus industry's turn to bemoan unfair competition.[44]

Amtrak competition around major urban centres was only the most publicised problem facing the bus industry. The continued growth of the airlines, especially local airlines which were still being subsidised, added a different kind of competition. The predominance of car travel continued undisturbed despite an oil crisis and fluctuations in the economy. Competition, if anything, was getting stronger and the buses had to work hard to retain their already small portion of the intercity travel market.[45] By 1976, fifty years after the establishment of its trade association, the intercity bus industry carried only 1.7 per cent of the total. Gone were the halcyon days of the Second World War when buses transported 8.8 per cent of the nation's long-distance travellers. Yet motor carriers still ferried some 340 million passengers in contrast to the railroads' 78 million and the airlines' 210 million. Buses were still a vital part of the country's transport network. Using their greater flexibility of movement and service, benefiting from the construction and improvement of national highways, and using new equipment supported by modern facilities, they offered both an economical scheduled service and a convenient and profitable charter and special service.

[44] *1974 National Transportation Report*, pp. 302–6; *The Intercity Bus Industry*, pp. 89, 90; *1926–1976: One Half Century*, pp. 6–10; *Bus Ride* 8, 2 (1972), pp. 23–26.

[45] Taff, pp. 493–94; *The Intercity Bus Industry*, p. 22; *Bus Ride*, 11, 1 (1975), pp. 28–30.

12

RMT: *History of a Merger*

James Knapp

Seventy-seven years ago, when three general railway unions merged to form the National Union of Railwaymen (NUR) in 1913, the leadership of the new union was optimistic that further mergers would follow. The obvious link-up was with the Associated Society of Locomotive Engineers and Fireman (ASLEF) or the Railway Clerks Association (now the Transport Salaried Staff Association – TSSA). Most members of the new union would have been astonished if it had been suggested that the next merger involving the NUR would be with the National Union of Seamen (NUS). Yet on 10 September 1990 the NUR and NUS merged to form the National Union of Rail, Maritime and Transport Workers (RMT).

From 1913 the NUR made regular overtures to both ASLEF and TSSA with a view to creating one railway union. Unfortunately, for a number of reasons but – it has to be said – basically sectionalism, the NUR was rebuffed. In 1982 the NUR achieved something of a breakthrough when ASLEF agreed to join the NUR in the Rail Union Federation. This provided a much closer working relationship between the two unions through regular meetings and joint decision making. The longer term objective of the federation is merger of the unions. The trend towards merger among unions generally is pronounced. Since 1979 the number of unions affiliated to the Trades Union Congress (TUC) has fallen from 112 to 79 in 1990. Pressure for merger has been mainly economic as membership of individual unions has fallen. The NUR's membership in 1979 was 170,000 but at the time of the merger with the NUS it had fallen to 108,000. Since 1979 the government's privatisation programme has fragmented the NUR's membership. The union now deals with more than sixty separate employers. Twenty-five years ago the practice was for the NUR to negotiate with British Rail and any major changes negotiated there – improved pay, holidays or reduced hours – were followed through on London Underground, hotels, workshops and other ancillary groups.

Changes in the structure of the railway industry have seen employment fall from 182,000 in 1979 to 126,000 at the end of 1990 with a consequential decline in trade union membership. Railways, however, remain highly unionised. In a situation where membership is falling the choice for trade unions is to cut back on services offered to members or to consider a merger. Over recent years there has been an expansion of services offered by many unions – including the NUR – into areas such as reduced rate mortgages, insurance, holidays and loans. While members still join a union for traditional reasons of mutual protection – and it was heartening to see NUR members' collective opposition to British Rail Board plans to break up the bargaining machinery in 1989 – members today also expect something more than the conventional 'death and orphan' or accident benefit from their union. Smaller unions cannot provide these additional financial packages.

The crisis of falling membership also hit the NUS. Again the structure of the industry has changed dramatically in recent years. In 1979 Britain's merchant navy fleet consisted of 1,042 vessels. At the end of 1990 it was just 398. During this time membership of the NUS fell by more than a quarter from 26,000 to 19,000. The main job loss among merchant seamen took place a decade earlier and coincided with the advent of containerisation. Prior to containerisation some cargo vessels carried a crew of perhaps eighty to ninety. The new method of cargo handling reduced this to twenty.

It was against this background, that the NUR and NUS began talks about the possibility of merger in 1988. The initial idea arose out of an informal conversation I had with the General Secretary of the NUS – Sam McCluskie – at the 1987 TUC. The more we explored the issue, the more apparent it became that the unions had common interests. Both unions organised workers employed in ports and docks and both negotiated with the same employers such as Sealink and Caledonian Macbrayne. Interestingly, on looking back to the origins of the NUS, we discovered that this union's first rule book and constitution was based on the rule book of the rail union the Amalgamated Society of Railway Servants – a forerunner of the NUR. Another link was the strike of seamen in 1911, which inspired railway workers to take strike action themselves over low pay. Members of rail unions cooperated so well during this dispute that pressure for one rail union became intense with the end result being the formation of the NUR.

A report on our informal discussions was put to the respective executive committees of the NUR and NUS and both organisations agreed to formal negotiations on a merger. Exploratory talks then began in two working parties – one dealing with financial issues, the other with administrative and structural matters – to consider in greater detail the practical consequences of merger. Both unions had a number of common benefits to be expected but offered different scales of payment and had different rates of contribution. Structurally the NUR's policy-making body was an annual general meeting. The NUS conference met biannually. There was provision for grades conferences – conferences of members employed in similar grades such as signalmen, workshops staff or traincrew – in the NUR's constitution but nothing similar in the NUS's rules. However, after detailed examination both working parties came to the unanimous conclusion that there was no insurmountable constitutional or financial problem to preclude merger.

Before we could get involved in drafting a new constitution the NUS received an approach from the Transport and General Workers Union on a merger with that organisation. The leadership of the NUS decided to ballot their members on the principle of merger and if this was accepted to vote on whether to merge with the NUR or TGWU. NUS members voted for merger with the NUR. Obviously different individuals had different reasons for voting as they did, but one of the strong positive arguments for the NUR was that we were offering a genuine merger – not a takeover – and seafarers would remain an autonomous group within the new union.

Following the welcome result of the NUS ballot, the two unions set about creating a new rule book and constitution. Basically the new rules provided for the general administration of the new union to be conducted by a Council of Executives. This was to be made up of twenty-one representatives of general grades (ex-NUR) on a general Committee and thirteen representatives of shipping grades (ex NUS) on a Shipping Committee. Matters relating solely to seafarers are considered by the Shipping Committee; issues of concern to rail, bus or other non-maritime members are dealt with by the General Committee. Policy issues in areas covering all members are decided by the two committees meeting as the Council of Executives.

254

The issue which probably created most controversy during the lead up to the merger in October was the name of the new union. If not exactly a household name, the NUR was one of the most recognisable of trade unions in this country. Indeed the union has always had strong international links and was highly respected among the international labour movement. Yet, from day one of the merger talks, it was accepted by both unions that we would create a new title. This would ensure that accusations of a takeover by the NUR could be rebuffed. It was also agreed that the new title would keep as much of the old titles as practicable, thus retaining some link with the past. There were other practical arguments for a change of name. The National Union of Railwaymen ceased being an organisation catering only for railway workers very many years ago. Docks, road transport and catering workers all had a place in the union. In this age of equity the very title Railway*men* was anachronistic at best and seen as sexist by many of our thousands of women members. Perhaps even more important, we were trying to crate a *new* specialist transport union. The constitution was designed to encourage mergers with other transport unions; continuing to call ourselves the NUR was not a credible alternative if we were serious about a new transport union.

The law required that members of both unions should have an opportunity to endorse – or reject – the rule book of the new union. Prior to this the NUR annual conference has accepted the principle of merger on two separate occasions and a special general meeting had approved the new rules. After seeking advice from the Certification Officer, both unions distributed voting papers to members' homes. The result of the ballot was announced at the NUR annual general meeting at Liverpool. This showed members voting three to one in favour. The participation level was 30 per cent, about average for postal balloting within the NUR. NUS members voted six to one in favour of the merger in a poll involving 25 per cent of members (see Table 4)

The National Union of Rail, Maritime and Transport Workers – RMT – does not yet have the aura or history associated with the NUR. But the leadership of the new union is convinced that we have developed a framework for a modern, forward-looking union equipped to serve transport workers in the twenty-first century. Both the NUR and NUS had a proud past. They gave magnificent service to generations of members. There is no doubt that many members had a strong sentimental attachment to the old unions but, as the ballot result showed, members recognised that the time had come for heads to rule hearts.

Table 4

Ballot on Proposed Merger of NUR and NUS

NUR

Ballot papers issued	113,006
Papers returned	33,902
Those voting for merger	25,178
Those voting against merger	8,700

NUS

Ballot papers issued	18,900
Papers returned	4,877
Voting for merger	4,229
Voting against merger	644

There is considerable scope for further mergers within the transport industry, we still have three unions organising in railways. Unfortunately, there is a century of mistrust to overcome between railway unions and we cannot do that overnight. The creation of the Rail Federation was a positive step which allow us to discuss common problems around the table. Disregarding economic pressures, the sheer sense of having one union for railway workers will eventually prevail. By forming the RMT we have broken the log jam among transport unions. I am totally confident that we will not wait another seventy-seven years before further mergers take place.

Index

List of Subscribers

John Armstrong
Prof. T.C. Barker
Prof. L. Barrow
Peter Barton
Lord Briggs
Prof. A.J. Burkett
Dr. Alan Campbell
Prof. G. Channon
R.S. Craig
Mark Dennison
W.A. Emmerson
Nina Fishman
Prof. Dick Geary
Dr. Clive Griggs
John L. Halstead
S. Harpur
Prof. G.R. Hawke
Prof. John Hibbs
G. Higham
Prof. E.J. Hobsbawm
C.A. Horn
Dr. David Howell
Richard Hyman
Bob Jones
Dr. I.J.E. Keil
A. Kemp
James Knapp
Prof. Y. Komatsu
J.E. Lehrer
Janet Livingstone
A.J. Lucking
Dave Lyddon
Dr. David E. Martin
Dr. R.B. McKean

Michael Meadowcroft
Prof. Gordon Mingay
Terry Monaghan
Margaret Morris
S.A. Munro
Andrea Panaccione
Dr. H.M. Pelling
Harold Pollins
Jason Reece
Peter Richards
Dr. R.C. Richardson
Michael Robbins
Dr. E. Royle
David Rubinstein
P.A. Ryan
Prof. John Saville
J.J. Seegers
Emma Shepherd
John Shepherd
Louise Shepherd
Mike Shuker
Andy Smith
R.T. Smith
Lord Soper
Susan Spencer
Richard Stevens
E.L. Taplin
Joe Tormey
Jesus M. Valdaliso
H.J. Vincent
Dr. M. Walsh
Esme Whiskin
Arthur Wrigley
Prof. C.J. Wrigley